LIBRARY AND INFORMATION TECHONOLOGY

Concepts to Applications

LIBRARY AND INFORMATION TECHNOLOGY

Concepts To Applications

Editor
Ramalingam

KALPAZ PUBLICATIONS

Delhi-110052

LIBRARY AND INFORMATION TECHNOLOGY
concepts to applications

(Library Science, Information Technology, Computer Science)

ISBN: 81-7835-010-6

Published in 2000 in India by
Kalpaz Publications
C-30, Satyawati Nagar
Ashok Vihar Phase-III
Delhi-110052
E-Mail: kalpaz@hotmail.com

Laser Typeset at A.S. Printers
Printed at Mehra Offset Printers, New Delhi

Contents

Preface

Library information technology is one of the major tool of tomorrow to shape our society and our institutions particularly our libraries. Our education and cultural infrastructure must change to meet the challenges, addressing them through new and creative educational techniques. In order for librarians and libraries to survive as a profession and as an institution, respectively, they will need to lead their institutions in building improved information technology-oriented infrastructures.

It has been evident for over half a century that libraries can no longer comprehensively collect in a wide variety of subject areas. Thus, a long history of cooperative networking and interlibrary lending has been die mainstay of satisfying ever widening and interdisciplinary subject material demands of research, scholarly and student users.

New publishing techniques such as CD-ROM, multimedia interactive computer works, machinereadable text files on the Internet, and collections of scanned materials stored in image and character formats are increasingly becoming key parts to library resources. These collections are accessed and controlled through specialized retrieval software and LANs with Internet connections. The new publishing formats and systems are pushing the envelope of the library community to supply and service clientele using these new mediums. The local area network, with its ability to provide wide CD-ROM access as well as institutional connectivity to both the library and to the Internet, is the underpinning communication system of today's forward-looking library. A host computer-based automated library system providing technical processing, online catalogue and circulation support is not sufficient in itself to provide all the information technology resources needed for today's libraries.

We can expect that the new century will bring further consolidations within the computing field. There will be fewer but larger corporate competitors serving libraries, just as there will be fewer but larger computer manufacturers. All of this progress still will not bring nirvana. Libraries will be required to invest in continually evolving technologies and the personnel infrastructures necessary to their effective operation and utilization. However, while these technologies are increasingly complex in themselves, their incorporation into commercial products should simplify the training and support needs across computing platforms for the long term.

Editor

1

Introduction to Computers in Libraries

The technological advances are discernible in the hardware materials used in the machine and its operational processes. The computer designed in different periods by using advanced technology has been specified by the term 'generation'; e.g., the pre-1959 computer is called the first generation computer; the computer designed between 1959 and 1964, the second generation computer; the computer of the period between 1964 and the late seventies, the third generation computer; and so on. In different generations, the material used in the computer have been changed for each and every part of machine-the memory, the arithmetic and logic unit, input/output processes etc. In the first generation computer, dating prior to 1959, vacuum tubes were used and all functions were performed in the central processor unit. In the second generation, dating from 1959 to 1964, transistors were used. These had considerable effect on the computer which gradually became smaller in size and lesser expensive in cost.

The third generation computer was built with integrated circuits by making use of microelectronics for the components introduced in 1964. The magnetic media were used for the memory storage. The fourth generation computer came into being in the late seventies using advanced microelectronic concepts to get further circuit densities. The new circuits were microscopic. The size became smaller still and the cost, less expensive. At the same time, the capability for storage and performance of the operational systems increased greatly. Modern technological advances had an overall impact on the computer hardware in all aspects-the machine, operations and the cost.

The primary impact on the machine was the diminishing of size. The earlier computer was large enough. The weight of ENIAC was 30 tons. It consumed much electricity and produced much heat. The second and the third generation computers became smaller and smaller as a result of the use of electronics and microelectronics. There are more than 50,000 integrated circuits in a modern computer, but the size is smaller than that of the earlier computer. The size of a modern computer has been reduced considerably by using a wafer-like material—the silicon chip. It is possible to pack over 2,00,000 components in one square inch of the silicon chip. It is expected that smaller chips will be able to accommodate even more components in future.

The chip is an extraordinary material for the computer hardware, because of its low cost, compact electronics and capability to embody the logic and the memory units. A large umber of microelectronic circuitry can be fabricated on a small chip which lead to 'very large-scale integration' used in a modern computer. A chip can store a very large amount of information, and so it is known as the memory chip A microprocessor is the 'computer on a chip' combining memory with logic functions. Using the chip the computer is becoming cheaper and more powerful, day by day. A computer stores a large quantum of data in the memory, much in the cache memory and performs complex operations for various computations. So, it should be perfectly reliable. The vacuum tubes were not so reliable. The transistors had also certain flaws. They sometimes broke off from circuit boards. The chip has no soldered wires and each circuitry is more compact.

The failure points are almost nil, and it has become most reliable. Furthermore, it is tiny and the electronic signals can move through it very quickly and thus save time. The probability of failure or committing mistakes is almost nil. Moreover, self-repairing computers are also being produced. The sophisticated magnetic media and the silicon ship brought about a major break-through in the storage of data and information. The magnetic media like the magnetic tape of offline service and the magnetic drum or disc for online service can hold more information than their counterparts in the earlier computers.

Magnetic cores are proved to be efficient storage media requiring less space and working with greater speed. They are inexpensive and compact in size. Millions of magnetic cores can be accommodated in a small cabinet. Random access is provided much faster. The time for access to documents can be measured in nanoseconds. The early chips could perform work with greater speed than magnetic cores. The large scale integrated (LSI) circuit storage elements were used. In modern chips, very large scale integrated (VLSI) circuits are being used. It has increased the storage capacity in a comparatively smaller space. Computers are becoming smaller in size, but of larger storage capacity owing to the advancement of hardware technology.

The speed in operation has become faster and the output, of greater reliability because of reduction in size. Now, least time is required by electronic pulses to travel because the distance is shorter in modern hardware. Thus, the speed of the processor has increased. The calculation time in the 1970's increased several hundred times more than what was in the 1950's. More than a million of calculations can be made in a second. The speed of the early computers was measured in milliseconds, i.e. thousandths of a second; the second generation speed was expressed in microseconds, i.e. millionths of a second and the next generations of computers in nanoseconds, i.e. billionths of a second. It does not come within human perception.

The computer job of ten hours in the 1950's came down to a few seconds' job in the 1970's and now the very same job can be performed in the tiny fraction of a second. This can be done also in a time-sharing and multiprogramming operation. The new innovations in hardware technology, particularly storage media, microelectronics, VLSI, etc., have reduced the cost of the computer. Not only the cost of machines is reducing, but the cost of maintenance and operation is also being reduced because of the low consumption of electricity compared to that of the earlier computers.

The cost of computer instructions has also been reduced because of greater speed. As the computer capability is increasing more and more, so the cost is becoming lesser and lesser. A wide range of general-purpose and special-purpose computers is being used in libraries. Computers are also available in various sizes and with various systems adaptable to various specific-purpose applications. Mainframe computers, mini-computers, microcomputers, microprocessors etc., are the types which can be used in libraries. These can be used independently or in interconnected systems with master-slave relationship or network relationship. Computerisation may be implemented as an integrated system with a mainframe computer or part by part with mini-or microcomputers to be interconnected in future. Such alternative make library automatic financially viable.

Planning and management also become efficient, cost-effective and result-oriented. Mainframe computers are usually host systems for several libraries or information centres. These computers are time-sharing and multiprogramming, and an usually multiprocessors, being composed of many computers including microcomputer. All these operate in a connected way under the control of a central operating system. Modern mainframe computer are capable of address and several billion positions or more of memory with hundreds of registers. These are more than 32 bits in length.

The channels between various parts of such a computer are capable of carrying upto 5 million bits of detain one millionth of a second. A mainframe computer has microcomputers to control specific hardware devices, such as printers, disc drives etc. These also help transfer of memory from one device to another through the bus. These microcomputer have central processing units with the large scale integrated memory system like the read-only memory or the programmable read-only memory or the programmable read-only memory.

RAM stands for Random Access Memory (RAM), and is a general-purpose memory to store data and programmes. It requires electric power to hold the content intact. So, it is known as volatile memory. In RAM, the location of the specific circuit is possible and can be accessed directly in the middle of the chip. One need not examine each circuit starting at the beginning and moving forward one by one.

While the chip is composed of specific circuits designed to execute a single programme, it is called Read Only Memory (ROM). Expect the designed programme, no other programme can be held by ROM. The entire chip must be replaced and redesigned for any change in the programming. But ROM is very much useful for any specific application, and when it is to be produced in large quantities.

The large scale integrated memory can be used for specific applications known as Programmable Read Only Memory (PROM). In PROM, chips are used singly for programming by breaking connections between circuits. PROM is very useful for specific programmes and can be used for specific routine programmes.

The disadvantage of PROM is that once a programme is recorded in the chip, it cannot be changed or revised. So a method has been devised known as Erasable Programmable Read Only Memory (EPROM) which is constructed not by breaking circuits, but by activating circuits between specific values within the chip and later de-activating the circuits with high intensity ultra-violet light. The chip for EPROM can be programmed over and over again without being replaced.

The instructions programmed in ROM, PROM and EPROM can be held for years together, and are known as non-volatile memory. The programming languages viz. BASIC, COBOL, FORTRAN, PASCAL, PL/1 are available for microcomputers. All the programming languages have their specific fields of application for different purpose. In library applications, Beginners All-purpose Symbolic Instruction Code (BASIC) is most widely used. The advantages are that it is easy to learn; and the programming is rather simple. Moreover, the scope is wider and all the terms used in the library are programmable with basic. With the knowledge of a few commands and by manipulating them judiciously, one can construct fairly sophisticated programmes with basic. It is possible to create numerous routines, subroutines and subcommands with BASIC.

The usefulness of basic in library applications lies in its capability to handle strings. It is not always possible to determine the lengths and the characters for bibliographic data, and so, the undefined length area of a string allows flexibility in data input. The original BASIC was limited in scope and command. But basic has been much developed since then. Now it is available in two modes-interpreted and compiled. The interpreted mode is better at the initial stage. It is slower, but helps the programmer to do his hob correctly. The compiled version is sophisticated and meant for advanced users. For online interaction, the compiled version in more effective.

The use of computers has been steadily increasing in Science and Technology since the Second World War. Most of the advanced countries of the world have made much advance in this respect but India has just made a start, especially in industry and business and there also these are witnessing stiff opposition from the employees and their trade because of the fear of retrenchment. However, their application is increasing day by day in science, technology, industry and business. Their recent conquest is railways.

Libraries are no exception to them. As the Library Authorities and Librarians are becoming aware of their potential uses, these are being put to more use. So much so that not only some courses in computer applications are being arranged regularly by the private sector, but they are finding their pride place in Library science courses also. For example, the syllabus of the Master's Comrse in Library and Information Science of Delhi University has included Computer use in Libraries as a part of one of the papers. It is hoped that their use libraries would increase in the years to come in India, thought not at a rapid speed, especially because of our socio-economic conditions and the prohibitive of their installation and maintenance.

A computer is a device which is capable of accepting information/data automatically, applying a sequence of prescribed processes to the information/data and supplying the results of these processes. It usually of input and output devices, storage arithmetic and local units and a control unit. Thought the first automatic general purpose digital computer, designed by the Havard university, was built in 1944 by the I.B.M. yet its technology dates back to 1833 when Charles Babbage devised an idea of a computer which was utilised by George R Stibitz of the bell telephone laboratories in 1930s for using telephone relays in the construction of a computing machine.

There have been very rapid changes in computer technology. First generation computers developed during 1954-59 had vacuum tubes. These were replaced by pea-sized transistors in the Second Generation Computers developed during 1954-64. The Third Generation Computers developed after 1964 used tiny chips sized transistors. The forth generation computers which will make use of "big integrated circuits have been developed in 1970.

There is a possibility of BIC to be replaced by 'GIC' i.e. Gigantic Integrated Circuits which will have the speed of more than one billion operation per second. These may have memory, equivalent to a million volumes of 500 pages each. These developments will have immense impact on the storage and retrieval of information in Libraries. It is estimated that in 1960 there were only 5,0000 Computers in the world whose member went upto 75,000 in 1969. Dr. Jerome B. Wiesner, former Science Advisor to the late President Kennedy of USA rightly remarked that the Computer with its promise of million fold increase in man's capacity to handle information, will undoubtedly have the most far-teaching social consequences of any contemporary technical development.

The potential for good in the computer and the danger inherent in its misuse exceed our ability to imagine. The latest development in the field of computer technology is the reported Soviet-patented high capacity computer called Recursion Computer which is capable of coping with sophisticated scientific and technological task, thousands of time quicker than the present Computers as the new computer is multi-processor. Soviet specialists, according to Prof. Mikhail Ignatiev are now developing Computers capable of performing 12.5 million operations per second for serial productions.

Another development in computer technology is the production of handy computers which will cut down home and office drudgery. It performs daily house-hold chores such as putting the lights off and on, protecting the homes, balancing the cheque books, reading one's pulse and helping in the preparation of breakfast. These minicomputer may be available even in pocket calculators or micro wave ovens, sewing machines or automobiles. These microprocessors which are ting and low-cost computers capable of performing jobs equivalent to those of room-size computers will change the whole picture. It is estimated that within less than 10 years, some limited use computers will cost between 5 and 10.

Voice-computers are in the air. As such the new computers will help people to overcome the fear of big brother computers. Similarly, special-purpose computers will cost between 100 and 1000.. The Computer can either purchased right away or in easy instalments or can be hired. No doubt, various computer manufacturing companies allure the prospective purchasers by stressing that the total cost of the computer can be realised in the form of savings and the cost of service for which additional staff has to be pressed into service. However, in view of the fast-changing computer technology and the increasing manufacture of sophisticated computers during last few decades many computers will become obsolete thereby putting the libraries to irreparable loss, it is but advisable that not only big computers are taken on hire basis but mini-computers and other turnkey devices should be made use of for performing specific jobs so that the risk-remains with the manufactures or it is mimimal and the library is assured of latest Computer to be taken into account in the respect include the following.

— Main-frame Computers VS. Mini-computers.
— Capabilities of various Computers, especially in relation to library applications.
— Reliability and Service of various makes of different manufacturing companies.
— Hardware and Software.
— Specifications and Accountability of various makes of computers.
— Amenability to national and international standards.
— Easy servicing and availability of spare parts.
— Warranty and Safeguards.
— Free training for hardware and software.

2

INFORMATION TECHNOLOGY IN LIBRARIES

Computers are of two kinds i.e., (i) Analogue and (ii) Digital. The former is useful for scientific work as it helps in calculating the accepted information according to a pre-determined pattern which may be mechanical, electro-mechanical or electronic. In other words, it helps in processing the information in a physical from i.e. in terms of weight, volume or electric current. For example, it can translate temperature, flow, speed, attitude, voltage an other physical variables into related electrical quantities and for this purpose it uses electrical equivalent circuits. The latter type of computer i.e. Digital Computer is a general purpose computer as it helps in calculating and processing the accepted data in digital form. In other words, it makes use of conventional letters, symbols and numbers for the purpose and is, therefore, suitable for processing of information in general and for various other commercial business and office applications. It is this type of computer which is used in libraries. The digital computer can be further divided into two types i.e., batch processor and Real-time Processor.

Batch processor processes the data accumulated into batches or groups over a period of time. It consists of the following four component units:

(i) The hardware i.e. the machinery which is designed to carry out instructions necessary to perform the assigned jobs.

(ii) The Inputs Units help in converting the data passed on to them into a standard from acceptable to the Central Processor.

(iii) The Central processor of the heart of the computer consists of the storage unit, the control unit and the arithmetic unit.

The data in the store section of the computer is governed by the software the programme i.e. a series of instructions which are devised by the computer manufacturer or by the computer users or their agents. The capacity of the central processor is measured in thousands of units which may consist of one character of a byte or a computer word.

The second part of the central processor of a digital computer is called the control unit because it not only helps in picking up one programme only at a time but also activates the necessary circuits so as to help other parts of the computer to perform the described jobs. However, a direct control over the operations can be exercised by the operator who comes to know as to what is going on inside the computer besides enabling him to key in massages necessary to run a programme.

The third part of the central processor is known as the arithmetic unit because it carries out arithmetic calculations such as additions, subtractions and comparisons.

The results of the foregoing processes performed by various parts of the computer are called output units which may either be in print or in machine readable print-on punched cards, paper tape or magnetic tape.

The backing store provides the filing system for the computer and consists of magnetic tape reels. The input, output and backing store units are together called peripherals i.e. those which are outside.

Real time processor

The Real Time Processor is designed to process a large volume of data. In this system, the units called *terminals* have a direct connection or *on-line* connection with the computer in such a way that data can be fed to the processor directly. Generally, the *terminal* is an electric type-writer through which the operator keys in information or interrogatories. In this system, there is no need of presenting this information on machine-readable media i.e. magnetic tape punched cards or paper tape because in it the programme can directly control the processing of data received from a terminal i.e. an electric typewriter besides adding it to the files on backing store or sending back to the terminal the data already available on file and that is why is called real-time processor because quick service even though the data is received from many terminals. As such, these two processors differ from each other on the basis of input and output units used by them.

The main advantage of a digital computer is its speed of processing the data. It carrier out the instructions of the programme in a fraction of a second. The speed of the peripherals expressed its one thousandth of a second or one millisecond while that of the central processor is indicated as one thousand millionth of a second or nanosecond. It is evident that the speed of the former is slower than that of the latter, the reason for it being than in the former electro-mechanical devices are used while in the latter electronic devices are made use of. It is claimed that computers can serve as a panacea fcr all the existing ills libraries since these can be made use of for performing efficiently all sorts of jobs from the procurement of the reading materials to their organisation and use.

In another words, these include the acquisition, classification and cataloguing and the circulation and use of the reading materials besides making provision for information and retrieval systems. The Computer-based book order System of the Michigan University library started with the use of 1401 Tape Computer and the present type of 360/40 computer. The system consists of the following processes:

1. The name and address of the book-sellers or suppliers are stored in a disk file and each one of them is assigned a number.
2. The book orders for the books to be procured are key-punched and each of the book-sellers is identified by the number alloted to him as stated in (i) above.
3. The orders are batched and sent to the data processing Centre on the campus twice a weak. On the following days, ten copies of the order forms are received by the library alongwith pre-punched cards in triplicate for each order and a list of orders according to each book budget a location besides an undated cumulative supplementary list representing all new orders placed in the library system and all transactions done against the orders placed earlier.
4. Out of the ten copies of the order forms, two copies are mailed to the book supplier and the third copy is field in the order by the order number, while the remaining seven copies are field in a separate file to be used for classification and cataloguing work.

5. The pre-punched cards serve various purposes, namely to indicate receipt of the book the need to pay the bill, to count the books added to the stock and to remove the order card from the order file in case the book is classified and catalogued.
6. The cumulative supplemental outstanding order file is passed against the budget allocation and statistics files every fortnight which helps in printing the up-to-date position of funds so as to help the Order Section Incharge to control new orders. In this way, two supplementary order tapes are printed every month for bringing up to date the master outstanding order file, indicating the position of each order at that time.
7. Letters for the unsupplied items are issued.
8. An Expenditure Statement is prepared monthly. It indicates the amount already spent up-to-date and the amount which is still unspent.

Advantages

1. Many repetitive jobs are performed at one and the same time, thereby reducing the number of staff members for the Order section.
2. An accurate, up-to-date-and automatic information is made available about the latest position of each book order placed there by helping to avoid unnecessary duplicate ordering.
3. An accurate up-to-date and automatic information is made available about the latest position of each head of the book fund i.e., how much amount has already been spent and how much is in balance thereby either to limit future orders or to accelerate the pace of orders so as to utilise the funds in time.

The Yale university library system provides for all the processes through which a book has to pass through the moment it is selected for purchase and is made available for use by the readers.

In the Cornell university library system, an order-search from is used for placing a book order which remains there alongwith the L.C. cards upto the time of receipt of the book. In case, L.C. card is not available machine generated orders for L.C. cards are produced automatically.

Besides in three other University libraries the On-Line Systems are in use. These include the "LOLA Library On-Line Acquisitions Sub-System Washington University Library "Rice University's On-Line Acquisition System and "The University of California at Irvine's On-Line Acquisition System".

The files system has been designed to perform all technical services and processes consisting of various separate sub-stems of which one is the Acquisitions sub-system performs the following seven functions:

1. Preparing an entry indicating request for purchase.
2. Preparing a book selection entry and its checking.
3. Preparing a book order and its processing.
4. Receiving the book.
5. Processing Bills,
6. Preparing a standing order plan.
7. Preparing a report of the books received.

The second system at the Rice University in based on MARC II tapes and holdings at eighteen libraries of the Gulf Coast which are cooperating in the project. In this system, when a suggestion for the purchase of a book is received, the above record is first checked up to know whether the book in question is already in one of the libraries. If it is there, a report to this effect is generated but if the book is not available in any of the libraries but if the information is available in the file, the order for the book is added to database.

Simultaneously, a multiple order from and receipt card in order to update the record are generated and the cost of the book is debited to book fund. In case the order relates to multiple volumes a card for each volume is produced.

If the information about the book is not available in the file i.e. data, the details of the order are included in the holdings and the non-order file. On receipt of the ordered book, a cataloguer work sheet is produced which is used to correct, and update the existing record before catalogue cards for the book are prepared. In this system, a teletypewriter, called CONTROLMATIC Model 37, is used to supply to the cooperating libraries the current information received from the Library of Congress besides the preparation of classified extracts and the card listing to be used by Book Selection as a book selection tool.

The third system at the university of California at Irvine makes use of IBM 360/50 along with a central core memory of 512 K. It consists of two sub-systems i.e. book found accounting and purchase order writing. The first sub-system is to record, process and make available financial information regarding the book fund. The second sub-system besides writing purchase orders is to debit automatically the cost of book ordered besides conversion of the foreign currencies.

The acquisition, processing and control of periodicals have been eluding a permanent solution due to their idiocyncrasies. In many cases, the periodicals have been controlling the librarian instead of the librarian controlling the periodicals. The latest method to bring them under control takes the help of the computer, which is considered by many a panacea for various ills of library jobs including those of processing and controlling of periodicals and serials. Though efforts to develop a computerized system were started in the 1940's yet the first important system was designed and developed as late as 1962 only which was fully put into operation in 1964. The earlier systems were using computers for keeping parallel records on manually-run systems, whereas the latter system discontinued their use.

The periodical's work involves the following main jobs:

1. Ordering and Bill Passing.
2. Receiving supply.
3. Claiming the unsupplied periodicals.
4. Completing the volumes and sending them for binding.
5. Classification and cataloguing.
6. Preparing lists of Holdings and Union lists.
7. Administrative Control.

To perform these functions efficiently, various computer-based systems have been brought into use. In India also, computer is being used for the acquisition, processing and controlling of periodicals. Most of these systems have the following components of records, inputs and outputs, with, however, minor variations besides converting the existing manual file onto a magnetic tape.

Inputs

i. Location Mark.

ii. Call number.

iii. Title.

iv. Periodicals holdings information with years and volumes.

v. Month and year of the latest issue received in the library.

vi. Source of supply i.e. either by purchase, gift or exchange.

vii. Fund Allocation.

viii. Supplier and his code number.

ix. Period of subscription.

x. Unique Identification number for each periodical title in the file.

xi. Frequency of publication i.e. number of issues per volume and number of issues per year.

xii. Expected dates of publication and receipt in the library.

xiii. The existing position of a periodical i.e. whether it is active or not.

xiv. Binding Code Numbers and other Binding Instructions.

xv. Expected dates of the receipt of TCI, i.e. Title Contents and Index pages.

A Mnemonic Title, i.e. Abbreviated Title is used for the purpose of checking the receipt of a periodical issue.

Outputs

In most of the systems referred to above, the outputs consist of the following:-

i. *Master File List* which is an alphabetical list of periodicals, by Main Entry, received in the library indicating details of periodicals holdings of the library, is meant for staff use.

ii. *Public Holdings Printout,* also an alphabetical list of periodicals by title or main entry which is meant for public use and consists of daily, weekly and monthly lists. These lists are very simple and contain only such information as is relevant to the users.

iii. Supplement printouts which include daily receipts to be cumulated weekly.
iv. Non-receipt And Claim List for all the overdue issues of periodicals.
v. Titles List indicating the list of periodicals received in the library and their location but without the information regarding the total number of volumes held by a library.
vi. Subject List for public use i.e. subject-wise list of periodicals.
vii. Shelf List i.e. A classified list of periodicals with information about holdings.
viii. Duplicate Lists i.e. lists of all periodicals of which more than one copy are received in the library.
ix. Cross-References List
x. Subscription Agent List.
xi. Active Titles List.
xii. Inactive Titles List.
xiii. On Order List.

Advantages

1. A Computer-based periodicals System enables a better access to the periodicals records to the staff.
2. It provides better service to the users.
3. It provides more accurate records.

Disadvantages

It involves huge expenditure for the conversion of the existing manually operated periodicals file onto the magnetic tape. Development costs of a computer system are exorbitant which are lost over a period of time.

The cost of continuing operation of computer-based periodical system is not less than that of the manual system. Rather, in some cases, it may be even double of the latter, although final estimates are not available. In the computer-based system the time taken for checking a title is not less than in the manual system. However the following few recent developments in the computer application to periodical systems which are under way may be helpful in improving situation:

The library of Congress MARC Serials Format will serve as a communication format for periodicals between a reporting library and a receiving library in respect of the following:

i. The national Union catalogue symbol for a reporting library.
ii. Periodicals Holdings information.
iii. The period of periodicals available
iv. Retention information.

Standard serial numbers

The second development is the use of an International Standard periodicals Number, officially called the American Standard identification Number, for serial publications which is specifically useful for periodicals checking work. This number is to consist of seven decimal digits besides an eighth check digit.

Periodicals standard format and arrangement

This format provides guidelines as to where and how the bibliographical information which is essential to identify a periodical should appear. On the front cover of the format, the following information is provided.

1. Volume number.
2. Issue number in Arabic numerals.
3. Date of issue.
4. Code number of the issue for the identification of a periodical.
5. An abbreviated title.

The use of computer in cataloguing e.g. MARC I Pilot project was started in November, 1965 by the Library of Congress. The main aim of this project was to distribute Library of Congress cataloguing in a machine-readable from to various libraries for the reading materials received by them so as to facilitate them to meet the explosion of knowledge and the increasing demand for easy and quick provision of required information.

The MARC II was completed in 1967 with the development of a new format capable of transferring bibliographical data to the receiving libraries. The system consists of the following stages:

1. It presupposes the existence of a centralized or co-operative classification and cataloguing system on the pattern of that of the Library of Congress.
2. It also requires that the participating libraries of the programme should install computers and appoint programmers in their respective libraries.
3. The Computer-Based MARC Cataloguing System consists of the following main sections or programmes:
   (1) *MARC Maintenance Programme* for keeping the MARC file up-to-date- by means of the weekly tapes received from the Library of Congress.
   (2) *MARC Selection Programme* for selecting entries from the MARC tapes, converting character codes, preparing a record in a format suited to an individual library and for printing two proof copies to be used by cataloguers of the library.
   (3) *MARC Correction Programme* for editing the selected entries preparing the proof copy of the edited list, punching cards for using in converting to paper tapes and for typing book

cards and spine labels in case a Flexowriter is used.

(4) *MARC Card Print Programme* for printing catalogue cards for the selected items may be presorted and alphabetized filing purposes.

(5) *Update-Generate Programme* for updating the Master file and generating the entries and changing for print files.

(6) *The Weekly Print Programme* for printing the weekly supplements for the printed catalogues and the list of new books by call number.

(7) *The Monthly Pint Programme* for bringing up-to-date the print files of the catalogues, and printing monthly supplements and a list of new books. These monthly supplements are cumulated to print the full catalogue.

Advantages of the system

1. A centrally prepared catalogue can be distributed to the receiving libraries in a machine-readable form.
2. In spite of increasing acquisitions the catalogue can be kept-up-to-date without employing additional staff.
3. The production cost of card catalogue on the computer is lesser than that of purchasing the Library of Congress catalogues cards.
4. The MARC tapes can be utilized for acquisition functions i.e. selecting and ordering and claiming unsupplied books without any additional cost.
5. The MARC tapes can be used for producing conventional card catalogue by the subscribing libraries as demonstrated by the University of Toronto.
6. The MARC data can also be used for producing book catalogues as demonstrated by the Washington State Library.

Limitations of the system

George Piternick points out the following few limitations of the Machine-Readable catalogue system:

1. The MARC record for any title is almost similar to the conventional bibliographic record, as such it inherits all its limitations.
2. The MARC format will be limited, at least for the next few years, to the English language books because the MARC character set is severally limited in respect of special characters and diacritical marks.
3. The time gap between the creation of MARC record and a catalogue record copy by the participating library which is inherent at present in the existing card production methods of the Library Congress, will not be removed until and unless both the cards and tapes are prepared from the same machine-readable record.
4. Expending on account of machine time by the participating libraries will go on increasing in view of the weekly shipment of about 1.200 records or about 62,000 records annually requiring 15,000 feet of magnetic tape.

Latest developments in the system

The COMARC project has been taken up by the library of Congress with the financial help from the Council of Library Resources. Under this project, the Library of Congress receives records based on Library of Congress Cataloguing representing those of selected libraries which have converted their catalogues into MARC format. These records are to be checked with the Official Catalogue of the Library of Congress for updating and redistribution through the MARC distribution system.

The Computer Output Microfilm (COM) was developed in the U.S.A. by Stromberg Carlson Company.

It used the Charactron tube for projecting the computer output onto an unexposed film at high speed. The Charactron cathode ray tube was invented in the early 1950's which was responsible for displaying the results of computer processing on the phosphor-coated face of a television screen. Later on, a microfilm was attached to the screen of a television so that the information given by a computer was recorded. This device was responsible for the invention of Computer On Microfilm.

The latest types of computers which were capable of recording more than 100,000 characters per second were responsible for the replacement of electro-mechanical line-printers were, in their turn capable of printing 1,200 lines per minute each line having a width of 132 characters. Further a COM is capable of recording photographically a full page at a time as compared to a line only printed by a line-printer.

A microfilm has another advantage over the paper in the sense that the microfilm has the capacity of storing more information in a particular amount of space as compared to that of his paper equivalent as the microfilm of 105 mm x 148.75 mm size can store 225 pages of text with the reduction ratio of 42:1 into this computer, microfilms having 16mm or 105 mm width are fied. The former are wound in spools or cartridges while the latter are cut into microfiche. The end product of a Computer Output microfilm is a magnetic tape which contains the requisite bibliographic information besides the concerned printing and format control codes provided for the final images. This magnetic tape afterwards enters the said computer machine thus exposing a master micro-negative through which a microfilm master is developed and duplicate copies are prepared from the negative through which a microfilm master is developed and duplicate copies are prepared from the negative.

Pre-requisites for maximum output

In the following situations, the computer Output Microfilm can be helpful in ensuring optimum output:

i. There is data file in a machine readable form.

ii. The facility of a computer is available.

iii. The data is of such nature which requires frequent sorting and reorganisation.

iv. The data is to be printed out in cumulated from for mass distribution.

v. The readers are ready to use the material in microfilm form.

Advantage of COM

If the library catalogue is to be produced in microfilm from instead of a book form, the following may be major advantages of using a COM:-

i. *Easy to handle* As compared to computer print-out the microfilm or micro-fiche are less bulky and thus are easy to handle.

ii. *Compact storage* Because of their lesser bulk, the microfiches & microfilms take lesser space as compared to card catalogue or printed book form catalogue.

iii. *Less Expensive Storage & duplication* Because of their lesser bulk, the microfilm or microfiche catalogues are lesser expensive so far as their storages is concerned. Similarly, duplication of microfiche is much less expensive than their master copies once the negative are available i.e. their cost ranges between one tenth to one-hundredth of their master copies.

iv. *Cumulations are less costly* As the catalogues are to be kept uptodate, so frequent cumulations are essential. In case of printed book form catalogue the cumulations take much time and are quite costly & still remain out-of-date, whereas the microfilm editions produced by computer are less costly.

v. *Requires no Binding* The microfilm edition of catalogues being self-contained require no binding and hence lot of money is saved on that count.

vi. *Takes lesser time* As compared to conventional printed book form of catalogues the production of up-to-date COM microfilm catalogues which are capable being used immediately takes much less time i.e. it takes between 24 hours to 48 hours only.

vii. *Less production and Distribution Costs* Not only the microfilms are lesser costly than paper but their distribution is also much cheaper than a book because these can be sent by air mail at lesser cost as their weight is light than that of the book.

viii. *Easy availability of microfilm* The microfilms are much more easily available as compared to paper.

Limitation of COM

The following are few limitations of COM when used for library catalogue applications:

1. ***Needs Costly apparatus***

   Not only the COM equipment is costly and is out of the reach of each library but it also requires costly microfilm readers at various and places.

2. ***Limited supply of COM apparatus***

   Very few libraries in the world have COM service bureaus. Hence they have very little utility for majority of the libraries. Moreover, their rentals are so high that majority of the libraries can afford to avail of their services.

3. ***Limited number of type founts and styles***

   Similarly, very few stylised type-founts are available

which restrict their use throughout the world. For example, except for few Japanese character sets, most of the COM machines use the Roman alphabet. As such, in the countries using other than Roman alphabet, the utility of COM machines is very much limited.

4. ***Preparation of paper copies is difficult***
In case paper copies of microfilmed matter are required it will cost much because the equipment for enlarging paper copies from film negative needs special equipment which is not only available at each point of service but is very expensive also.

However, these limitations of COM can be overcome. The COM machines are being used by various libraries for other library purposes also which include the maintenance of circulation records in process ordering information for acquisition and feeding cumulation and publication of catalogues directories and yearbooks etc.

The OCLC started in August 1970 is a non-profit Corporation which was originally planned to be a network of academic libraries but now it has more than 700 user libraries with 1200 terminal including types of libraries including one national library i.e. the national Agricultural Library. Major portion of its budget is composed of fees received from non-Ohio Libraries i.e. in 1974-75, more than 62% or 1,213,330 out of a total budget of 1,956, 981 came from non-Ohio Libraries. It is an line system. Its data base consists of the LC MARC records, catalogue entries contributed by its member user libraries.

Advantages

1. The system is very effective as the response time for title searches was 25-30 seconds.
2. Since it has adapted the battelle System the OCLC

enables its users at remote places to search the central catalogue by author, title and subject approaches.

3. Its common products include computer line-printed catalogue cards besides spine and book labels accession lists and OCLC catalogue tapes for the purpose of producing COM catalogues.

The new systems which will provide genuine on-line cataloguing include the following.

(i) Washington Library network.

(ii) The university of Chicago Library System.

(iii) The New York public Library System.

Many computer-Based On-Line real-Time Circulation Systems have been devised during 1960's beside many other data collection and batch systems. These include the following.

(a) The State University of New York at Buffalo's Real-Time Library Circulation system.

(b) The Illinois State Library On-Line Circulation control System.

(c) The on-Line Circulation Control System at Midwestern University.

(d) The Bell laboratories Library real-Time Circulation System.

In the first system an IBM 2741 typewriter terminal and the CDC 6400 computer are used. It needs borrower's Identification card but does not require any book card.

To issue a book the borrower's identification card number and the call number of the book to be issued are passed into the computer by means of the typewriter and the typed matter is inserted in the book. Thus completing the charging of the book, this transaction needs 20 seconds. This system handles more than 300,000 per annum at the State university Library of new York at Buffalo. It has the capacity of hooking into the system of the branch Libraries circulation work. In this system the computer can be asked through the terminal of find out the position of any item. Moreover, overdue notice and circulation statistics can be processed automatically. In this system the master circulation file consists of charged books only instead of the shelf list or other record of complete holdings of a library.

The second system which came into operation at the Illinois State Library operates on an IBM 1710 system using IBM 1031 terminals as inputs. It needs punched book cards and borrower's card. For issuing a book, the borrower's card and the book and card are inserted in the badge section of the terminal. To find out whether the borrower is a valid borrower, the programme calls for the master file of borrowers. In case the borrower is a valid user, his number and the information about the book are transmitted to the computer for final editing. After final editing, the information is put on the daily transaction pack in consecutive order to facilitate its further processing after few hours later on. Thus the issue work of a book is complete and the book is handed over to the borrower after due date slip is inserted in the book. At the time of return of a book its call number and cutter number are checked from the book card and the reserve list and the returned cards are arranged in consecutive order with daily returns pack. If a book being returned is already reserved by a borrower the computer sends the information to the 1033 printer terminal which provides the call number, Cutter number, borrower's number and the date of reservation of the book. After, it, the returned book is handed over to the Reservation Assistant for further action.

In the evening the computer lists and punches one cards for each transaction of the day besides sorting them into Dewey Cutter and serial number orders. After this, a programme for updating the record is called in the computer for merging the sorted transaction with the master circulation record. This programme called CIRCUP takes up the transactions one by one for necessary action. In case of a discharge of a book it removes it from the master file but if it is a case of an issue of a book, it adds the information to the master file.

The programme called DUE NOT prepares a new master file whenever it is updated besides printing the daily statistical information in the classified order by Dewey Decimal Classification. This system is not only capable of printing the overdue notice for borrowers alongwith their mailing addresses, but also provides monthly statistics about the use of library. In this system, the book ID cards are generated from the shelf list kept on punched cards but it has not been made to serve as a basic record for circulation purposes. It is claimed that in this system the average cost per transaction comes to about 32 percent besides cutting down the number of staff members employed in the circulation section from twenty-two to nine only. Further this system works on a time sharing basis. In other words an interrupt feature controlled by 1026 controller, allows the central processing unit to work only when the information to be handled is fed into it.

For issuing a book the book card and borrower's card/badge are inserted into IBM 1031 data collection system. Before the issue of the book, the processing of the computer is interrupted for finding out whether the borrower is a valid borrower which takes about second of CPU time. If valid the printer 1033 prints a book slip to be inserted in the issued book. Thus the book is issued. The total time taken in charging a book is about 10 seconds of returning a book, the information about its reservation if any is passed on to the circulation

Assistant automatically because of the on-line updating of the circulation file.

Advantages of the system

This system automatically provides to the circulation desk information about the reserved book borrowers membership validity due date of return of the books fines due and other statistical data besides printing a daily circulation file. Like the Illinois State Library's circulation system, this system also does not use the shelf list as the basic record for circulation purpose.

The real Time circulation control system invented by the Bell Laboratories called BELLREL is one of the latest in the series. It uses 360/40 computer to which are linked by Dataphone the terminals kept in three different libraries. Each of the three libraries keeps two terminal with keyboard, printer and card read facilities. In the system, a Union list of all three libraries is maintained which can help in finding out the position of every book stocked in the libraries of the system i.e. indicating whether a book is available in a library and can be got issued. Similarly, Direct Access Files maintained in the system provide information about the total book collection of a library i.e. shelf list and the position of the books issued and reserved. The system can performı 22 transitions related to issuing, returning and reservation of books besides other queries about them.

The system batch processes daily issue lists, pre-due and over due notices, lists of books in great demand and other related statistical information. It is claimed that the system can handle more than 300,000 transaction annually. However, in charging it takes about 23 seconds which is more than that taken by the three other systems described above and many of the manual systems.

A Computer-based classification system is being

experimented at the Documentation Research and Training centre, Bangalore. It is based on Colon Classification Schedules. The following procedure is followed for the purpose.

1. The schedules of Colon Classification are transferred on tape which include the schedules of Basic Classes Special Isolates and Common Isolates.
   For this purpose a punched card with 80 columns is used which provides the above-mentioned information a follows
   (a) Basic Classes 1-8 columns
   (b) Basic Subject Terms 9-40 columns
   (c) Number of reels of tapes locating special isolates schedule 41-48 columns
   (d) Indication for card sequence 49-80 columns
2. The Kernal term of the document to be classified are fed into the computer.
3. In the synthesis procedure the compotents of a required class number are picked in the sequence in which they should be synthesized manually according to the set principle and postulates.
4. The computer assigns automatically the appropriate class number to the document in question.

Computer Based Inter Library Loan Systems

In order to facilitate the provision of material requested on inter-library loan basis, the use of computers and other latest telecommunication devices in being made increasingly in U.S.A, UK and Canada. These include the following devices:

1. Tele fascimile transmission.
2. Long Distance Xerox
3. Tele type.
4. Telex.
5. Computers.

The following are the important systems in operation which make use of one or more the above-mentioned electronic transmission devices for inter-library purposes:

Intrex

It is a device of facilitate speedy fascimile transmission of full texts of books, journals reports and other research materials requested on inter-library loan basis.

A. H. Robins Library Richmond Virginia Projects

The system started at the A. H. Robins Library, Richmond, Virginia makes use of the following equipment for processing inter library loan requests:

(i) IBM 360 computer

(ii) Four part Form using NCR Paper

(iii) Worksheet containing the names of its four major suppliers.

Other systems

(i) LDX; University of California

The LDX is a telefacimile system which provides 135 lines per inch and electrostatic printing on paper. Only single pages can be transmitted. It is a costly system. But it is speedy one.

(ii) University of Nevada Experiment.

(iii) Teletype

There are about 1000 libraries which use own teletype machines. Under this system, the massage is typed on teleprinter alongwith punched tape equipment. The message is produced in a visible form 100 words a minute.

In U.S.A, the first teletype was installed in 1950 at the Racine and Milwaulkee Public Libraries while in Europe, such a system was installed in 1955 at the Manchester Central Libraries. In Canada, the

Scarborough public Library got the equipment in 1967.

Telex

The system of Telex is being increasingly used by libraries in the United Kingdom. More than 150 libraries have already provided this facility which include about 8000 libraries in their network. The rent is nominal i.e. about 5sh 6d. This is being used increasingly by the national Lending Library for Science and Technology, Boston, Spa.

A Computer-Based Information Storage and Retrieval System consists of the following two phases:

Storage, Feeding and Storage of Information In the Computer

It consists of classification and cataloguing of the books and other reading materials forming the input of the system and transferring the catalogue entries on to the magnetic tape and getting its print-out, if required. This catalogue on tape is to updated by adding new entries and correcting the existing entries, if necessary, and getting a print-out of the updated catalogue.

Retrieval-search, selection and answering the Query

The second phase consists of (a) preparing the Reader profile record i.e. the recording the Readers Queries and transferring them on to the tape and updating them, (b) arranging a dialogue between the reader and the computer through the language of the system, (c) selecting the bibliographical details of the relevant books from the catalogue on tape (d) transferring the selected entries on to the magnetic tape, and (e) getting a print-out of these entries, providing a copy to the reader and transferring them on punched cards if necessary. In this process the following may be used:

1. Computer-There are different kinds of computers

which might be used in the system e.g. IBM 360/50 and 360/67, ICL 1903 etc.

2. Magnetic Tape, punched cards or punched paper tape.
3. Magnetic tape deck, Card reader, line-printer, Electric typewriters.

However, these may vary from one system to another depending upon various kinds of input items, the kind of catalogue the kind of vocabulary of the kernel ideas used for identifying subjects of documents and readers queries the kind of computer used or available and the kind of output required.

Advantages

1. Facilitates retrospective and selection of documents as and when demanded by a user.
2. Provide periodically current awareness service i.e. Selective Dissemination of Information.
3. Facilitates the acceptance of reader's queries in the language of the system.
4. Provide the reader with a documentation list or a retrospective bibliography for his use.
5. Provide the service in an automatic and speedy way.

The following are some of the important Information and Retrieval System which are in operation in various parts of the globe:

1. Defence Documentation Centre (ASTIA) Arlington, Virginia.
2. Medlars.
3. Western Reserve university centre for Documentation and Research, Cleveland.
4. US Naval OTS, California's Uniterm Indexing.

5. University of pennsylvania Institute of Cooperative Research.
6. National Bureau of Standards U.S.A.
7. Technical Information Centre, Electronic and Radar Development Establishment, Bangalore.
8. Autometed Data Processing System, INSDOC, New Delhi.
9. German Computer Centre of Machine Methods in Documentation, Frankfurt.
10. Ship Analysis and retrieval project.
11. VINITI
12. JICST
13. Technical Information Department Lockheed Aircraft Corporation Marietta, Georgia.
14. Documentation on Patents at Shell International Research Maatschappij, NV., The Hague.
15 Indian Institute of Petroleum Dehradun, U.P.
16. IBM Information Retrieval Satellites at the IBM Technical Information Retrieval Centre, Armonk, New York.
17. LC MARC System. It provides information and retrieval service also.
18. Project MAC at the Massachusetts Institute of Technology.

Information system and library network

In this respect, the United States of America has made much progress besides the United kingdom and some of the European countries whereas India has yet to take concrete steps in this regard except that the government of India has decided to establish NISSAT.

Critique of Computers

It is claimed that the application of computers to libraries would usher in a new era of progress and development as it will bestow the following advantages:

(i) It will make everything effortless.

(ii) It will perform the jobs with the speed of light.

(iii) It will help save money.

(iv) It will help transferring computer programmes from one place to author without extra expense.

(v) It will help in economising in future programming because programmes can be converted to later generation service by sharing computers with others.

(vi) It will help in saving money when many separate processes are integrated into a system.

(vii)It will provide better and more service to the readers.

Disadvantages

Among those persons who are sworn enemies of computers, the name of Ellsworth Mason is worth mentioning. Ellsworth mason, while discounting all the so-called advantages of computers, strikes a note of warning to those who want to use computers in libraries in the following words, Anyone who computerizes at this ;point time is hitching his wagon to a falling star... Computerizing library operations at present and projected costs and with foreseeable results, is intellectually and fiscally irresponsible and managerially incompetent.

Thought refuting most of the charges of Ellsworth Mason against computerization of libraries, Mrs. Henriette D. Avram, agrees with him in principle when she states that Mr. Mason certainly is correct in criticizing much of what has been done in library automation but is wrong to draw the conclusion that all efforts are misdirected doomed to failure. A poorly designed project does not prove that library functions cannot be automated; it proves that a disaster is a disaster. It is true that large amount of money have been expended and there have not always been positive or meaningful results.

Remedies

Lawrence Auld suggests the following ten practical and useful ways for preventing failure in library automation and for making it a success.

1. Motivation based on clearly defined goals;
2. Effective communication between librarians and computer people;
3. Logical and complete analysis of the system carefully executed programs, and abundant documentation;
4. Constant feedback of the system's day to day operations to the systems analyst and programmer;
5. Flexible and adaptable programs.
6. A competent computer operator;
7. Computer machinery capable of performing the tasks required;
8. A high priority for computer services to the library;
9. Adequate budgetary support' and
10. Positive long term commitment by top management both now and in the further.

The first Indian computer was developed and built in 1956 art the Tata Institute of Fundamental Research, Bombay with some imported components while the second computer was built by the University of Jadavpur, Calcutta in 1963 in collaboration with the Indian Statistical Institute Similarly the Bhabha Atomic research Centre, Bombay has developed a small but high-speed digital computer for real time applications.

At present in India many public and private sector firms have started manufacturing computers. These include besides others the Hindustan Computers Ltd..., New Delhi and the Delhi Cloth Mills and Data products. Delhi. It is claimed that the Business Computer No HCL--8C manufactured by the former corporation costing Rs. 83,500 can repay its cost within two years besides providing various direct and indirect benefits. The computer industry is likely to get a boost due, to the recent policy-decision taken by the Government of India to reject the proposal by the American multinational computer firm IBM to continue to operate in India as a 100% foreign equity company under the foreign Exchange regulation Act besides establishing a computer Maintenance Corporation under the control of the department of Electronics to take over the servicing and repair activities of foreign computer the British company ICL has already agreed to dilute its equity. However, it has been reported that IBM has decided to wind up its business from India within the next six months.

The number of computers in India went up to about 250 in 1975-76 ranging from the small-sized Honeywell 400 to the largesized IBM 370/155. Twenty-nine universities in 17 States of the country have computer facilities which include IBM--1620 (5), IBM 360 (2), IBM 1130 (6), TDC--316 (8), TDC--12 (6), R--1020 (1), and B--5700 (1), besides, the Himachal Pradesh University Simla has procured for its Department of Physics a mini computer Model No. 1101 manufactured by the Delhi Cloth Mills and Data Products, Delhi which is being used mainly for mathematical and scientific calculation. The important institutions which are at present making use of computers for information processing include the INSDOC, New Delhi BARC, TIFR. PRL, DRTC, IIT NIC; and IIT. These institutions use the following of computers:

IBM 360/44; IBM 370/55;

IBM 1401, IBM--7044, IBM 1620;

ICL--1901, CDC--3600 and Honeywell--400.

Similarly they use the following programming Language

PL/1; SPS, COROL; Autocoder

FORTRAV IV

However these different types of software programmes in various types of computes cannot be used without modifications. In the Government of India the names of the following five Departments are worth mentioning which have been using one or the other type of computer for various types of application from the years mentioned in brackeds:

1. Planning Commission.
2. Registrar General of India.
3. Institute of Agricultural Research Statistics.
4. Department of Statistics.
5. Meteorological Department.

In short it is evident that since mid-fifties computers in India are not only being used increasingly in performing various jobs in libraries information centres and Governments Departments but are also being developed and built by public and private sectors. As future is bright in India especially due to the establishment of various such, their national and Regional Information Centres viz NISSAT DESIDOC besides about 600 Local Information Units located in the various government departments, industrial organisations and other R and D establishments, Steps are also being taken for establishing sectoral Information Centres, especially FOSTIC, ICA, NICL, and MTIC besides various other industries. Whereas the first computer was installed in mid-fifties of the century at the Indian Statistical

Institute, Calcutta mainly for the scientific and research purpose while for business purposes the first computer was installed in India by a U.S. oil firm, their number went up to 170 in June 1972. 15 are installed in Bangalore 46 in Bombay, 18 in Calcutta 20 in Delhi while remaining 68 are installed in other places in the country.

Further out of a total of 170 computer installations 80 are used by business and industry while the Government, educational institutions research establishments and public, utility services and other organizations use 14, 20, 21, 23 and 2 respectively. This information has been revealed by a study undertaken by the NITIE which was sponsored by the United Nations Industrial Development Organization. The complications of managing the sensitive and complex demands of the computer in libraries re infinite and incessant.

Coupled with the fact that the computer in the hands of those derived from English stock tends to invest them with the emotional state of a Latin behind a driver's wheel this condition accounts for the fact that, even after twenty years, library computerisation not infrequently resembles the Place de l'Etoile during rush hour. While the basic problems of freedom from careful cost control, and decisions based on institutional egofulfillment rather than users' needs are still with us to a considerable degree, whatever its degree of success, the widespread application of the computer has brought changes in the way that libraries are run that were not anticipated.

The immediate impact on library management came with the creation of the computer unit in the library, which began in the early 1960s. Computers were introduced into libraries with all the subtlety of a spear thrust in the groin, or the crash of a satellite in a back-yard swimming pool. Their rise in library economy coincided with the post-Sputnik decade, which spewed forth on education in the United States and elsewhere a flood of gold undreamed of in human history. Unlike the River Alpheus which cleansed the Augean stables, this flood left tidy barnyards all over the land hip-deep in sharn. In retrospect, despite the material advantages which remain as residue, the 1960s was he most destructive decade of this century.

Computers came to libraries straight out of the technology of industry, and brought with them the mentality that characterized industry during an extremely confused and self-defeating period, marked in my experience most dramatically by the production of the Boeing 747 airplane. Repeated public statements by the presidents of all major airlines agreed without exception that this airplane could not justify itself economically (ten years before oil prices jumped), but conceded they would all have to buy them because they were the latest technological development, and they had to get with it. Why they had to get with it, and what they were doing in business in the first place were never discussed. This mentality of getting with it, totally disregarding cost justification, led to the observation in 1972 by one of our leading economists, Kenneth Boulding, that although productivity, in our economy had been increasing from two to four percent a year for a century, it had hardly increased at all in recent years, when at least 100,000 computers were being used in industry. His conclusion at that time "Automation seems to be a total fraud. There is not the slightest evidence of greatly increasing productivity in manufacturing processes."

The year before, a survey of 100 American companies in eleven industry groups by a major New York consulting firm showed conclusively that investment in computers did not give a company any significant competitive advantage; in fact four of the eleven industry groups showed a negative correlation. The conclusion: companies that did well were not those with lots of computers but those with able management in depth. Nevertheless, during the 1960s the computer industry was riding high, wide, and handsome, and in the process generating some of the most repulsive personalities of the century.

At one time IBM home office managers would acknowledge privately that their salesmen were completely out of control, selling the moon with each computer, and the number of bankruptcies that attended the installation of computer processes in smaller businesses was alarming. These miracle-mongers swept into university computing centers on a wave of large academic budgets and pin-headed university president (who at that time in the United States tended to resemble industrialists in intimate ways), and they early brought pressure on the libraries to surrender to their lures. Their formula was simple, if brash-we can do anything you are doing in the library faster, better and much cheaper. Their persuaders were simple, if harsh-brass knuckles and billy-clubs. Librarianship was heralded as the whale-oil industry in petroleum times, and libraries were condemned as mismanaged, neanderthal units, dark blotches on the bright electronic screen.

Early specialists in library computerisation were for the most part recruited from the commercial world. They brought with them these simplistic views and attitudes and a very large burden of ignorance about library operations. They seemed to specialize in yanking fish out of water to teach them how to breathe the air. Quite understandably, they were accorded the enthusiasm usually reserved for Martians at a high-church picnic or burnoosed Arabs in Grosvenor Square.

From the beginning the computer unit in libraries was viewed as a foreign body, destructive to the larger organism. In time, events proved this to be the case, and this first wave of computerisers was dashed on the rocks of its own ignorance-ignorance of library operations and the demands on them, ignorance of the complexity of computerizing bibliographic projects, ignorance of the complex variations that existed in seemingly repetitive operations.

Discouraged and discredited by repeated notable failures, this first wave left or were replaced in library operations within a few years. During their tenure, there existed nearly total antagonism between them and the library staff, which they managed to keep in turmoil nearly constantly. There was no possibility of integrating them into the library in any managerial sense. The positive result of their failures was an understanding of the high degree of complexity involved in computerizing library operations.

The second wave of library computer specialists as kind of rebound tended to be librarians who had some experience with programming. In most cases, they did not have exposure in depth to an understanding of the computer, generally had not worked in other kinds of computer operations, and very few of them had high skills as programmers. They generally worked together with programmers from industrial backgrounds. This was the situation when I surveyed computer operations in eleven major university libraries in 1969, when every university of significant size had its in-house computer staff, some of them larger than ten.

On the whole the shortcoming of this generation of computerisers was inadequate programming skill, and, with the reduction of library budgets, in house-computer staffs largely disappeared in the early 1970s, although the last large staff of its kind persisted at the University of Maryland until 1978. Although this second wave of specialists was far less antagonistic to librarians, they still were held at a considerable distance, partly because they were thrust into library operations by library directors and partly because of the long drawn out agonies inflicted to their colleagues by programming methods that they prevailed.

The computer unit was still something 'out there', and if it no longer was engaged in guerilla warfare with the library staff, it nevertheless seemed to work largely at night in mysterious ways, and to slip things into operations that were not completely understood, often not needed, and even worse full of what were called 'bugs', for which there never seemed to be any truly effective exterminator. Though no longer considered the enemy, the computer unit existed for the most part despite the library staff, and could have done just as well, or badly, as a department of the university computer center.

There was much raging in the literature during this period of computer fumbling against the inherent rigidity of librarians who hated change and were obviously evil in many other ways, when you come right down to it. Re-reading these articles demonstrates how alienated computer people felt at the time, and rightly so. In thirty-five years of librarianship, which falls short of the introduction of the typewriter but encompasses the advent of microfilm, we have never seen any worthy librarian who did not embrace any new tool or machine that clearly helped do what he was doing. By its very nature, every library pullulates daily with change of every kind; nothing goes on the same from day to day in any operation, and the problems and demands shift constantly.

There are few other agencies in the spectrum of human affairs so constantly involved in change. But at least until quite recently, librarians tended to be discerning, and if the tool or machine was not obviously useful it had to prove itself before being accepted. The fact is that computer efforts in libraries from 1958 to 1970 contributed almost nothing to library computerization except disruption of library processes, fantastic waste of money, and a heritage of bitterness through arrogance that has disappeared only in recent years.

The Ohio State University Library circulation system we believe is the only significant in-house computerized system that has remained more or less intact until the present day, and it came on line late in 1970. By the end of 1970 OCLC was still in a batch card production system, BALLOTS (now ARLIN) still in its programming stage, the University of Chicago system, (offspring of the atomic bomb) was still under cloak-and-bagger cover behind vault doors, and MARC (the dinosaur with tiny brain that may yet devour us all) was still building up to solidity. The first interactive bibliographical system MEDLINE, which began in February 1972, was, in retrospect, the only highly successful library computer operation developed up until that time.

The achievements in library computerisation, then, are the product of the last seven years, and it is useful to speculate the changed conditions that made them deviate into sense and begin the Modern Age in library computerization, for which any sane operation would have waited before plunging. First and most important of all was the radical drop in library support that began to hit us in 1970 and has increased to the present day. It shook out the monkeys from the orange crop, and within three or four years stamped out library computerisation as cottage industry (every library it on IBM company).

The fact, blatantly obvious in the failures of the sixties, that skilled computer programming is one of the rarest commodities in the world (and rarely, seen in a library setting), began to be recognized, and we looked for help to the few large computer operations outside where it seemed to have focussed. The second factor, for which we had to look to England for guidance, was realization of the impossibility of local collection autonomy, and the promise of the computer as an information transmitter in a country as large and complex as the United States (conditions which influenced developments in Canada and Australia as well). This emphasized and in some ways exaggerated the importance of central production sources of basic library computer needs. Networking was in (and that rhymes with 'C' and that means Computers).

Third was the early success in producing the bricks with which we all were building-catalogue cards-by OCLC, in an area of service which we all were accustomed to buy from a central source. While MEDLARS had preceded OCLC in distributing a widespread computer service, it was remote because it serviced only doctors. But OCLC reached real people-librarians-at a central point of their existence, and we quickly learned to love it, despite its additional costs, and to look to centralized production for a whole range of our computer needs. Enter BALLOTS, WLN and a whole series of new actors to provide that lovely element, competition, so long absent from our economy, which is now getting intense. Fourth was the development in the Library of Congress of a totally computerized cataloguing system, which came very slowly and at a cost that no one has ever dared to look at, for fear that it would overthrow our national government, but with national implications. Its totality now threatens to engulf us, as discussed below.

With a new set of props under their foundations, libraries could now look sensibly, with much smaller resources, at what they could produce locally, with programming done outside the library, and the present status of the computer unit and its relationship to the management structure of the library emerged. It tends to exit in two conditions. In one condition the computer unit controls decisions on library computerisation, with the advice of concerned departments, and is itself the equivalent of a department. In the other condition, control over computerization is dispersed among the library departments, and the computer specialist provides centralized technology as a staff officer of the library director. Neither condition is totally satisfactory, and different kinds of tensions result from each.

The computer unit or computer specialist in either case represents a new type of power level within the library organization. It is central to the entire operation, a pivotal unit, with no counterpart in previous library history. It can impose changes by design or inadvertently on departments with which it is not working directly, through the interaction of parts of systems and how they are affected by adjustments in the system.

The computer specialist is never as fully integrated into the library structure as other unit heads can be. For these reasons and others, the most successful computer units seem to be those headed by a librarian, with extensive knowledge of library procedures, who has accumulated the requisite systems and programming knowledge, although we know one spectacularly successful exception to this rule. Since he generally does not do the programming, academic knowledge that enables informal interaction with outside computer programmers will suffice. This kind of a specialist can minimize the impact that changes in computer applications make on library procedures and adapt them to desirable library needs most precisely. He also, since of the same stripe, will be more approachable to his colleagues and be engaged more intensively and more often in useful conversations with his colleagues about their work, totally aside from any practical need they have for his expertise.

Computerization has changed many relationships between departments in libraries. Its largest effect is the tilt in power balance between technical processes and public services divisions, which had been reasonably evenly distributed previously, in favour of technical processes. The most dramatic instance of this shift in my experience has been that registered in the Library of congress, where the proposal to close their card catalogue precipitated a major battle between the two elements that was finally resolved in favour of technical processes. Evidence of this shift is seen in the emergence in the past five years into high levels of library administration, including the directorship, of librarians whose career had been in technical processes, formerly a rare occurrence. Within the divisions the independence of the separate units has been considerably loosened.

Departments formerly based on rather clearly defined functions have now had those functions changed on the basis of new procedures generated outside of their unit, and to a larger extent than ever before the library organization is beginning to be described in terms of processes that are heavily overlapping in their reach. Boundaries have been blurred, and tensions have arisen over control of various aspects of computerization, such as the nature of processes and the demands they will impose on the department, the kind of hardware and software to be used.

The nature, location, control, and scheduling of computer terminals are often a matter of bitter dispute.

Like elevators, they are far more economical if arranged in banks, but their cost strictly limits the number obtainable. All of these factors have greatly increased the amount and constancy of negotiation necessary to conduct relationships between departments.

A typical battle in American libraries occurs in locating the bank of OCLC terminals, which are likely, especially early in the use of the system, to be used by cataloguing, acquisitions, serials, inter-library loan, documents, reference, and even rare book librarians. While the early promise by computer-flappers in the early sixties was that every man could be his own terminal, with access to world information easily achieved by this point in time, there are a limited number that can be obtained by a library because of their cost. The matter of cost is the most frustrating aspect of the entire range of computers in libraries. We know that it can do wonders for us in the hands of competent computer managers.

The computer, in fact, presents the only longterm solution to the two most pressing problems in the entire range of librarianship-short-life paper of books, which is rapidly heading for shorter life with economic trends in paper manufacturing that are irreversible, and even shorter-life bindings (ironically called 'perfect bindings') for books, about ninety percent of which are held together by plastic smeared on the edges of loose pages at the present time. These crack after seven or eight circulations, and twenty years from now any library committed to preserving books over time will be a mass of loosely-tied sheets. The computer, of course, could store all of our texts, and pump out on demand either microform or hard copy, but the costs of doing so are astronomically beyond our reach.

The promise of locating terminals everywhere,

which of course is the highest desideratum in any information system, cannot begin to be realized, either now or in the long-term future in the declining state of library budgets. The future will see us with fewer terminals, rather than more, and struggles between departments for control will become even more acute.

All departments affected by computerisation (which includes most of them) become dependent on outside technology experts with the introduction of the computer, and this has markedly reduced their autonomy. While this often is not an entirely bad thing to happen, because departments can become rigid, it is futile to assume that basic decisions about what a department is doing and how it does it can be made better outside the department than in it, or better when having to accommodate the needs of other departments than when decided entirely on internal needs. An automated circulation system, for instance can have an impact of considerable depth on the budget, priorities, and scheduling of acquisitions, cataloguing, and collection management, that is to say, it can rearrange their use of staff and funds, and churn up long standing policies that have emerged from years of negotiation and adjustment between departments within the library and the entire range of academic experts on a campus.

The affected departments do not expect the circulation department to have an impact on them, and there is a tendency to resist or reject the new demands that should logically result from circulation information analysis. Nowhere in the costing of computer operations in a library is any account made of the cost of the time required for negotiations and the toll of these tensions on efficiency of departments placed in this new and far less secure matrix of organizational relationships, but it has to be a noticeable cost. Branches pose special problems to the main library in any dispersed system, and they are a special element in the interdepartmental relationship changes that follow computerization.

Branches tend to go their own way to a large degree. They have their own support constituency in their academic specialists on a campus whom they can bring to bear on the library and instruction. They are not constantly viewed, as internal library departments are likely to be, by staff passing through the library. Changes in their conditions to service can occur without being detected by the main library, and they impose large demands on the main library's central services for processing and information. With computerisation, the branches become far more dependent on the main library. While they may gain access to the records of the entire library system collection, which is highly desirable, this may be in the form of microfiche catalogues which they may not like. They also will lose their card catalogues.

However, centralization of the locus of collection records, if on line to branches with provision for defining whether materials are available, can remove a large burden of the curse of branch libraries to students, who are driven mad by the dispersal of books among libraries for reasons that seem insane and on a rationale that defies acceptance. The branch libraries under a campus-wide computerized circulation system like that of Ohio State University, become access points for searching the entire system and reserving books for pick-up, greatly broadening the use of materials in all the other branches and in the main library.

The intolerable delay of a minute by telephone to determine current periodical holdings, which led nationwide to branch library check-in records duplicating the main serials record, yields to sense when the delay is only ten seconds by computer. So critical have fifty seconds become in this century!

Computer application tends to standardize methodology in the branches, making transfer of staff easier and cheaper. In public library branches that must respond to rapid change in public demand for the most recent books, easy turnover of book stock is possible with a centralized computer catalogue and computerized check-out of books to the branch, instead of local card catalogues. It is also possible to generate management information about the branches for the library administration that will inform it more sensitively on a timely basis of what goes on in the branches, making them more amenable to central policy control. In general, computer applications tend to make the branches less autonomous, but in the near future we should see the processing of all their materials return to the branches, as it is facilitated by the system. Although a the present time few libraries have more than a few operations computerized, throughout the land most library departments somewhere or other have tried their little trotters at some from of automation.

Early on, some of the wildest computer money was squandered by enthusiastic fools with keypunched brains in converting shelflists to machine readable form with no foresight about what was required for multiple use of these records, and no insight into the requirements for proper bibliographical standards.

Enormous sums of money were spent in keypunching, and the resulting carloads of IBM cards lying around in closets throughout the land have scarcely been used and are mostly unusable. The University of Toronto library reports being confronted by "five separate files which had strong family resemblances but were not really compatible," resulting from keypunching that went back to 1965. Before the volume of MARC records at the Library of Congress grew large enough to dominate the scene, most computerized cataloguing records fell far short of standards for reasonable bibliographical access. The data base at OCLC still suffers from the fact that early entries into their computer from some libraries were not subject to quality control.

At present computerized cataloguing information is produced almost exclusively by the few large central on-line data bases and bought by local libraries, who enter any local records not already in the data base as well as deriving records from it. When these data bases reached the critical mass that met most of the demands for current cataloguing in smaller libraries, their use increased greatly. This point was reached when two or three of the larger research libraries joined the system and began adding their records to those generated by the computer center. The rapid formation of regional networks with multiple members was accelerated by the need for smaller libraries to have contracting, access lines, and hardware procured by a central agency, and membership in such centers as OCLC has more than doubled in the past four years. The ease of joining these systems has tended to slow the development of local on-line mini- and micro-computer systems, which pose many problems identical to those handled to badly during the first decade of library automation. Because of the mass of information in the card catalogue, in the development of local on-line systems the card catalogue may be the first to be converted or the last.

The impact of automated cataloguing on the staff of cataloguing departments has been beneficial, since one of fits early results was the eradication of inefficient hand-cataloguing operations, of which there were many.

The reason why libraries that joined OCLC early could show immediate cuts in staff was that many of them had cataloguing departments with very low productivity. Professional cataloguers who had been performing work easily accomplished by the support staff, practice that had stubbornly outlived the surge of acquisitions of the 1960s, were immediately obsolete and professionals now are restricted to original cataloguing. Except in those libraries expect in replicating inefficiencies, where professional cataloguers are used at computer terminals to summon catalogue cards.

There has been retraining of the support staff, and some reduction of total staff in the cataloguing processes. Radical staff cuts in previously efficient cataloguing departments have not occurred.

On the managers of cataloguing departments there have been new demands requiring considerable ability to understand technological processes, radical new demands for training programs, increased demands for supervision and work-flow adjustment, and infinite patience in coping with the peculiarities, changes, and failures of the on-line centers. These managers, once proudly suspicious of the flawed nature of humankind which generates the chaos in which they flourish, have now become total believers in the new magic-that once the button on the terminal is pushed the catalogue cards will inevitably come and that all the cards required in the card-set will inevitably be present in the alphabetical cumulations they receive from remote computer centers.

These changes have resulted in cataloguing processes that are more expensive than efficient hand-cataloguing, but which produce much faster processing of the current flow of acquisitions to the shelves. The cataloguing department has become a much more central department than formerly, because it is the closest in need to the data base terminals. Its high priority demands on these terminals make it a host department to other departments using the terminals in most libraries.

This department has experienced the largest change through computerization of any large library department.

Processing department, which is often absorbed into the cataloguing department, spent most of its time before computerized cataloguing maintaining files from which were drawn the bibliographical base for production of catalogue cards, an din producing the proper number of catalogue cards, in a variety of ways. This process has been entirely eliminated, and the largest cuts in staff produced by library automation have occurred in this unit. There still remains the task of filing cards in the various library catalogues, and the magnitude of this task is leading to the closing of library card catalogues in the large research libraries throughout the land.

No satisfactory substitute for the card catalogue has yet been found short of local production of catalogues in microform or on-line access to local computerised catalogues, a process that is still excessively expensive. This new condition has reduced the requirement of extremely high typing skills and high bibliographical skills in the staff of this department, making replacements easier to select, in a unit that characteristically has a high staff turnover. Order department has been computerized in both its bookeeping and its order placement functions.

One of the earliest applications of the computer to libraries, often generated by self-seekers outside of the library was to bookeeping records of the order department, which are fairly simple records subdivided into allocations of the book budget by categories. While this is a simple, commonplace computer operation in business, we have seen more of them in libraries that did not seem to work effectively than one could imagining.

By now, most of them have been straightened out, but in libraries that programmed their own systems, departure of the librarian programmer has generally left behind an undocumented system that had to be reprogrammed. These systems involve payment of vendors through code numbers assigned to each vendor, and payments to the wrong vendor occur not infrequently. Fortunately, our bills do not run into millions. These systems often make out the order forms, but the multiplecopy hand-typed order form is still in common use.

In the 1960s systems were designed to track the exact stage in the order process that each order has reached, but low use of this information has not justified its cost and effort.

At present the on-line cataloguing data banks are used by order departments for verification, which has greatly speeded up the search process. New processes have required staff retraining, but there has not been much change in the size of the staff. However, the nature of the searching, which formerly required educated, intelligent, and bibliographically skilled staff has changed, making it possible to recruit at a lower level of skill for these positions although they have not yet been downgraded in most libraries. The new demands on the manager of this department require heavy interaction with the computer specialist, negotiation for the use of terminals controlled by others, and heavy dependence on outside sources for program maintenance, re-programming, failures of the reporting schedule, and incorrectly paid bills. Like everything caught up in the forefront of the wild enthusiasm of early computerization, the butchery that resulted often made even computers run blood. At one time information generated at this point was made the basis for all other computer applications in the library from cellar to attic, with disastrous results. In 1969 saw one large research library operation that updated its circulation print-out only once every four days because of the cost of paper. In the same year, we assured at one university that computerization had for the first time given them the ability to produce totally accurate circulation records.

Computerised circulation demonstrates nicely some of the basic weakening of control that can come in a library that automates.

The library at the present time almost always depends on an outside computer for processing its data. It is not rare for these operations to wipe out completely the entire circulation record. While this can be regenerated to some degree of approximation by using previous computer tape records, there is no possibility of ever recovering completely from such a disaster. One library was about to shorten its circulation period from three weeks to two weeks, only to discover that the outside agency that handled its data was about to change to a new computer. This required total re-programming of every operation serviced by that computer, and two-and-a-half years later, when the computer operation had been converted and the library circulation system had worked its way into the re-programming schedule, it was possible to change that circulation period.

A prime example of that fact that although the computer initially can be a great accelerator of change, once imposed it becomes a powerful agent against change.

The difficulty of managerial control over programmers was demonstrated in one system that generated a daily Computer Output Microfilm circulation record. When you located a specific call number, it would tell you the date it was charged out and the date it was due, but both in Julian Dates, which completely defy normal human understanding. The record, you see, had been generated for the machine and not for the public although it was intended as a public record. This system also made it impossible to place a hold on a book currently charged out.

Although very small high school and public libraries that could in no way justify it either on functional or cost ground computerized their circulation records to get with it, there were nevertheless valid reasons for computerizing this operation in larger libraries. The volume of circulation had so swelled the bank of circulation cards in larger libraries that adding and retrieving information from them was ponderous. In addition, the process of defining overdue books and issuing recalls would churn up the files for days. The computer eased both of these problems. It also imported new problems-the difficulty of the user finding the circulation record by himself (either in a wad of print-out paper or on microfilm), the lag in updating the filing of newly charged out books (in large libraries three or four thousand on busy days), which can reach two or three days if the timing of the system misfires, and errors in records caused by system lapses in collecting or discharging data.

At present, most computerized circulation systems are remnants of local programming (some still the relicts of wild-and-woolly local library programming), and they yearn toward on-line systems, the simple and obvious condition for the solution of circulation record problems. Few can afford them. In the interim, light-pen collector systems are being used more and more, but instead of using packaged software programs (with known effects and predictable costs) these often are subjected to local programming, with all its attendant evils. Computerised circulations systems, once past the gargantuan task of keypunching cards for each book in the library, have eliminated the staff formerly used for filing and overdues, and have greatly eased the space-crush at the central circulation desk. They require very little staff training, and have imposed no great demands or the department manager.

Except at times of re-programming, when dislocations in the records (until de-bugged) are so frequent and irrational that he must become a psychiatric social worker to avert hysteria on his staff, and an international diplomat to smooth the ruffled senses of library users.

Once the shortcomings of computerized circulation systems have been absorbed by the manager, this operation becomes easier to manage than previously, since it involves far fewer workers, and so sizeable new problems. This department has become the center for three kinds of computerized information services-on-line bibliographical data bases, specialized analytical programs of statistical sources, and local service information in public libraries (occupational or carpool information, volunteer clearing houses, elected officials list and the like). These sources have in some libraries divided reference service into two sub-units for information sources and for in-depth traditional reference service.

There are now about 300 on-line data bases available for purchase. Larger libraries tend to subscribe to two or three of the most comprehensive in their fields of greatest demand with others added, as specialities and finances dictate. They are all extremely expensive, and the main-line bibliographical services are computerized versions of printed indexes with only slight extension of their coverage. Their virtue is the saving of time involved in manual searching of indexes, a factor of importance to advanced research workers.

Costs of using them tend to be passed on to the user, which eliminates use by the ordinary library user or by the staff, useful as these services could be in routine reference work. They require extensive training, study, and experience in depth of veteran professional reference librarians, preferably educated in a discipline (science, social science) in the area on which the data base focuses.

There is a certain amount of prestige connected with this retrieval that enhances the status of the librarian engaged in it. The use of COM catalogues, spread around the university, or on-line catalogues with multiple terminals, reduces the use of reference departments for card catalogue assistance, which is provided at the other access points in the system. The extension of reference power that will be possible with the advent of on-line catalogue information accessible in all the ways now possible at the card catalogue, and with expansion of ways of approaching the data base, must wait for the day when libraries can afford such services.

The added computerised services have been assumed by reference departments without additions to staff and at a time when, indeed, public service staffs are being cut all over the country. They have required transfer of skills from the lower level users (typically at the student level) to the research level user at a time when services to students is deteriorating at an alarming rate. They have imposed no perceptible burden to managers of reference departments, and have equipped them with the new magic carpet-a computer terminal, to achieve which some good librarians give up librarianship. The man in the catbird seat, the runner between the redoubts of staff and higher administration has been affected by computerization more than the rest of the library put together. In the first place he is completely without choice as to whether or not to use it. In the view of one of its exponents, "technology does not permit the luxury of not using it." At the present time, it even forbids reasoned judgment in its application. In any sensible social or economic condition, decisions about whether to use technology or what kind to use depend entirely on what you are trying to achieve and what you should buy to attain the largest library service at the level of quality you require. In a condition where magic and witchcraft predominate in any of their manifold forms the arcane rituals must be applied, though they kill the body. With the radical decline of personal confidence of librarians who shudder at the thought of being labelled obsolete, not 'with it', defenders of `the old manual system' and other cock-a-many nonsense, the magic words branded on our bosom are 'change' (for all changes are obviously good) and 'technology' (for machines are undisputed friends of man, ousting the dog from this once honoured status).

But once it is used, the Director is not off all of his hooks. There were more sound and mature directors squeezed out of their positions in the late 1960s in disputes over computerization than you could count. Ironically, they were fired for being on either side. If they did not apply the computer, because they saw the messes in library computerization throughout the land, they were pressured by the local computer boys and the administration; if they did apply the computer, with the level of results usually attained at that time, they were pressured by their agonized staff and users. The budget squeeze of the 1970s made university administrators look at the costs of what they referred to as 'free' computer time, and prudence in approaching the computers was allowed. In addition, as recounted above, programming had moved out of the library and conditions of choice had improved. The pressures on the director became less irrational. After all, any fool can join OCLC, and no one can possibly object to catalogue cards.

However, at the present time the directors of research libraries are heading into a major decision with very long term implications for the entire library, depending on which cataloguing data base they will choose to contract with. On this decision will depend a whole range of computerized processes for their library's operations (managed by an outside source), the scope of bibliographical retrieval possible within their library, and their standing in the research library community. In some libraries this also will involve major commitments of budgets. This decision now emerges from what seemed to be a simple decision four years ago of where they would buy on-line computer-produced catalogue cards.

Outside sources, as of this date, cannot to all of the work in the library, and dealing with local application of what is always an unruly technology presents the director with some of his most difficult problems. In many ways the director is the prisoner of his staff, dependent on them for information to cope with the bewildering range and numbers of complex problems that continually expand before him. However, a director with broad experience in library operations (and we are getting very many now who have very little) can review with some degree of sophistication the information supplied by most library specialists and question them when necessary.

In the case of the computer unit, however, this is virtually impossible, leaving this operation to a large extent on the honour system. The director is far more dependent on the technologist's expertise than on any other unit head. For reasons which range from frivolous to profound, the computer head's decisions are questioned by more peers in the library than are those of any other librarian. The director is left to unsnap these department rivalries. In many cases, the internecine disputes lead to hiring an outside consultant to help make decisions on a level above the emotional entanglements within the staff.

The ability to manage with any degree of sensitivity the development of a computer program in terms of its time-table, its economy of machine time and storage, its documentation (so others can run it), the avoidance of program-play (a speciality of professional programmers), and cleanness of the program to minimize misfires is almost never within the scope of the director. Someone else controls it, in the library or elsewhere. Consequently, there is a looseness of control over the computer unit that would be inconceivable in the case of any other department. And yet, this relationship is crucial in a library, especially in one dedicated to rapid change, since application of the computer can produce more change in less time than any other factor in existence short of total budget withdrawal. If the changes are not good, the resulting difficulties can take five years to repair. For all these reasons, some of the younger library directors who are beginning to emerge here and abroad are those with deep experience in computer applications.

Management information, which the computer can generate by the mile, is not used very much and generally not used effectively at any managerial level in libraries at the present time. The ability of the computer to identify exactly which books have circulated is not often used at a time when radical constriction of books budgets requires precise information about what kinds of materials to buy. At the director's level the computer is used for accounting purposes, but for cost accounting, work-flow scheduling, staff balance, collection management, resource allocation and budget preparation it is used sporadically and often very badly. A recent visit to a library discovered a monthly statement of management data about three inches high on the director's side table, including more statistics than anyone could digest and correlate in three days. Yet when the director produced for me his per-volume cost for cataloguing a book, an extremely useful statistic to have, we recognised it as being somewhat less than the cost for he catalogue cards produced by OCLC alone, the system he was using.

We believe that slowness of movement into this important area of information is the result of poor results in programming that most of us have experienced in the past. Many of the director's problems with the computer, including early detection of poor performance, could be relieved by one-line information systems, whose costs still place them a considerable way in the distance. Smaller operations, such as public library branches, with small demands for information storage can move to on-line micro-computers more easily than large and complex libraries with huge information demands, and to some extent this is happening, although movement into computerization by American public libraries has been very slow.

A sizeable portion of the library budget has been transferred to computerization and the staff to run it. Almost without exception, this constitutes additional costs, even after deducting cost savings resulting from the change. Only one major voice, Dr. Gordon Ray, President of the John Simon Guggenheim foundation in New York, has been perceptive enough to state in public that computer operations will have to be funded at the expense of conventional library services (at a time when these are being cut). This balanced view of what is giving way to supply computerized processes is seldom applied, and cost considerations seldom play a major role in decisions on library computerization. Costs experienced in system developments have a way of over running cost estimates by the experts by 60% not infrequently.

This looseness of careful cost control in such decisions is best illustrated in the application of the computer to new academic libraries that began in the 1960s and even now are drastically short of collection strength, without regard for what could have been done with the money by forgoing computerization. This use of computerization as a public relations cosmetic to disguise basic inadequacy is illustrated in such cases as the Australian library 1,500 miles from the nearest substantial collection, supporting ten Ph.D. programs on a collection of 60,000 volumes, which boasted of being computerized up to the ears. Or tiny public libraries in remote areas of the Rocky Mountains who have been forced against their better judgement into on-line systems using expensive terminals which have been foisted on them by the State Library. Or the proud report that 70% of English university and polytechnic libraries, most of them with inadequate collections, are using on-line bibliographic search services which are extremely expensive. These are computer diversions from library inadequacies. The sloppy management, or non-management of the costs of computers in libraries is not as bad today as it was ten years ago, but in the present state of library funding here and abroad, many of us should have been hung long ago for some of the things we have done. The lynchings still may take place. Computer costs are now visible enough in many library budgets to be targets for cuts by university administrations in the budget squeeze besetting the academic world.

Computerisation tends to divert more money into equipment than formerly occurred, and as we become more dependent on on-line access from multiple consoles this will become increasingly the case. As we move into microcomputers, where obsolescence is a daily rather than an annual fact, even more money will have to go into equipment replacement, and nothing short of short-term contracts at a fixed annual price on a lease purchase basis will be practical.

A final factor in the library budget is the competition generated against it on academic campuses by the computational computer center that serves faculty information needs. This is the only other large information source on campus, and it has a power base in the science and statistically-oriented social science, and language teaching faculties, and at the same time is critically important in generating research rant proposals. These departments have fairly consistently had better response to their budget requests than libraries in this country.

The critical change in the library-campus department relations brought by the computer is in our dependence on an outside computer, generally the one that handles administrative data for processing library systems. This dependence on an out house computer has reduced the library's control over its own operations to a noticeable extent. We are dependent on their choice computer on the skills of their programming staff on their schedule on changes in their program systems, and on breakdowns resulting from volume of which the library is a small part. This outside computer tells us almost without exception that our work will be done on a batch system, interactivity as we need it being far beyond their capacity. It is a constant thorn in the side of all systems.

The demand by state legislatures for rapid response to requests for what they consider to be accountability data, which they always consider to be statistical and the mounting volume of such requests has been a large factor leading computerization in libraries. Yet the ability to respond has created additional demands for information, ad has made public academic libraries even more subject to political control at a time in our history when this has become noxious. Legislatures have decreed by fiat a 20% blanket cut in all state computerization budgets. They have removed computer budgets from separate departments and centralized them in one local computer unit, with little knowledge of and no regards for the consequences. As computer budgets grow larger and state financing tightens as is likely to be the case in most states in the next few years they will be prime targets for a sweeping cut. All of these factors make for reduced control of the library over its own operations.

The very large computer systems with profound implications for libraries are MEDLARS, MARC, CONSER, BLAISE, OCLC, WLN, ARLIN, the University of Toronto system, the Canadian National Library system. Suddenly librarians are confronting big business, which these systems all are. Previously, it this occurred at all, it was on terms such as Blackwell North America's blanket order programs, that gave a wide range of choice. Instead now a choice must be made among systems, all of which impose very large demands and have large rigidities which must be absorbed, if the benefits are to be obtained. This new situation, in which most libraries of any size are involved has considerably decreased our control over our own operations. Suddenly someone else is controlling how they will be done.

The networks which are the offspring of computer tie-ups and which are leading rapidly to a national library network again require the surrender of local autonomy with no clear realization of what balance of benefits and obligations they will produce. Already the grounds on which these stand are being shifted after a few brief years. Because of data base networks, the functions of the main bibliographical centers in this country are changing and their importance is decreasing. The centrality of OCLC is being eroded by the networks, and will erode further with the incursion of WLN and ARLIN aggressively into the field the latter two requiring total acceptance of their bibliographical structure and procedures.

Looming above all is the impact of the Library of Congress on the library economy of the entire country. For a long time its handling of library cards on while we have depended since 1902, has become less concerned with its clients and more concerned with its own internal operating problems. With the completion of computerization of its cataloguing processes and the expansion of its comprehensive coverage of books published, it has now become totally free from major influence by the entire library community and has gone is own way. For some time its subject headings have been changed to suit computer reading rather than user needs. Now that shortened budgets have made it totally impossible to break away from the bibliographical data that it generates, LC is imposing a radical discontinuity on practices of the past than within a year will churn up the entire academic enterprise to furies of frustration. While early in its development of computerization the library of Congress presented the glowing picture of their catalogue totally on-line. The financial realities dictate that the catalogue generated up to the present will not be computerized. The early promises of pushing a button to change the subject headings on all pertinent records when new subject headings, more in tune with changing times and terminology, were appropriate turn out to be something we cannot afford to do. Instead, we are confronted with a split catalogue that at the same time will consist of author and subject entries that break radically from practices in establishing these formerly. It is impossible for libraries of any size not to accept these changes, and equally impossible to prevent the Library of Congress from making them.

The loss of control over our operations involved in this development is immeasurable. Academic libraries ill spend the next five years trying to make their faculty believe that we in no way connived in the chaos that descended upon us on January 2, 1980 and trying to make them believe that there is some point in continuing to support our budgetary requests, and that money hitherto spent on libraries should not be diverted to some other more useful corner of the campus. It is the ultimate take-over of libraries by government, but not even that because LC will not have even token responsibility for any of us. After all, we are completely free not to use their cataloguing data directly through networks if we so choose, even though financially it is impossible not to do so. While the computer has helped us perform some of our tasks in libraries to a large degree its potential to help us has not been used, largely because of the extreme rarity of high quality programming skills and what was produced by lesser brethren in the past. Computerization has led to some reductions in standards in the error rate in circulation and bookkeeping records, in unchecked catalogue cards and has virtually eliminated prompt and accurate repair of errors when detected. The sum of what of the computer has done for us in the library has increased our total costs over efficient hand operations. Our achievements in the past seven years have consisted in getting up operating systems that work and in operating participatory networking data bases bit to only a slight degree a re we doing things whose end results differ much from what we were doing before. As one commentator on the computer scene put it "It's like hitching a rocket to a wagon."

Balanced against these achievements have been major losses in control over own operations caused by dynamics of the computer in our libraries, In its connections to networks, and in national computerization policies largely uncontrolled by libraries. While libraries in the further may be managed from a remote center, local management has been greatly impaired. For a number of reasons among which the computer looms large, libraries will become in the near future less satisfactory for more people than before and their importance in their institutional setting will gradually decrease.

In this fast changing world information technology and information management are going to play an important role. Information has already been recognised as one of the basic resources for the socio-economic development of a country. Information has now rather acquired the status of the most sought after resource of the resources. The newly emerging 'high tech' disciplines such as computers, tele-communications, biotechnology, etc... are given importance because they store, generate, manipulate, communicate information.

We are experiencing the impact of the new technology on every facet of information handing. The advent of digital computer has opened up new possibilities in information management, and it is likely to change the information infrastructure by merging itself with other related technologies. The increasing use of computer systems for the control of management of information important implications for our thinking about information. And this information processing, storage, and dissemination with the aid of computer is probably called the Information Technology.

When the first computer, called ENIAC, was developed in 1946 it was a huge as it used electronic tubes with a slow speed and clumsy peripherals. It was the first generation computer. However with the development technology the tubes we re replaced by thee transistors and later the integrated circuits etc. and consequently the size of computer has been considerably reduced, while the processing speed has gone up marvellously. The computer systems we have in the late eighties or rather at the end of the eighties are based on Large scale Integration and very Large scale Integration. And with the availability of the microprocessors, we in India are on the way to developing computer networking.

In India computers have already invaded the library and information field and some of the liberties in the special and research organizations have introduced computer systems to automate some their functions. These functions include book ordering and acquisition, cataloguing serials control, circulation, generation and publication of bibliographies, indexes, and other documentation lists. The application of the computer system can also be extended to storage and retrieval of bibliographic indexes, and other documentation lists. The application of the computer system can also be extended to storage and retrieval of bibliographic information, and SDI services. The first computer in India imported from the UK, was installed at the Indian Statistical Institute, Calcutta in 1955. And in the first decade since as many as 16 computers were installed in different parts of India.

The first indigenous computer was designed in India in 1964 by the ISI, Calcutta in collaboration with the Jadavpur University, Calcutta. This was the introductory phase for computer systems in India, and since then India did not look back in the field of computerisation. During the period 1965-72 the process of computerization speeded up with the installation of 170 more computer systems, although most of them were imported from the Western countries. Then the ECIL, Hyderabad took over the responsibility and installed as many as 94 indigenous computers during the period 1973-78.

Meanwhile, the Government of India gave the responsibility of the computers to the Department Electronics which looked into the question of computer acquisition and evaluation. In 1975 the Government of India set up the national Informatics Centre at New Delhi, and two years later NICNET which now is proposed to be extended to each state capital and district level. Besides, many more computer networks have been established in India during the last decade or so. These include, in addition to the NICNET, the INDONET it is the commercial net work for the country as a whole. We have the RAILNET it is the computer network for the railways; OILNET computer network for oil sector; EDUNET computer network for linking educational institutions; another related one is ERNET computer network for education and research purposes; IANET-computer network for Indian Airlines etc. Besides, there are others which are being developed as the BANKNET for the banking services: STEELNET for linking steel works across the country to form a communications network etc.

The following operations of the library functions can be speedily processed by the computer These are outlined briefly.

A. Acquisition

(i) Duplication checking

(ii) Preparation of order lists.

(iii) Sending orders to book supplier/s

(iv) Monitoring orders and follow up action

(v) Verification with order file and invoices

(vi) Maintaining state of funds, budget control etc.

B. Cataloguing.
   (i) Duplicating cataloguing cards
   (ii) Preparation of authority file/subject headings list
   (iii) Sorting, checking, and filing of catalogue cards
   (iv) Automatic generation of added entries
   (v) Generating the monthly accession lists
   (vi) Developing centralized and cooperative cataloguing system.

C. Circulation Control
   (i) Registration of members
   (ii) Charging and Discharging of documents
   (iii) Updating the records file
   (iv) Prepation of reminders
   (v) Maintaining statistics
   (vi) Information retrieval etc.

D. Serial Control
   (i) Ordering of serials
   (ii) Receipt and updating the record file
   (iii) Receipt to vendors/publishers
   (iv) List of holdings
   (v) Preparing list of additions
   (vi) Preparing list of binding

E. Documentation and Information Retrieval
   (i) Indexing of micro and macro documents
   (ii) Thesaurus construction
   (iii) Abstracting work
   (iv) Compilation of union catalogues/lists
   (v) Bibliographic work
   (vi) Searching and print-outs of queries of users

In addition to what has been outlined above, more library operations can be manipulated with the computer system to achieve efficiency, effectiveness, and to reduce per unit costs etc.

Now let us have a cursory look at the advantages which can be accrued from the computerisation. The application of computer in libraries has enormous advantages. The various functions of a library can be extended further for the benefit of the users. Not that computerization will solve all the library problems with which it is infested today, but certainly it has great many potentialities as we have just seen above. If the librarian will be able to improve over the existing set of library services the image of the library and that of the librarian will definitely go up.

3
Online Computer Service

Online operation provides the intimate human-computer relationship having a two-way interactive communication. Offline processing means that the user is not directly connected with the computer at the time of operation. Most offline operations are conducted in batch mode which is a method of processing data in blocks or batches and a stack of searches are run in a single unit. Online output or display is made by the visual display terminal looking like a small television set equipped with a manual keyboard. Since it is interactive, input can be made by means of the same keyboard which may not be faster than ordinary typing. But the output display is very fast and silent. The cathode-ray tube makes the screen line, and the characters of displayed information become visible by an electronic device. The terminal displays alphanumeric characters. The output or the answers flash on the screen one after another, as they are registered in the memory. If an interrogation is made in the wrong way, it flashes an asking mark. The visual display unit is easy to use and read. It may be continuously used for a long time. The creation of the permanent record is not possible by the visual display unit unless the matter is printed by the connecting printer.

Online computer systems are usually 'real time' systems. Such a real time computer interacts with processes external to its system in real time, which means 'as they occur'. The intake data are processed on arrival at the computer system and summarised instantaneously on the display screen as output.

The real time processing operation is in a parallel time relationship with the on-going activity and producing information instantaneously to be useful in controlling the current activity. Since non-perceptible time is the only factor in the real time operation, a real time operation is made in the online system. But all online operations need not be real time ones.

In the real time system, answers are instantaneously to be used in influencing the process underway. In the real time operation, parallel time relationship is essential with ongoing activities. Information retrieval is instantaneous by controlling the dynamic activities. In real time processing, many remote stations may be connected directly by the high-speed communication system with the central processor, and several stations may be operating simultaneously. In modern computer system, 'remote computing' is possible. In such a system, input facilities can be located at a long distance from the main processor of a computer system.

Communications in between the input and the output peripherals and the main computer can be maintained by a telephone or microwave transmission. In this system, several widely separated units located at different places can utilise the central computer facility. Usually, in such a system, appropriate programming is made, so that a computer can handle both local and remote demands. The data entered at a remote online terminal are stored in the main computer memory and processed according to programmes designed for the particular purpose.

When the central computer system pays attention to each remote terminal, all or several, in a specified time and operates simultaneously in a specified sequence instantaneously, it is called the 'time sharing' system. Each remote terminal gets the output in turn but considering the computer speed, a very small fraction of a second not perceptible by human sense, it is felt that the output is instantaneous.

In a time sharing system, each user has access to the computer when-ever he wants it. He can have access to a part of or the total storage of the main computer memory. He may even be assigned a storage area in the main computer and there he can keep his own programme for future use. In a time sharing system, a number of independent terminals located at various places is provided direct access to the central processor or the main computer.

The system allows multiprogramming at a very high speed with one or more terminals. Special purpose time sharing computer systems are more and more being used in libraries both for library and information services so that a large number of users can use the system in various ways for different purposes. Either the housekeeping jobs performed by the library staff or storage of data for information retrieval or current awareness service for the information scientist, or browsing over the library catalogue for information retrieval by users-any of or all such services can be rendered simultaneously by a time sharing computer system. Several terms are used to mean such a system. These are remote access, multi-processing, multiprogramming, multi-access and the like. The term 'multiprocessing computer system' is specifically used where the computer becomes an integral part of a complex operation rather than an instrument used for computation or processing.

In the multiprocessing computer system, a single central processing unit having several input/output terminals is not used, but two or more central processing units are interconnected that serve all the input/output terminals of the system. In such a system, many programmes may be operated simultaneously and complex jobs may be performed. Online access may be available to local databases or external databases across geographical barriers.

The searching is made through an online terminal connected, via the telecommunication network, to a host computer or a series of computers. Within a locality, a terminal can be hardware to the computer. For distant communications, a telecommunication network is required via either leased or dial-up lines. When a database is needed through an international telecommunication network, access is made through a local node of network using a telephone. The local node is usually a minicomputer that transmits messages through a large computer network. Usually, within a country, the ground communication is made via coaxial cables and microwave communication channels suitable for the computerised data network. The satellite-earth stations are used for satellite telecommunication.

The satellite control earth stations, equipped with the ground communication equipment, such as, the antennae, the tracking and telecommand equipment, communicate via the ground-satellite-ground communication via a satellite is the recent speediest channel of communication. There are many online system networks for access to many databases over the telecommunication network both for current information and retrospective databases. Millions of document abstracts, serial titles, indexed data and information contained in thousands of documents may be available through a telephone call and a tele-typewriter, which is a device almost identical to an ordinary typewriter with additional keys for communicating with a computer.

The electrical signals from the tele-typewriter are converted to audible signals that move through the telephone line and then the process is reversed for the messages on their way back. These simple communication media have a profound impact on the communication technology, and tremendous progress has been made in respect of rapid access to any quantum of information. The earliest attempt for access to the computerised database was made in the mid-sixties by the US National Library of Medicine with the introduction of the batch processed database on medical science known as MEDLARS. The provision to MEDLATS online is known as MEDLINE.

The provision for access to online databases on a commercial basis was introduced by Lockheed under the name DIALOG and by the system Development Corporation under the name ORBIT Online Retrieval of Bibliographic Information Time. Both Lockheed and SDC provide an enormous range of materials with a large number of data bases. Another commercial organisation is Bibliographic Retrieval Services started in 1976 in USA. Several other online library systems in the USA are OCLC at Ohio, BALLOTS at Stanford university, WLN at Olympia, RLIN.

In Canada, the largest online computerised library system is UTLAS. In Britain, the largest online system is BLAISE. BLAISE offers online services through a large number of databases under various names and styles, such as MEDLINE, SDILINE, TOXLINE, CHEMLINE, CANCERLINE. In Europe, online access is available to ESA and DIMDI.

The North American telecommunication networks are TYMNET and TELENET. They have more than 200 nodes in Europe and other parts of the world. The nearest point to India is at Hong Kong. These networks provide access to almost all the major American online services. EURONET provides online service to EEC countries mainly, but it is begin extended to other countries also buy interconnecting with the host computer systems for such countries.

In India, online interconnection with ESA has been made on an experimental basis. Online searching is performed through an online terminal. The user must have a clear idea of the request, a chosen database and the online system with operational capability. The search comprises a series of keywords together with the Boolean or weighted-term logic. The search strategy of the search statement should be framed before logging-on. When the communication is made by logging-on, the data of system will be displayed on the screen of the terminal and the user will be requested to select the required database.

As the search proceeds, the interaction between the machine and the user goes on, and the user gives a series of commands to which the computer responds. The terminal is the visual display unit which has a cathode-ray tube (CRT) display. A modern terminal is fitted with a continuous printer because it is necessary to get continuous printed record of searches. The printer is capable of working in parallel with VDU. The terminal is connected with the computer. But in between the terminal and the computer, a telephone connection is essential via a modem. Modem means 'Modulator Demodulator'. The function of a modem is to convert the digital messages, which both the terminal and the computer understand, to messages which are understandable trough the telephone. A similar device is connected with the computer at its end of communication. The computer must be connected with the telephone line like the standard telephone set. The telephone line should be a direct outside line, so that the connection is not interrupted by ordinary telephone calls and other noises in the line. While in operation, the printer prints the hard copy of the search.

If the connection is for long distance international search, the telecommunication networks make the connection with the help of the nearest connection node. When the public telephone lines are used for connecting the computer, it is known as dial-up access. A better but expensive system is the leased-line telephone connection, which connects the computer directly and the lines are used only for the computer connection.

Online selective dissemination of information service has been possible owing to random access searching and random access memory to keep users' profiles. The current information is made input under specific areas as required, and the prepared existing files are updated at regular intervals as and when needed to prepare the data files for SDI. In libraries and information centers where SDI services are offered, an adequate number of profiles is maintained and online profiles are developed by the input and editing systems.

SDI service sets are a series of unique data sets of references of information with each set matching with one profile. These unique data sets may consist of reference numbers only or full bibliographic citations or full bibliographic citations with supplemented abstracts.

These may be from various sources, but are arranged logically. If a user has a terminal, he can get the SDI service directly online. If he does not have a terminal, the online SDI service output may be supplied to him by online printouts. The SDI service is a personalised information service. It is a sophisticated form of current awareness service on a selective area basis, so that the user can get up-to-date information for a specific purpose.

The service requires a tremendous speed for collection, storage and retrieval of information, and an online system is best suited to get the desired result. Computerises SDI service was initiated by H.P. Luhn in the early 1960s, while he was working in the IBM corporation. The titles of the documents used in the chemical abstracts were provide on magnetic tapes in 1962. The institute for scientific information first started SDI service on a commercial basis known as Automatic subject citation alert. Since then, the computerised online SDI service has been being widely used. Some of the SDI services are : Canadian SDI operated by the Canadian institute for scientific and technical information and used in India; computer assisted information retrieval system used at the Leatherhead food research association; storage and information centre; Agricultural system for the storage and subsequent selection of information used at ICI. The U.K. MEDLINE centre situated at the British Library lending division offers the SDI service on the MEDLARS database. The online service is called SDILINE. It offers both MEDLINE and SDILINE with updated information.

In the mid-sixties, the National Library of Medicine in the USA produced the printed Index Medicus. The data were kept in the computer-readable form and the files were known as Medlars. These databases were generated files of computer-readable bibliographic description in the batch process for access to offline searching. The database of Medlars is available on online search service and the service is known as Medline which was wet up in 1973. The software is known as Elhill. The national library of medicine offers online bibliographic search service now with more sophisticated software. It has also several online search services on medical information in several specific areas besides medicine in general.

Sdiline contains the latest month's references to be used primarily for current awareness. Toxline consists of ten separate collections of secondary information in the fields of toxicology and environmental pollution. CHEMLINE is an online dictionary file which enables the users of TOXLINE to describe chemical substances before beginning a search. The mesh vocabulary file contains information on all terms in the mesh thesaurus and it can be searched online. The online system with the search language DIALOG is a commercially accessible online database operated by Lockheed information services at Palo alto in California, USA. It uses an IBM 360/65 computer with the software DIALOG. The software was prepared from the Recon soft-ware developed by lockheed for the national aeronautics and space agency, USA.

The online services of dialog comprise more than seventy databases on a wide range of human knowledge from agriculture, engineering, technology to humanities, social sciences, the arts, public affairs, management, economics and information science. It has databases, both bibliographic and non-bibliographic, American and European. It charges access fee, telecommunication charges and prices for printouts of retrieved references. Some of the databases are AGRICOLA, LISA, METADEX, SCISEARCH, SOCIAL SCISEARCH, CA condensates, COMPENDEX, ERIC, etc.

DIALOG is an outstanding, successful online system and a principal leader in the online service. With wide publicity in Europe it created a tremendous impact on computerised library and information services in Europe, and it has made significant contribution to online service in Europe. It has consultation facilities and it offers a wide range of boolean search options according to the requirements of users. DIALOG contains over 16 million bibliographic citations available online, and these are constantly being reviewed and updated. A dialog search is expressed through search words or thesaurus terms with the commands like EXAPAND, SELECT, COMNINE and TYPE. The command or instruction is made input through an online terminal keyboard for processing by the computer. The output is displayed on the screen and then the searcher can proceed can proceed with the next command or can modify his search by the interactive method. It has online current awareness and selective dissemination of information services.

The system development corporation is also a pioneer like lockheed for commercially accessible online services. It is located at Santa Monica, California, USA. SDC and lockheed are the two largest online database organisations in the world. Both of them prepare purpose-built software and render online services through international telecommunication networks to many countries. SDC prepared a software package for online searching in 1968 known as orbit. It has over fifty databases. It uses and IBM 370/158 computer.

Orbit facilities and capabilities are constantly being reviewed and improved for purpose-oriented user needs. Some of the databases available through ORBIT are ACCOUNTANTS, AGRICOLA, BIOSIS, CAS 77, CHEMDEX, ENERGYLINE, ENVIROLINE, ERIC, INSPEC, NTIS, TITUS. etc. For user orientation ORBIT user manual and orbit quick reference guide are most useful. ORBIT has over 12 million bibliographic citations online. Both DIALOG and ORBIT can be accessed via TELENET, TYMNET and other networks.

The European Space Agency (ESA) operates network links with many computer installations in various European countries. Its UK node is located at the technology reports centre of the department of industry in Kent. It offers access to the space documentation service of esa. ESA formerly used the software package known as RECON, and the online database was known as ESA/RECON. The information retrieval service of the European space agency used ESA/RECON. At present, the version of recon has been revised and the software package is now known as QUEST.

The ESA/IRS database system provides access via online process to more than twenty databases mainly on nuclear and space sciences. IRS uses and IBM 360/65 computer located at Frascati near Rome. IRD can be used through the linking of leased line network by member countries. The department of Industry, U.K., provided a dial-up technical information service known as DIALTECH introduced by the Technology report centre in 1976. This service extended facilities to any user in the UK to dial the node at TRC and be connected to the ESA network having head-quarters in Frascati. The node at trc in kent is a minicomputer and the search method is QUEST. The information retrieval service at Frascati can be accessed online from various locations via telecommunication networks like TIMESHARE ESANET and others. The database includes INSDEC, CONPENDEX, NASA, POLLUTION and the like. The simple access through the ordinary telephone lines to large databases in computer-readable from has been possible, and can be used online. The operational information retrieval service network of the European space agency is the largest European network. It is now known as ESAANET. It serves usually the west European countries. ESANET is planning to provide ready and equal access to scientific and technical information for all member countries of the European economic community through international telecommunication networks.

Online data service and information exchange can be possible among all the member countries. This will also lead to an efficient and coordinated information management system having connection with EURONET, BLAISE, INFOLINE and other online system networks. Euronet is a European online information service operating to offer access to a large number of databases and the sharing of resources among the member countries of the European economic community. It envisages generation of databases in the member countries, as well as access to online databases across geographical boundaries of the member countries. The countries are interconnected by the online system for sharing of information and online information retrieval.

A system has been devised known as diane which offers online search service using the packet-switching data transmission network, with such latest technology, information is transmitted in 'packets' by switching operation. It is fast, reliable and effective on available lines, and it makes automatic corrections of transmission errors. A large number of databases created in the member countries and other online agencies, such as MEDLINE, DIALOG, ORBIT, CANCERLINE, INIS, ISDS, NASA, etc., is available in EURONET. A common command language has been devised that will help the existing sophisticated language as an alternative.

The system of packet switching ensures more efficient use of available lines, a large range of terminals compatible with the network and the most effective and efficient service transmission errors are corrected automatically and the network provides alternative routes. It is also inexpensive. EURONET is interconnected by a large number of European host computers and makes them accessible from any part of the continent. Many host online computer networks are interconnected in EURONET, such as BLAISE, INFOLINE, ESA IRS, information retrieval service, DIMDI, and online host systems of other member countries.

TELENET is an online network operated by bolt, Baranek and Newman in north America. Lockheed and the system development corporation databases can be accessed via this network in the European countries through trans-Atlantic telecommunications.

TYMNET is a network operated by timeshare inc. The network having online services is based in north America, but it has telecommunication access to several nodes in Europe. Lockheed and sdc databases can be accessed also by this online network to European countries. Both the online networks, telenet and tymnet, were implemented in the early seventies in north America and were accessible to Europe and other counties of the world. They have more than 200 nodes in north America and several nodes in Europe in London, Paris, Rome, Viennna, Geneva, the hague, breussels, Frankfurt and other cities, as well as in other cities in Asia and south America like hong kong, manila, Singapore, San Juan etc. Through these nodes, the searcher can dial and have online access to principal databases.

Online databases

In the library sense, an "online bibliographic database" is generally understood to mean a collection of records held online in a rapid-access computer disk store. The online file is usually derived from the machine-readable version of an abstracting or indexing journal. Bibliographic records held in this form are not, of course, directly useful to users and it is the function of online "systems" to make the details held on these disk files accessible to users. Quantitatively, while this can be matched in hard-copy form by a few very large libraries, it represents for most libraries a resource-pool far larger than anything they could possibly hope to afford as shelf-stock, particularly in disciplines not close to their main subject field. In online information retrieval the searcher uses a computer terminal usually linked by telephone to a remote computer. The computer stores the database of bibliographic records on rotating magnetic disks always available for immediate access. The database can be searched and re-searched using special computer programs which allow the searcher to carry out a two-way conversation or dialogue with the computer.

Online retrieval offers many advantages, the following being particularly noteworthy:

- In-depth searches of computer-held files can be carried out at a speed which no human can hope to match.
- The user is an active participant and can instantly adapt his request to the reality of what is actually in the reference file-perhaps very different from what he expects-and also readily recover from errors in the formulation of queries.
- Databases can easily be re-searched, using new clues.
- The user has easy access to an extremely wide range of indexes and databases, many of which may not be available locally.
- Databases searchable online often offer a far greater number of access points than the corresponding printed indexes.

— There is almost no need for the irksome note-taking so typical of many conventional searches.

Information retrieval from databases

This volume is concerned with databases per se, and not with retrieval. However, for the benefit of readers not familiar with online bibliographic searching, two searches briefly illustrate the general nature of this method of searching the literature. Both searches demonstrate the ease and flexibility of online searching.

The search to find references on depth profile studies in ion microprobe analysis proceeds as an interactive dialogue between searcher and machine. The searcher first Selects candidate search terms and then combines them into a search statement, the Boolean logical operators available to him being:

— A + B OR logic: only one of the terms need be present to cause capture. It is allowable to type the word OR

— A x B AND logic; both terms must be present to cause capture. It is allowable to type the word AND

— A - B NOT logic; captures reference with attribute A but not attribute B. It is allowable to type the word NOT.

The search is carried out in sequential steps as follows:

(a) User connects his terminal to IRS host computer.

(b) User calls for connection to File 08, INSPEC, containing Physics Abstracts. IRS confirms connection.

(c) User asks system to as Select records on DEPTH PROFILE? IRS reports that 543 records meet this specification.

(d) User Selects records on ION MICROPROBE ANALYSIS. There are 1039 captures.

(e) User Combines searches 1 and 2 to obtain a smaller subset containing references that may be directly relevant to his enquiry.

(f) User samples result, telling system to Type search 3 result/in format 6 ('short')/and to display 5 references.

(g) User calls for fuller details of the fifth displayed title

(h) User disconnects from the IRS system.

In practice, the choice of adequate search terms and the way in which they are combined are essential parts of good searching. The first search term links the name of the company with the drug name/major/ingredient/ medical indication. The second term is the drug trade name. The third specifies the phase. The fourth and fifth terms cover various combines the five previous sets to produce an answer set containing 26 documents.

The point that while most would-be searchers can carry out searches online, only the skilled searcher is likely to know the many factors which may affect the search result as examined at the terminal. Online retrieval therefore displays a not-unexpected paradox; online searching is easy-online searching is difficult! The pre-selection of terms before combination in the fashion is presented here for the sake of simplicity; skilled searchers can, of course, enter complex search formulations directly in one step if they wish. It should also be noted that all online search systems offer many powerful searching, point-out, and mailing facilities.

Readers wishing to supplement the above very brief description are referred to the very adequate body of literature that now exists on the topic of retrieval from online bibliographic databases. For example' many of the 35 books listed under the heading "Books on online retrieval" in the General Index address the topic very directly.

There is continuing growth in availability of SDI services from most online suppliers. Generally, the user's interest profile is held in an online file and matched against the incoming information. The resulting list of current references matching the user's profile can as an admirable way to keep up-to-date. Developments in the supply of SDI services are taking place so rapidly that this Directory makes no attempt to provide details since they would be misleading by the time this text reaches the reader. Up-to-date details can easily be obtained from the main suppliers. However, some idea of the wide range of databases from which SDI service can be drawn can be seen which shows a selection of DIALOG files with automatic SDI capability.

The word "database" is often used outside the library and information field to describe any set of computer-held structured records which can be approached using search keys, and that the word "databank" is sometimes used synonymously. In the field of library and information science the words database and databank are now usually taken to have the following meanings: a database generally provides details of bibliographic references which the searcher uses as keys in order to consult the original source literature to obtain the detailed knowledge he is seeking.

Increasingly, the online record will contain an abstract, or indeed full-text detail, which answers the enquirer's question without reference to other documentation; a databank, on the other hand, concentrates on factual information and generally gives a direct answer without further reference to original source documents. For example, a statistical tabulation of the output from British coal mines over the last century can easily be loaded into an online file; at a later time a question concerning the output in a specific year produces a specific numerical quantity which the enquirer can immediately use as a "fact". Online databases are usually a by-product arising from the computer-production of conventional printed indexes. Typically, the databases producer/owner makes available magnetic tapes for lease or for sale, usually in a format based on, or deriving from, the producer's, in-house requirements for the production of the printed abstracting journal.

The magnetic tapes supplied by database producers are often leased/sold at prices which in terms of a unit-record are very cheap indeed. For example, the METADEX tapes are available at $5-$20 per record. But of course the in-house record can be expected to be nearly 100% germane to the interests of the creating body; bought-in tapes will clearly contain much redundant material. "Downloading" from a service supplier's online database, having selected wanted references, clearly has many cost and effort advantages in cases where it is legal to download.

Overall, the immense size of producers' production costs is little appreciated by users; VINKEN estimated the global costs of abstracting and indexing publications for eventual storage on databases at $80 million per year. An online service supplier on receiving such tapes will generally use an in-house reformatting computer program to read the tape and reformat the data-elements as received into a new format appropriate to the online inverted file and retrieval programs used by that specific online service.

4

LIBRARY NETWORKING

The typical university library has access to both host-based resources and distributed computing sites via typical desktop computers or more powerful UNIX-based workstations. This composite of application support reaches beyond the capabilities of any single integrated library system itself.

We will examine some basic local and wider area networking concepts to tie this interoperable environment together. The decade of the eighties saw the maturation of multifunctional library automation systems, the acquisition of microcomputers and local workgroup software, and the implementation of LANs in our libraries.

The decade of the nineties has produced further fine tuning of these automated library systems, with increased emphasis on workstation-based distributed applications, i.e., client/server designs, and inter-connectivity and interoperability of these systems through worldwide internetworking. First, let us examine the Internet.

The term "INTERNET" denotes the collection of

networks that has evolved out of the Advanced Research Projects Agency (ARPA). This ARPA network uses the Transmission Control Protocol (TCP) and Internet Protocol (IP) for its architectural basis. The term "internet" (lower case) means any collection of networks that uses the TCP/IP protocol suite and is based on the Open Systems Interconnection (OSI) Reference Model. Currently, the Internet encompasses over 2,218 distinct networks, according to the tables kept at the DDN Network Information Center. The Informational Sciences Institute (ISI) does much of the research, standardization and allocation work of the Internet. Information services for the Internet are provided largely by SRI, International. Each independent network connected to the Internet has its own operations center. For example, the ARPAnet was operated by BBN, under contract from DARPA. All of these interconnected networks use the TCP/IP protocols and incorporate layered architectures based on the OSI Reference Model. Every major research network worldwide now has some sort of connection to the Internet. Accessing these resources for basic service requires use of three pieces of software on your microcomputer or host system. These are Telnet, TN3270 and FTP. Telnet software, allows a host-connected terminal or microcomputer on a LAN to emulate a Digital Equipment Corp. VT100 family terminal, or in some cases another emulation, in order to log on to another network-attached computer.

The TN3270 program provides similar services, except that the emulation is for IBM computers using the IBM 3270 emulation for IBM 3178/3278 terminal models. FTP is a program that implements the file transfer protocol, which allows a user to send or receive ASCII or binary-type files to or from a remote host, using commands that are relatively host independent and that support locating the appropriate file source or destination. Further services require Gopher client software to access these numerous Gopher information servers.

Similarly, the World Wide Web (WWW), which uses Hypertext to provide information, requires a client such as Mosaic or Cello for Windows 3.1. Gopher servers worldwide are indexed through a service called Veronica. Similarly, Archie servers index major anonymous FTP file repositories on the Internet. WAIS is another locational service to find various Internet accessible resources. Gopher servers often provide a connection to these search servers, or they may be accessed directly. Your connection to the Internet will be through one or more networks operating in your institution area.

The internal network workings are defined in a set of documents called Request for Comments (RFCs). If you have an issue to bring before the Internet, you can write it up as an RFC, to be considered for formalization. Jon Postel is the RFC referee to whom any proposal is sent. He will electronically broadcast the RFC for comment by anyone who wishes to use Internet electronic mail. These RFCs can be classified into five groups: required, suggested, directional, informational and obsolete. An example of a required RFC would be RFC-791, which defines the Internet Protocol (IP). Because it is required, it must be implemented on every connected host computer. Suggested RFCs such as RFC-793, Transmission Control Protocol, are generally implemented by network hosts, since they do impact on useability.

Directional RFCs are ones that have been discussed and agreed upon but not widely applied. An example is RFC-937, the Post Office Protocol, which was not felt to be widely needed. However, if a site feels certain protocols are needed, then they should implement them according to the agreed upon RFC. Informational RFCs contain factual information about the Internet and its operation. For example RFC-990 tells how numbers are assigned for the numeric IP addresses for each host on the Internet.

The last category, obsolete RFCs, is needed because RFCs which supersede earlier ones may not be completely understandable by themselves as they may not include the whole model, only the changes and their rationale. Another part of the Internet that users should know is die Network Information Center (NIC). The facility is available to all Internet users.

Network and telephone may be used to contact the NIC, with the most prevalent contact being electronic mail on the network. This is done by using the Telnet software facility to access nic.ddn.mil. Anonymous FTP is used to retrieve selected documents. For IP address and domain name assignments, one must contact the NIC electronically with a message to hostmaster@nic.ddn.mil. The way most people keep up to date on network news is to subscribe to one or more mail reflectors. These are special electronic mailboxes which broadcast received messages to those subscribing addresses.

The NIC provides a registration service for mail reflectors in the files netinfo: interest-groups 1 .txt; netinfo: interest-groups-2.txt; and netinfo:interest-groups3.txt. How does all of this message traffic get to the appropriate destinations? It does so by using a standard unique IP address. The path to this address is controlled by routing schemes through gateways that pass on the message between connected networks comprised by the Internet.

The IP address is allocated by the NIC above via an application template by email to the above NIC address. These addresses take the form of four decimal numbers separated by periods. Each number is the value of an octet of 32 bits, e.g., 128.39.7.90. Addresses have different meanings for these octets, depending on the net organization, i.e. one net with lots of nodes or a hierarchical site of nets with fewer nodes each. Thus, there are Class A, B and C networks. Class A networks have the first octet as a network address and the remaining three as a host address on that network. Class B networks use the first two Octets as a network address and the last two as the host address. Class C addresses use three octets as the network address and one as the host. All Class A networks have now been assigned, so that any current applications must choose Class B or C.

There is an infrequently encountered Class D for multi-cast-type networks that may seen more frequently in the future. Also, for purely experimental networks, there is a Class E experimental format. Since these IP addresses are not very easily remembered by humans, a symbolic name register was set up at the NIC where the IP address was to be equated to a text form address such as "lambda." However, with the Internet expansion, a domain-based symbolic name in the form "sun.min.stk.edu" is more commonly used by users when sending messages or accessing remote computers.

The root of this tree is the rightmost group of characters. In the example above, "edu" is the domain service educational institutions, "sun" is the actual computer's name and, within the subdomain method of allocation, ."min" is a subdomain within the institution "stk." Root name servers are contacted by software on the user's machine, called a resolver, to determine who is responsible for these first-level domains. What root server to contact is an installation parameter.

The resolver finds out who provides "edu" or another domain's services. Then, it contacts the "edu" or other domain name server, which supplies it with a list of addresses of servers for the subdomains, such as "stk" above. Next, the subdomain server similarly gives another portion, such as "min," until the final subdomain returns a list of addresses of interfaces on that host, e.g., "sun" in the above example. With this background on the Internet, it is time to consider the utility of the Internet to libraries as well as some resources of interest to librarians and information specialists.

The early developers' conception of the Internet was of a pathway between a few supercomputer sites connecting fewer than 100 systems across the United States. The growth of the Internet as a much wider utility really took off beginning in 1989. In just a few short years, the following benefits of Internet growth have been amply demonstrated:

— Direct search access to the major research library catalogs in the developed world, with more additions each year
— Ability of one institution to provide its clienteles access to a remote service provided by another information provider
— Access to rapidly expanding numbers of scholarly journals in electronic form and electronic archive sites for collections of these electronic publications
— Mail reflectors, or in the language of BITNET, Listserv's or Usenet's News Groups, devoted to hundreds of topics, allowing concerned communities to have continuing interactions that are rapid and dynamic compared with annual scholarly meetings, telephone conferencing or conventional mail
— Data transfer among researchers that can be accomplished in minutes or hours instead of days or weeks,
— Archive sites to serve as repositories for much public domain or shareware distributed software,

accessible to Internet connected users just as microcomputer bulletin boards have made such resources available to the modem-equipped community

— Worldwide electronic mail, including gateways between such disparate commercial services as MCI Mail or CompuServe

— Ability of users to secure accounts on remote computers for specialized software or other resources, with a savings in telecommunications costs since each Internet connected site pays for the line charge to its regional network hub

We can look forward to the Internet's functions being taken over by the National Research Education Network (NREN), following the enabling legislation Congress passed on November 22, 1991.

On that date a final compromise version of the High Performance Computer Act was sent to the White House. This act is now signed and forms the basis for President Bill Clinton's initiative on the National Information Infrastructure Act of 1993, which describes further initiatives to bring about the NREN. This legislation provides funding authority for two-thirds of the NREN to the National Science Foundation and the remainder to an interagency group under the White House Office of Science Technology Policy. Although George Bush signed this legislation when he was president, it is likely to be still several years before the beginnings of NREN are in place to provide expansion of services beyond the present Internet community-largely higher education, think tanks, high-technology industry and governmental sites. Groups such as the Coalition for Networked Information are taking an active voice in pushing for NREN and Internet expansion as well as providing more organized resource information for users.

Internet-connected host computers provide Transmission Control Protocol (TCP) services to their users through the NCSA Telnet software. This program allows a user on one system to emulate a terminal on another system, usually a Digital Equipment Corp. VT100 family terminal, although several other emulations are sometimes encountered. For systems that are either IBM or compatible mainframes, where IBM 3278 terminal emulation is the norm, the TN3270 software is used. Its services are similar to those of Telnet. UNIX-based computer systems provide these programs as part of the UNIX operating system facilities. Sun Computer pioneered UNIX as an operating system of choice for engineering and scientific workstations. Other competing workstation manufacturers such as Hewlett-Packard, IBM and NeXT Computer also use UNIX and provide this TCP protocol.

The third piece of software used across the Internet is the File Transfer Protocol (FTP) program. This allows either sending or receiving an ASCII or binary-type file, independent of various proprietary file transfer schemes. It also allows access to whatever directory and subdirectory structure may be present on the host computer being accessed, using a common command set that frees the user from having to know the specifics of each system. Thus, one command, "cd," for example, allows a user to change to the proper directory to either find the file desired or to receive the file the user wishes to upload. This command means "Change Directory" and can be used independent of the type or brand of host computer connected to the Internet.

For the microcomputer user-either MS/PC-DOS or Macintosh-Telnet, TN3270 and FTP are available as public domain programs, usually supplied by campus computer centers but also downloadable by FTP from several Internet servers. If such systems are connected directly to a campus or institution-based backbone network having its own IP address registered with the DDN NIC, all of the systems connected will also have their own unique address within that network and will be able to access Internet resources without any host computer intervention. These LANs can be provided a numeric IP address and their own English alphabet domain name form. An Ethernet card is used in these microcomputers and the above software can be used in appropriate format for these systems.

To complete such a connection it is also necessary to obtain the correct packet driver software for the Ethernet card. A number of these have been developed at Clarkson University and constitute the Clarkson Packet Driver distribution also available from sites distributing the NCSA Telnet software. These Clarkson drivers have now been taken over by Crynwyr and are being distributed as the Crynwyr drivers Before connecting to your backbone network, be sure to cheek with your network administration as to what specific Ethernet cards perform best with your backbone and to obtain the correct Crynwyr packet driver for that card. For example, at the University of Minnesota, where connections to the campus Ethernet backbone are via the Etherjack/ IOBase-T connection, Western Digital (now SMC) Ethernet Cards (WD-8003 series) and their corresponding Crynwyr packet driver are preferred for performance on this form of Ethernet backbone. As an alternative, ODI type drivers can be used which enable both Novell ipx and TCP/IP to be used together. These ODI drivers are supplied by the Ethernet card manufacturers.

The staff of computer centers, while they may have had some RFC's tucked away, usually had little to offer in the way of helpful descriptions or addresses of archive sites or specific resources. Also, if you did not know the electronic mail address of your recipient you could not send that party mail electronically on the Internet. Unfortunately, this latter situation still presently holds true, although it is easier now to find out the IP address or the domain-based symbolic name for a given computer site. There are some valuable guides to various Internet resources that have been compiled, and these should become familiar to all who would use the Internet for more than electronic mail services. For Internet beginners, Brendan P. Kehoe has produced "Zen and the Art of the Internet: A Beginner's Guide to the Internet. This is available for Anonymous file transfer from various sites, but the author can be contacted at Widener University via the Internet, using the address brendan@cs. widener.edu.

The mother of Internet guides is a collection of indexes by Robert Elton Maas. As of December 23, 1991, his indexes were in version 0.16. The first part of this collection is called "maasinfo.topindex." It contains addressing and accessing information to 52 resources, including files available only by Internet FTP or electronic mail daemon. He does not include any files that are only available within Usenet News groups or dial-up, modem-accessed bulletin boards.

Maas has built this index with contributors of resources, who receive a waiver of a shareware payment in return for their contribution. Surprisingly, although resources in the hobby bulletin board networks like FidoNET or RBBSnet are not included, Maas is reachable for short messages over FidoNET, with the address ROBERT.MAAS@F212.N 143.ZI.FIDONET. ORG or as rem@darkside.com. Typical of entries in this index is the following entry:

> "INTEREST. GROUPS (800K) The famous "List of Lists", every known open mailing list and digest on the Internet and Bitnet, in alphabetical order. (Mail to: i interest-groups- request@ nisc. sri. com to add

or delete an entry to that list.) (Bad news from nisc@nisc.sri.com (Steven, for the SRI NISC: INTEREST.GROUPS is not updated with any great frequency at this time.)

To: LISTSERV@NDSUVMI

GET INTEREST PACKAGE (511 K, old version?, split into eleven pieces)

To: mail-server@nisc.sri.com

Send netinfo/interest-groups (817K, split into 23 pieces)

FTP ftp.nist.sri.com (192.33.33.22) netifo/ interest-groups (80OK)

FTP noc.sura.net (192.80.214. 100) nic/ interest groups (800K)

FTP csuvaxl.csu.murdoch.edu.au (134.115.4.1) pub/library/listof. lists (80OK)"

The above entry assumes the reader knows how to send electronic mail from his or her site on the Internet and how to use the FTP software to get files.

The second part to this index of indexes is maasinfo.docindex. This is a bibliography of online tutorials and other useful documents for the user to learn how to use many available Internet and BITNET resources. For example, one very useful document is the Inter-Network Mail Guide, which describes how to send electronic mail from one network to another, such as from Internet to CompuServe or MCI Mail, given that you know the local address of your recipient. To obtain this guide written by John J. Chen, you can send the email message GET NETWORK GUIDE to LISTSERV@UNMVM. Or you may FTP to ftp.syr.edu (128.230.1.49) for networks/doc/ingmail.txt. The third part is maasinfo.hownet. This briefly describes how to get started using various network services.

The fourth part is called maasinfo. archie. It explains

a file-finding database service called " Archie. "If you know the file name, "Archie" will find the FTP site. Several other smaller files complete maasinfo, such as maasinfo.mactexed, which lists shareware and public domain text editors for the Apple Macintosh computers.

Another Internet resource tool is the NNSC Internet Tour, a Macintosh Hypercard stack. It is a rather general introduction but contains some valuable leads to data archive sites. The mainly UNIX network called Usenet, which is one of the Internet connected networks, has many news groups, since this is its purpose. These are similar to the BITNET Listserv or the Echo Conference in the FidoNET electronic bulletin board network.

Each of these is devoted to a specific topic and has some sort of moderator that makes sure that relevant discussions are the norm. These Usenet news groups are listed in act. news. newusen, compiled by Gene Spafford, and it can be obtained via anonymous FTP to pit-manager.mit.edu (18.72.1.58) in the directory: pub/usenet /news. announce. newusers/list_ of active_newsgroups. Edward Vielnetti (emv@msen. corn) has revised the Spafford list, and this is available by FTP from ftp.cs. toronto.edu (128.100.3.6) in pub/emv/news-archives/ listofnewsgroups.

There are other lists of discussion or conferences on the Internet. For example, BITNET Listserv fists can be obtained by sending an email message to either of two different sites. The first is to LISTSERV@DARTCNIS I, with the message SEND LISTSERV LIST, or via anonymous FTP to DARTCMS 1. DARTMOUTH.EDU. (129.170.16.19) in SIGLISTS/LISTSERV.LISTS. The second is to LISTSERV @ NCSUVM, with the message LIST GLOBAL, or by anonymous FTP to utar 1 vml.uta.edu (129.107.1.6) in directory bitnet/listserv lists.

The "Directory of Scholarly Electronic Conferences"

overlaps with the previous two lists. It is compiled by Diane K. Kovacs (dkovacs@ kentvm.bitnet) and can be obtained by sending a message to LISTSERV@KENTVM @ or LISTSERV @ BROWNVM or LISTSERV @ UOTTAWA. The message to any of these sites should read:

GET ACADLIST README
GET ACADLIST INDEX
GET ACADLIST FILE1
GET ACADLIST FILE2
GET ACADLIST FILE3
GET ACADLIST FILE4
GET ACADLIST FILES 5
GET ACADLIST FILE6

For researchers and librarians, the ability to access remote library catalogs through Telnet or TN3270 connections makes possible a workable window to certain worldwide resources heretofore accessible only through a direct on-site visit. The first key to this resource class is Art St. George's 1ntemet-Accessible Library Catalogs and Databases. " It is available from many sites via anonymous FTP.

It also can be obtained by sending the email message GET LIBRARY PACKAGE to LIST-SERV(@UNMVM. One ftp site is ariel.unm.edu in directory library/internet. library. The second key to this resource class is Billy Barron's catalog, which lists over 100 libraries. Quite good logon instructions and other information are this list's strong points, though there is some overlap with the St. George guide. Billy Barron may be reached at billy@unt.edu, and his list may be obtained by anonymous FTP to ftp.unt.edu (129.120.1.4) in directory library.libraries.txt. A Companion BBS list can be obtained via the e-mail message GET INTERNET BBS sent to LISTSERV@TEMPLEVM.

Dana Noonan is the author of a shorter and more concise list of library catalogs accessible via Telnet or TN3270. This list can be obtained by anonymous FTP to hydra.uwo.ca (129.100.2.13) in directory libsoft/ internet_libraries.txt.In addition, Peter Scott is the creator of Hytelnet which is a Hypertext guide following the form of the Barron list. Peter Scott's address is aa375 @ freenet.carleton.ca. Hytelnet lists Internet and Britain's JANET-connected libraries, campus-wide information systems and other database resources.

To keep up to date, subscribe to the HYTEL-L listserv at bytel-l@kentm.kent.edu. Finally, three is Richard Duggan's CATALIST which is a Hypertext version of the Barren guide that runs under Microsoft Windows 3.1. Duggan may be reached at duggan@brahms.udel.edu. Anonymous FTP will obtain this list from zebra. acs.udel.edu in the directory pub/ library. The filenames are cat 10.exe, fullcat.exe and readme.txt. Since one of the basic activities you will want to perform on the Internet is file transfer through the FTP protocol, Jeff Linder has created "File Transfer Protocol-Basic Primer." Obtain it by sending the e-mail message GET FTP PRIMER to LISTSERV@TEMPLEVM.

These are the major resource guides to the Internet that you will want to examine. Others can be located that describe specific services or sites. Many of these are rather dated as they have no fixed scheme for updating, so their authors update when they feel like it and not necessarily when there are a lot of accumulated changes.

Other internet facilities

There are over 800 sites on the Internet that offer anonymous file transfer and serve as servers for distributing software programs, particularly programs in the public domain. Since over one million files exist, finding these can be difficult and often rather frustrating.

McGill University programmers have created software for a server called Archie, which maintains catalogs of many of these sites and their files. It is updated monthly, so it is reasonably up to date. The best way to connect to an Archie server is by Telnet or, Gopher, although command line and X-windows clients do exist for many systems and email access can be done via FTP by mail servers such as BITFTP@PUCC for BITNET-only users. Some currently operating Archie servers are:

archie.ans.net	(New York)
archie.rutgers.edu	(New York)
archie.sura.net	(Maryland)
archie.unl.edu	(Nebraska)
archie.mcgill.ca	(Canada- first Archie site)
archie.funet.fi	(Finland)
archie.au	(Australia)
archie.doc.ic.ac.uk	(Great Britain)

Log in to an Archie site by typing "archie" and after a greeting you will see an "archie >" prompt. Enter Help as a command to receive instructions on using the "prog" command to search as well as Archie's other commands. Another feature of Archie is the Whatis database, which gives names and synopses of over 3500 public domain programms on the Internet.

Another program of interest is Gopher, whose first server is available at the University of Minnesota by Telnet (VT100 emulation) and by special MS-DOS, Windows 3.1 and Macintosh client programs. This Gopher and others offer databases and news groups, with University of Minnesota resources and computer-related information and electronic books and directories of some Internet resources special to this mother Gopher server at Minnesota. Gopher can be reached at consultant. micro.umn.edu. Log in from Telnet as "gopher." If you are coming in via an A-NET connection from an IBM host, log in as "anet." The VT100 emulation is not very good on this server when compared to the software for MS-DOS and Macintosh which is distributed by boombox. micro.umn.edu. Over a thousand Gopher servers are now operating on the Internet.

Gopher clients are available for Windows 3.1 from NOTIS, Inc. (WinGopher) and as shareware from several popular FTP sites (HGOPHER v.2.4, BCGopher). VERONICA (Very Easy Rodent Oriented Net-wide Index to Computerized Archives) servers index the contents of Gopher servers. They usually limit the maximum number of items retrieved to 200 and are accessible through various Gopher servers. Sometimes the menu choice is "Search Gopherspace" instead of actually using the VERONICA name. Another index server is provided by WAIS (Wide Area Information Service). It searches collections of data, i.e., databases, on the Internet. Someone has to create an index for the server to use in a search. It uses a relevance score to order its search results and is not a Boolean system.

To directly use WAIS, you can use a Telnet client to log into think.com or nnsc.nst.net. At the login, type "wais" to run a character-oriented interface. There are several client programs also available from popular FTP sites. Some Gopher servers provide WAIS search connections or implement WAIS-type indexing on their Gopher server content. The World Wide Web (WWW) is a hypertext-based knowledge system with linking capabilities to other systems and resources similar to Gopher.

The Hypertext pages are created with Hypertext Markup Language (HTML), and Internet resources are tied through Uniform Resource Locator (URL) addresses. WWW was developed at CERN in Geneva, Switzerland.

NCSA has developed MOSAIC as a Windows-based client for WWW access. Another promising WWW client for Windows is Cello, developed at the Cornell University Legal Research Institute.

Local area networks (LANs)

Local area networks create a building or floor-level network connecting personal computers or workstations to shared resources provided by computers acting as servers. Also, for smaller LANs peer-to-peer networks can be set up to provide printer and program sharing. Windows for WorkGroups, Novell Lite and LANtastic are the most popular of these. These dedicated servers on a server-based network, such as Novell 3.12, can be file servers supporting multiuser applications, special work group software or communications servers acting as gateways to remote host computers or other networks. They can also provide sharing of high quality or specialized print or other output devices and storage media such as CD-ROM or WORM units. Electronic mail systems are another obvious benefit from LANs.

Multiple LANs can be interconnected for institution-wide networks that might span a metropolitan area or reach across a country or even the world. The metropolitan area network (MAN) and wide area network (WAN) build on the local area network concept, i.e., to enable data transmission between computer users and their computing resources for rapid communication and computer-based solutions to applications that could not be approached without these facilities.

Major LAN architectures

Basic LAN technologies were actually conceived in the early 1960's when the earliest networks were built. These included IBM's building of American Airlines' SABRE airline reservation network, connecting 60,000 video terminals all over the United States to six large-scale computers in 1964. However, the first real computer network was the SAGE (Semi-Automatic Ground Environment) system for the U.S. Department of Defense. It was designed in the early 1950's at the Lincoln Laboratories of the Massachusetts Institute of Technology. By 1974, Xerox Corporation's Palo Alto Research Laboratories (PARC) developed the Ethernet local area network protocol. It was a refinement of a protocol invented earlier by N. M Abramson. Ethernet is the most widely implemented LAN, with its original specification based on a coaxial cable transmission medium. Currently, it can also be implemented using a thin coaxial-type cable called ThinNet or unshielded type 5 twisted-pair wire under the 10-BaseT specification.

Today, Ethernet handles 10-Mbps transmission rates on conventional LAN media. Implemented on fiber optic cable in backbone configurations, it can support 100-Mbps transmission rates. This is the 10-BaseF protocol, which is composed of 10 Base-FP, for passive fiber, and which uses an optical splitter at the hub, and 10Base-FB, which defines Ethernet as a fiber backbone network. These are being proposed as revised chapters of WEE 802.3, which is the Ethernet protocol standard. AT&T developed STARLAN as a LAN that can be implemented with either coaxial or twisted-pair cable. Its 1-Mbps transmission rate makes it a relatively slow LAN but one with excellent reliability.

Datapoint Corp. developed ARCnet in the mid-1970's on coaxial cable media. It is the easiest to install and the least expensive to implement. It has a limit of 75 users per network and a 2.5-Mbps transmission rate. It is very reliable and is appropriate for smaller workgroup architecture. Its major drawback is its limited connectivity with bridges or gateways that are available with Ethernet or Token Ring architectures.

The last major LAN architecture is Token Ring, originally developed by IBM and now available from many other suppliers such as Proteon. It has been implemented in two variations: the original 4-Mbps and the newer 16-Mbps transmission rate. The 16-Mbps Token Ring uses IBM's premises wiring system or special type 1 shielded twisted-pair cable, while the lower speed version can be implemented on type 3 unshielded twisted-pair cable.

Many Token Ring adapter cards for 16-bit bus systems are available as a 4/16 arrangement, permitting the card to be used with either speed network. Token Ring is moderately difficult to install, works best with the IBM premises wiring system and is the highest cost LAN to install. These combination 4-MB and 16-MB Token Ring cards are much more expensive than 10-BaseT cards. Today, the most popular physical LAN strategies are Ethernet in ThinNet and 10-BaseT versions and 4-Mbps Token Ring from IBM or competing vendors.

There also are some special-purpose LANs that use wireless technology and some nonserver peer-to-peer-type networks, such as LANtastic, which allow resources on one LAN-attached computer to be shared by other LAN-attached computers. Photonic's PhotoLink is an example of an interesting wireless LAN that uses an infrared light beam to transmit and receive signals using a line-of-sight technique for the infrared light beam units. Microsoft's Windows for Workgroups v.3.11 is rapidly gaining market share in the peer-to-peer market.

MANs and WANs have ben made possible by the development of fiber optic cable technology used in fiber-distributed data interchange (FDDI) backbone networks. In these situations, different protocols may be supported such as Digital Equipment Corp. DECnet, which is based on Ethernet; OSI; TCP/IP; or Novell's IPX to link LANs into MANs and WANs. Value-added networks, such as GTE Telenet, Tymnet or Uninet in the United States and Datapac in Canada, also provide connections for WAN traffic.

The development by AT&T of TI service, which is a 1.544-Mbps telephone line equal to 24 leased lines with redundancy, and its even faster T3 line transmission have made it is possible to handle relatively high speed computer-to-computer traffic. Another advancement, which was conceived some time ago, is the Integrated Services Digital Network (ISDN) which is designed to provide telephone, data, and video signals for service providers to offer video, security, database or videotext services to an organization. ISDN is now finally taking off in the marketplace after a very slow start.

The International Standards Organization (ISO) pioneered the Open Systems Interconnection (OSI) Reference Model, which is a description of a layered communication protocol for computer-to-computer networking. Libraries embraced this reference model very early, as the Library of Congress Linked Systems Project was implemented as closely to the reference model as the then-current hardware and software technologies and products would permit.

Some deviation was necessary as some definitions had not yet been developed or accepted as standards, nor were commercial programs available for implementation at each of the layers. With the experiences of other network architectures and with lessons learned from actual implementation of the OSI Reference Model, there will be revisions to incorporate more emphasis on internetworking, as has happened with the Department of Defense network model. An excellent collection of articles on the OSI situation is in *Library Hi-Tech* 8(4): (1990). Layer 1 is the physical interconnection level. It is implemented in the RS-232C physical serial device interface standard. Layer 2, Data Link, is specified in the Institute of Electrical and Electronics Engineers (IEEE) Standard 802 series.

The ISO, under its 802 group, has accepted these WEE standards. The IEEE LAN Standards Committee 802 has approached this layer by defining logical link and medium access control, with work still being done on layer 3. ISO 802.3 defines Carrier Sense Multiple Access/ Carrier Detect network protocol, which is Ethernet's scheme to prevent contention on the network. ISO ,802.4 and 802.5, respectively, define Token Bus and Token Ring techniques,, the latter used in IBM's Token Ring network.

Currently, the Simple Mail Transfer Protocol (SMTP) handles layers 5 to 7 for Internet messaging. Telnet and FTP also handle layers 5 to 7. It will be quite a while before the full OSI protocol suite will replace TCP/IP on the Internet; however, current network directions indicate that eventually some modified OSI layered architecture will form the basis of many computer-to-computer networks and also be supported along with Novell's IPX and IBM's Netbios on LANs. As Digital Equipment Corp. and IBM move to develop OSI Reference Model-compliant products within their DECnet and System Network Architecture offerings respectively, these products will also change for the better.

There are two specialized networks that have been devised. The first is the Manufacturing Automation Protocol (MAP), developed by General Motors Corp. It uses the IEEE 802.4 Token Bus standard for its lower layers and the OSI Reference Model for its upper layers. It is designed for process control and factory floor automation. The second is Technical and Office Product System (TOPS), developed by Boeing Computer Services.

It uses either WEE 802.3 or 802.5 at its lower layers and the OSI Reference Model in the upper layers. Advanced Peer-to- Peer Communications is IBM's term for its Logical Unit (LU) 6.2 service. LU 6.2 provides basic internetworking services where applications communicate as equal partners, sharing management responsibilities. Any LU 6.2-based application can initiate a session with another LU 6.2 remote partner. These partners negotiate the roles that each will assume.

Low-entry networking allows this without mediation by the mainframe computer, although on older hierarchical SNA network sites, the mainframe must still mediate LU 6.2 sessions. The IBM Document Interchange Architecture and System Network Architecture Distribution Services (SNADS) are examples of LU 6.2 applications. They closely match the CCITT X.400 Message Header Support standard. It is this latter standard, along with CCITT X.500-Directory Recommendations, that enables interlinking of computers and electronic mail into a worldwide system, independent of specific computer manufacturers' hardware.

Today's large LANs often are an interconnection of different vendors' hardware and software, since networks grow over time, usually from a series of LANS designed to serve workgroup solutions. For example, a library may have installed a series of LANs to solve current problems. These might be for printer sharing, access to CD-ROM or access to an integrated online library system. When the number of networks is relatively small, interconnection is relatively easy and it costs about the same to connect each additional network. In this figure, when the network can no longer be supported at a reasonable cost, the complexity barrier is reached. Beyond that point, the network would be severely constrained and unable to grow or even continue responding to users' or libraries' needs. For these connections of disparate LANs, there are two technologies-bridging and routing-that can provide a solution based on accepted standards.

Since traffic bottlenecks at the point of LAN connections are often a problem, proper utilization of these technologies can assure satisfactory performance. A bridge is a device that connects separate networks into a single logical network. A router connects separate networks into an internetwork in which each network retains its logical identity as a separate network segment. In terms of the OSI Reference Model, a bridge operates at the data link layer 2, while a router operates at the network layer 3. If extended network length is needed in a building, it is possible to incorporate devices called "repeaters" between LAN segments. These repeaters operate at the physical layer 1 of the OSI Reference Model. Repeaters merely regenerate signals to accommodate extended wire lengths.

A gateway device is essentially a protocol converter and can operate at any layer of the OSI Reference Model. Bridges work with device addresses and use these to determine what to do with data packets. Since information about paths or routes through the network is encoded in network addresses and these are accessible only to device operating at the network layer, the bridge is a relatively simple device and therefore its cost can be kept low. Since routers operate at the network layer and know the network in both network address and path terms, they also "know" which path is the shortest or other details affecting choice of path. Because of this, routing software is more complex than that of bridges, while the actual hardware device itself may be the same.

Today, the LAN suppliers build in the functionality through the software, creating more flexibility for network designers. The OSI Reference Model and the

TCP/IP protocol are both vendor-independent standards for fully interoperable internetworking. The products available in the interconnection market break down into local-and wide-area products. Devices meant for local use permit connection to local media and network backbones. These may be coaxial, twisted-pair or fiber-optic media.

Local-area devices can connect dissimilar media of two networks. Wide-area devices are equipped with two or more long-distance communications ports and at least one local port. These long-distance connections typically are leased point-to-point lines with speeds of 19.2-kbps to 2.048-Mbps capacities. How basically does a bridge work? It uses source and destination addresses to create a database. These devices "learn" on the basis of source addresses and they "forward" on the basis of the destination address. They also perform a "filtering function" if the destination address is on the same network segment as the source, the bridge automatically discards it. This prevents unnecessary traffic congestion on the bridge since only packets destined for the addresses on the other network segments pass over the bridge.

If a destination address is not in the database, the bridge forwards the packet in a flooding" process, sending it to all network segments connected to its ports except the port where the source address is assigned. Once the packet is received by the correct destination, this information is then added to the database.

Current router products are capable of handling multiple protocols through appropriate software. Protocols that do not contain a network layer, such as Digital Equipment Corp. Local Area Transport terminal connection protocol, IBM's LU 6.2 and IBM's Netbios, are not able to be handled by a router. These can be passed only by a bridge or passed through another network to a network destination address capable of handling that protocol. The router database contains a "routing table" with the actual path to be used.

Although some devices in environments requiring absolute security are handled by the network administrator through routing tables built into a static routing setup, the more common method is a "dynamic routing," where the router itself broadcasts information when it detects network changes. Presently, institutions usually construct a fiber-optic FDDI type backbone having 100-200 Mbps bandwidth. This FDDI can be installed as a growth vehicle on the same fiber used in an Ethernet/802 fiber-optic backbone LAN.

Certainly, the future in data networking is to increase the bandwidth to accommodate heavier traffic. This implies an eventual extension of FDDI to the desktop in one scenario and might result in new LAN architectures that will extend the ISDN concept. 100-Mbps LANs will be needed to operate multiimedia LAN applications involving sound a graphics.

Automated library systems benefit from more standardization, both in data processing as well as applications. With standardization, it is practical for system developers to produce products with more acceptance and broader appeal. For the library, it also means that investments in information technology will use common and accepted parameters. This will ensure a wider choice of systems products for the future, with more preservation of hardware and software dollars already invested. For example, standards such as ISO 2709, which provides a magnetic tape record layout standard for data interchange, forms the basis for placing USMARC records onto magnetic tape, while USMARC defines the data element and logical layout of the actual bibliographic data. In a far-reaching way, other standards adopted by the National Institute of Standards and Technology (NIST) or Federal Information Processing Standards (FIPS) and those of other bodies, such as the IEEE, affect library information technologies. Now, let us examine the major player in developing American National Standards affecting library and information retrieval applications.

National information standards organization (NISO)

NISO develops standards that, when adopted, become American National Standards (ANS). Its predecessor organization was known as the American National Standards Institute Subcommittee Z39 (ANSI Z39). Thus NISO's adopted standards carry the identification number Z39.xx, with the xx denoting the specific standard number. As of January, 1994, there were 29 active and adopted standards in force.

Some current standards are in the process of revision, since every five years standards must be examined for possible revision and revoked or reaffirmed if not to be revised. Three new draft standards were being balloted. Z39 standards have increasingly addressed issues that have been brought out by the use of computer and communication systems. Early standards were directed at items such as Z39.4-Basic Criteria for Indexes or Z39.5-Abbreviations of Titles of Publications. New standards are exemplified by Z39.58-Common Command Language, Z39.67-Computer Software Description.

Several standards currently having a wide impact deserve specific mention here as they will affect current and future library systems. The first of these is Z39.50-Information Retrieval Application Service Definition and Protocol: Specification for Open Systems Interconnection. This is actively being implemented by major bibliographic utilities and system developers. The sixth meeting of the Z39.50 Implementor's Group at OCLC on September 810, 1991 saw over 25 organizations attending. They have developed a list of proposed enhancements for the next version of this standard, i.e., version 3, Version 2 has been adopted and version 3 is a work in progress. ISO's Technical Committee 46 also began working on its version 3 of their corollary standard. Z39.50 is the application layer protocol by which two computers can communicate. It offers the promise of designing intelligent front-end programs that will help and mediate access by users.

Implementation of Z39.50 may be done using TCP for the immediate future since TCP is widespread, whereas full OSI support is commercially lacking. As of December 6, 1991 there were three interoperating Z39.50 implementations in test operation. These are Pennsylvania State University (PSU) on a VAX 9000 under VMS, University of California, Division of Library Automation (UCDLA) on an IBM 3090 under MVS/ESA and the University of California, Berkeley (UCB), on a DEC system 5810 under Ultrix v.4.2. In each case of interoperation an Init and Search cycle was completed and MARC records were returned. PSU was a server to UCDLA and UCB clients in one series.

UCDAL was a server to UCB as a client and UCB was a server to a DLA client. Given the nature of this work, one thing can be assured. That is that later versions of this standard will be functionally improved since this sort of protocol technique requires staged development based on some experience. In 1994, all the major library automation system vendors are working on Z39.50 compliant clients and many also on servers. Several vendors have released commercial production versions of their products.

Also of considerable importance is Z39.58-Common

Command Language. For library users and librarians, given the wide interconnection of library systems now possible, it would be nice if one set of commands could be learned and become the common basis for searching these disparate systems. Given the eventual trend toward graphical user interfaces (GUIs) as exemplified in current microcomputer software and workstation user interface shells under UNIX, it is only a matter of time that host-based library systems will also incorporate such GUI facilities, most likely adopting one of the UNIX GUIs such as X-Windows or MOTIF.

When that occurs there will need to be some GUI Standard, but most importantly, there will need to be a translation from the GUI to a common command language set if systems are to become more hardware and platform independent. Therefore, Z39.58 becomes an important cornerstone to the eventual emergence of future standards covering GUI approaches. This will assure the widest interoperability and interconnectivity on the application level for all bibliographic systems.

Z39.2 defined a format for bibliographic information interchange. However, another important thrust is being made through ANSI X12 organization electronic data interchange (EDI) work. The Data Interchange Standards "Association-linc..is the major group responsible for X12 EDI standards development, and the Book Industry Systems Advisory Committee and the Serials Industry Systems Advisory Committee are actively working with publishers, agents and library system developers to develop EDI between libraries and their material suppliers.

Orders, claims, quotes and other financial and status data are all amenable to being facilitated by EDI application. Standards development is a consensus process within the various standardization bodies. For example, anyone can propose a standard for NISO consideration. NISO's Standards Development Committee and Board of Directors examine proposals for new standards.

If the review is favorable, which takes three to six months, the proposal is sent out to NISO's membership representatives for vote as a new work item. Then, it takes another three months for balloting, and if the proposal passes, NISO's Executive Director appoints a committee chair and together they recruit the committee members. That usually takes six to nine months more. Thus it is normal to see the initial standards development process for a new standard to take from 20 to 36 months, at which time a draft standard enters a three-month comment round to NISO member organizations or anyone else wishing to comment.

Comments necessitate revision, which usually takes a further 12 to 18 months, with balloting on the resulting draft another three months. If the standard passes, the resolution phase begins. In this phase any "Yes, with comment votes and any "No" votes (with their stated basis) are examined and resolved. This typically takes about six months. Once NISO has consensus, it passes the standard to ANSI for review, publication, publicity and implementation as an ANSI Z39 standard. This usually takes another nine months to complete. Thus, it typically takes 5 to 8 years to produce a standard from its original concept to final adoption. Then, every five years, the standard must be reviewed for possible revisions and reaffirmation or revised and reballoted. NISO had 57 voting members as of January 1, 1994.

NISO is the U.S. Technical Advisory Group (TAG) on the work of ISO TC/46 and casts the U.S. vote on these ISO standards. There are ISO standards that are implemented in their U.S. form via Z39 standards.

Subcommittee SC4 deals with computer applications within information and documentation. There are nine other TC/46 subcommittees and some of these are Common Command Language, Transliteration, Data Sets (EDI/X12) and Electronic Publishing. There is active participation by NISO in these developments.

The ANSI X.3 committee handles various telecommu-nications standards. With the increase in internetworking of systems, this work is integral to systems we envision in this decade. An exciting new development is the formation of the Coalition for Networked Information and its Architectures and Standards Working Group, which is working on standards for referencing networked information objects. A number of ad hoc solutions to identifying and referencing these resources have been, developed, but these present major barriers to assuring full future interoperability.

The Coalition's intention is to submit this work to the Internet Engineering Task Force as a draft RFC and also to NISO for adoption as an ANSI Z39 standard. The Museum Computer Network has its Computer Interchange of Museum Information Committee (CIMI) developing protocols for exchange of museum information. This protocol would carry a variety of data types such as text, binary, image and graphic. It would support real-time, interactive and batch modes of operation as various applications might require.

5

MULTIMEDIA CATALOGUE

The librarian's need may arise from the need for a stock record for purposes as stock-checking, statistics, accounting, and calling up of items not received. Strictly speaking, these last are not catalogue uses, the basic object of a catalogue being the exploitation of stock by users, whether directly or indirectly. However, as we know, much of the data for housekeeping purposes is the same as that used for exploitation. Inevitably, with the use of a basic set of data for various purposes, there arises the concept of an integrated systems approach, with the use of a computer for selecting from a comprehensive store, and manipulating the data to specific ends. From the user's or librarian's housekeeping point of view, entries for documents in a particular form could be selected, manipulated and printed out in whatever order was required for the purpose. An essential need is to be able to list all materials in a particular form, eg filmstrip. In turn, this means that each physical form must not only be represented, as in standard, eg AACR, cataloguing practice, but also it must be a field on its own, and with a tag to facilitate its use as an access term.

Nowadays AACR is justifiably regarded as working basis for much full bibliographic cataloguing, and its structure is usually assumed in MARC formats, whether for book or for nonbook materials. AACR does include provision for spelling out some physical forms a potential tags. Phonodisc could reasonably be made a field, with its own tag. Similar provisions apply for other physical forms starting with the stem 'phono...', such as phonotape and phonowire. It should be possible to enable a search to be made on the stem 'phono' to facilitate retrieval of all sound recordings, whatever their physical form.

Incidentally, in the example given above, the full stop (period) has been omitted at the end of the author heading, and following 'Phonodisc', despite its being, inconsistently, included in the code. However, by accident, the code may have provided a means whereby nonbook, as differentiated from book, forms of material might be retrieved by computer, the full stop acting as a searching and retrieval device for most 'special' materials as opposed to conventional materials. According to AACR, other special forms are not so conveniently indicated by a potential field attached to a uniform title.

A problem exists for music scores, which are not designated as such in headings or uniform titles, although in some instances the word 'score' occurs in the collation. Yet another problem occurs even when a potential field is suggested in AACR; this is when there is a possible difference of opinion over a term to be used. This would not pose much of a problem for locally generated data, but it could cause some degree of difficulty at least it locally generated entries using the 'British English' term had to be merged with, say, LC generated entries, which naturally would use 'American English'. Similar types of problem are manifested by the many other forms of document, when it comes to computerised manipulation and retrieval of selected forms, as well as of subjects.

Computerisation is the only feasible hope of achieving a multiple-access approach to both information as such and special forms of presentation. We wish to sum up, at this point, that not only a multi-media catalogue may be needed, but also that a generously multi-approach catalogue is needed. There should be approaches along the lines of a principle which we feel Cutter would have approved. Potentially, in one sequence, one could approach or trace information according to, not only author-type and title headings, but also subject headings and physical form headings; subject headings could consistently be subdivided according to form of presentation. As we have said, such a complex manipulation of data and approaches can be realised only through the use of the computer. Some libraries are already computerising, or planning to computerise, their bibliographic data on special materials. In some cases, systems are being, or have been, introduced for certain individual forms, depending on local need, eg the Library of the Western Australian Institute of Technology has a multiple-approach computer-printed catalogue for slides. At the time of writing other media have not been planned for in this particular instance.

Despite some academics' pipe dreams of an integrated systems approach, there is a lot to be said for experiment with a single medium. Problems relating to programming, computer storage, and access can be identified and solved comparatively inexpensively. However, we suggest that such achievements should be regarded as research and development projects rather than as ends in themselves. A most important aspect of such an experimental project is actual use of the resultant catalogue or index. In a comparatively 'closed' situation, as in the library of an educational institution, potential users of such a system can be canvassed and their comments recorded and analysed. Such a catalogue use study, if carefully planned and executed, could be extremely helpful as a pointer towards the potential exploitation of a comprehensive system. When libraries reach the point of finally appreciating that so-called 'special' materials are not so special that they may be rejected as 'normal' stock, or if actually acquired hidden away and largely avoided, it should be possible for multi-library catalogue use studies to be made. From these could emerge an idea of what library clienteles really need in relation to special materials.

Judging by one experiment, in Pearl River Public Library, New York, when a multi-media catalogue—and even stock-integration—policy is implemented, the users readily respond to such facilities: 'Users do like to find related materials on a given subject on one place'. Admittedly, as the article says, 'one situation does not connote a trend'; but we suggest that this situation is at least a symptom of the, as yet, unrealised potential of once-'special' library materials.

Just as normal monographic materials are being recorded on centrally produced computer tapes, as it happens MARC tapes, so there is more and more talk of doing the same for special materials. Also, as is commonly known, there are central computer stores, regional, national, occasionally international, of bibliographic data relating to articles, reports, etc. in certain subject fields. These can be searched on demand for specific subject requests. At the moment, MARC tapes for monographic materials are sold to interested libraries to use as they think best—or apparently, at present, to be merely accumulated with a view to future use.

As one useful by-product, MARC tapes are used centrally as a basis for the computer output microfilm production of the 'micro-microform' Books in English by BNB. There is not as yet a convenient facility for libraries to draw upon a national, let alone an international, central computer store for only the data which they require, either for documents which they have in stock or for searches on demand from users. However, there is a proposal, and presumably a hope, for setting up such a central, national, store, in Britain, to be tapped on demand for certain special materials.

The proposal is put forward in what we suggest could become a most important report issued with the authority of the National Council for Educational Technology. The Gilbert Report is confined in scope to audio-visual materials used in education. However, education and modern teaching techniques are probably the main stimulant to the increase in use and acceptance of at least the large audio-visual sector of special materials likely—or even unlikely—to be encountered by most librarians.

Further, the report interprets 'education' in a broad sense, and some documents which might formally be dubbed 'recreational' are likely to be embraced by its proposals. This interpretation does not affect the variety of physical forms, but it could affect the size of any central store established, and this in turn could mean that any local library's stock of nonbook materials may stand a reasonable chance of being as well comprehended by the central store as, say, a general library's book stock might be covered by MARC tapes.

We hope that the new British Library when it emerges will have copyright coverage at least equal to that of the Library of Congress. To return to the Gilbert Report, with its attempts at cumulating such data as is at present available in Britain, we have to appreciate that, at the moment, a large variety and types of records would have to be drawn upon to realise the hope of a comprehensive collection of bibliographic data on nonbook materials.

It is anticipated that such information could be reconciled, and incorporated consistently into a central store, without the central cataloguers having to sight the actual documents. This situation may, at first sight, seem to be analogous to that of compiling union catalogues of, say, books, or serials. However, in such cases, it is usually expected, or at least hoped, that entries have been compiled by professional cataloguers and, at least to some extent, according to a standard recognised code. We feel that Gilbert possibly minimises the technical difficulties in such a process. However, we feel that such a process. However, we feel that such a project is possible, and that bibliographic niceties so dear that such a project is possible, and that bibliographic niceties so dear to some—dare we say, conservative—cataloguers must give way to the immediate need of producing data of use to many libraries. To digress, but with a purpose, we might recall that some BM cataloguers seem to have wanted to delay indefinitely the photo-printed BM catalogue while they indulged their penchant for bibliographic perfection on the bibliographic information needed all over the world.

We had the privilege of meeting Sir Frank Francis, then BM's director, in the early 1960's and he commented that, in effect, he had to get his cataloguers to eschew academic bibliographic niceties and to get on with producing a catalogue for real live use. Librarians must have in mind not colleague-cataloguers' academic criticism, but the ultimate use of their product in document and information retrieval. In short, if any minor errors emerge—hard luck. The main concern should be use of the data to enable documents to be identified and exploited by users of libraries all over the country or even the world. In sum, then, we support the layman's proposition of integrating data from whatever source so that it can be drawn upon in real live situations. We do not apologise for this apparent tirade: there are still far too many cataloguers who derive more satisfaction from the use of a square bracket than from the knowledge that they are serving users' needs for information today, not in three months' time when they finally have finished their games and pass on their toys to a vague depersonalised public whom—through unfortunate library management—they never meet.

So, then, we keenly recommend the concept of the centrally accumulated data base hoped for in GILBERT, and we further hope that people can be found to do the accumulating, assimilating, and production for use of such information. However, to realise such a hope, two needs must be borne in mind: (a) an overall organisation; and (b) a detailed organisation for the manipulation and output of bibliographic data according to the needs of requesting centres, assumed to be libraries which receive and formulate enquiries. (a) is worked towards by a system as reproduced from GILBERT. This includes four components: (a) the actual producers of documents; (b) central cataloguing agencies; (c) a computer store; and (d) printers for producing usable hard copy as required. It is technologically possible for (c) and (d) to be parts of the same apparatus: a lot depends on the physical type of product expected in reply to an enquiry, and the type of physical presentation acceptable by users.

A single enquiry might be satisfied with a 'one off' computer printout, but a resource centre's own complete catalogue may demand a more sophisticated physical presentation. (a) is further enhanced by the system reproduced from GILBERT. The essential advances of this system on the previous diagram is that it introduces the real users of nonbook materials, and it shows how they are integrated into an information retrieval system ranging from producers, via a central store and enquiry-coordinating service, through catalogue agencies, and back to enquirers.

A major component of this system is the Central Bibliographic Service, linking libraries and similar information service centres with a computer store and with cataloguing agencies, and, ultimately, with users of nonbook materials—the final objective of the exercise. So far, we could envisage the service as providing computer-printed lists for individual enquiries. However, this concept would, in effect, put the cart before the horse. Before individual searches are initiated, it is reasonable to expect general lists to be searched, in much the same way that Index medicus may be searched manually before a MEDLARS search is initiated by computer.

The report, then, envisages a printed bibliographic service, which corresponds to the records of normal books covered by BNB or—in the film world—works covered by the British national film catalogue. A noteworthy quotation from GILBERT is that 'no significant problems were encountered, and that there is every reason to suppose that the MARC system can be used for the cataloguing of NBM. The inference is that all nonbook materials could conveniently be catered for in the MARC format, and presumably entries for all forms could be integrated into once catalogue.

The sample catalogue entries would be part of a so-called HELPIS system: Higher Education learning Programmes Information Service, as an adjunct to LERMISTOR: Learning Materials Information Store. But, confirming what we said earlier, the range of types of materials and of actual documents prepared for the system make it seem likely that the actual store of bibliographic data, and the spadework which would go into programming in the broadest sense, would encompass a lot of the work of all sorts needed to make the hole system operative. It may be useful at this point to try tu consolidate the main components of creating the type of integrated system envisaged in the report as a whole, and as demonstrated microeconomically by its sample Catalogue of materials available for exchange produced in March 1971 and including a variety of audiovisual materials.

First the documents have to be made, and, as with printed monographic media, they come from a great variety of organisations, and may range from commercial materials for national or even international distribution, to perhaps items locally produced for use in just on educational institution. An example of the latter—local products—which comes to mind, though in fact Australian, is a series of video-taped lectures made in the Princess Margaret Hospital, Perth, for the education of nurses. A decision must be made somehow and somewhere as to which documents are to be recorded in the central system.

A sort of parallel situation in letterpress materials might be the locally printed-or typewritten—reports on research, eg higher degree these, produced by the thousand in colleges and universities. Such products may be merely academic exercises or they may transpire to embody an original contribution to their subject and therefore have value in a broader context. We then come to the need for all such worthy documents to be catalogued, adequately and according to a generally accepted method.

An obvious need is that documents on one subject but in varying physical forms and from a diversity of origins must finish up with a uniform subject heading, whether verbal or codified. This operation would call for the recognition of a uniform subject approach if it were to cater ultimately for a wholly consistent integrated record at the projected central store.

Then comes the need for items' entries to be selected and to be notified to the central store. Approaches and description need to be either consistently expressed or given fully enough in whatever form for consistent records to be brought together accurately at the catalogue compilation centre. The problem of integrating dissimilar entries for similar documents is as old as the compilation of union catalogues, and goes back to at least medieval England when a union catalogue of the manuscripts in monastery libraries was compiled. The problem is vastly intensified nowadays because of the fantastic increase in the quantity of documents, and in the present context it is inevitably exacerbated by the variety of physical forms. A J Wells has stated 'The largest single problem in system terms arises at this point since there is no unique identifier for each item which would provide a ready means of eliminating duplicate standard descriptor fields from the file. This is a major problem since the same item may be input into the data bank from any or all of the agencies. Inevitably here we must bring up the fact of standard book numbers, and further, international standard book numbers.

There is an obvious need for some form of unique identifying tag for nonbook materials, just as there has developed a system for normal books in several countries, eg Britain and the USA. To plan and execute such a system would involve a lot of planning, and in fact we find it hard to envisage it being carried through. Presumably a prefix for each form would be required, as well as a unique number for each document.

A unique identifying system does already exist for

sound recordings in disc form, even though the notation used, assigned by manufacturers (i.e. publishers), is often complex. It is conceivable that at least commercially produced documents could be subjected to the same type of routine to which publishers of books seem to have responded so well in those countries not using standard book numbers. The next stage is the assembling and editing of bibliographic data at the relevant centre and its feeding into the store, say in computer disc form of facilitate the random access envisaged. This stage necessitates the allocation of tags and fields in a uniform way: this is why we have inferred that initial compilation of data should be made, if at all possible, according to an accepted code for author/title and description and according to a standard system for the subject approach. UDC is the most widely accepted system—whatever faults it may have at present.

An advantage of UDC is that it has built-in symbols for various types of physical form, which can be represented either through the use of the colon for linking 'main' notations, or through the addition of symbols, to represent physical forms. We suggest that in a central store the use of 'main' notations would represent the type of flexibility required for access according to physical form, as well as the obvious requirement for access according to the subject of a document. Further, experiments have demonstrated that UDC—despite its occasionally awkward facet indicators—can be computerised.

The inputting of bibliographic data might, we feel, be the most difficult part of the operation—possibly even more difficult than locating information in the first place. However, experiments with MARC-based formats seem to indicate that the project is viable. Input would embrace the functions of both bibliographic-oriented and retrieval-oriented catalogues, as we call them. This means that bibliographic detail in description and approaches would have to be as detailed, minute, and varied as might be needed by any user of such a system. If, for example, the system were to be completely acceptable and useful, it would have to embrace 'depth indexing' as well as the more conventionally expected approaches and detail.

We now come to the ultimate objective of the system: use. It is envisaged that the data base would be drawn upon in four main ways:

(a) Machine-readable data, in the form of magnetic tape, could be obtained as required by user-libraries and resource centres, preferably using 'Standard Nonbook Numbers' for access, but the system should cater for other approaches such as conventional author/title headings a s commonly cited and as arrived at by the application of, say, AACR. We reiterate here that work is in progress on a new comprehensive nonbook code in Britain, but at the time of writing this had not been produced. A decision would have to be made as to which code would be implemented, in the same way that users of MEDLARS must conform to the index language used as tags for medical subject terms. If a decision could not be reached, there would need to be additional fields to cater for tags according to the two or more codes used, either in the form of added entries or as references, at act as s sort of translation system between apparently rival headings. However the store would be structured, the resultant tapes would be used by local libraries and centres to construct catalogues for their own stocks, selecting whatever details and approaches were relevant to their needs.

(b) The central store could be used for printouts resulting from searches initiated by local libraries, etc. in response to requests for comprehensive information according to any approach: subject, physical form, author, collaborator and so on. Such a function would be similar to that performed by various data banks in selected subject fields at the moment. It is envisaged that such searches would be made mainly in subject areas, with physical forms as a further basis for selection depending upon the availability of apparatus for use of the various media. But it could also be used in support of, say, experiments, or programmes for entertainment or education, using a particular medium, an obvious example being the moving film, or 'motion picture', or 'cinema' depending on the approach term used in the system.

(a) and (b) could overlap in that a local centre may acquire magnetic tapes to use in local specific subject and/or form searches.

(c) A more sophisticated application approaches the limit of accessibility to data stores usually envisaged, in that a local centre could possibly be on line to the central store. We know that mainly, according to our observation, on-line systems seem to be operated by industrial and commercial organisations. So, it is technologically feasible that a similar system could be used for objective information retrieval via a local community-oriented service. This seems a logical next stage of development leading on from the, now common, linking of libraries and information at the local centre—screen display, facsimile printing, or normal printout—would depend on local facilities.

(d) Finally, comes the vital factor of location of required documents. In this respect, the central store would serve as a union catalogue. A field in the store indicating local holdings would need to be established, but this could be a fairly routine matter. It could also serve as an approach for printing out of local holdings. A notation could be established to ensure that various degrees of 'local-ness' could be identified. As already mentioned in the context of subject and form approaches, UDC might be implemented here, using its 'place' numbers. Of course, union catalogues could be printed out as required.

Despite the lists produced in the US by NICEM (National Information Center for Educational Media), there is not in progress any system attempting to do all that needs to be done. We feel keenly that the time will come when either such a system has to be realised or we shall lose contact with nonbook-based information and its sources.

6

LAN Software

The LAN-based LAN workstation system provides for growth and remote connectivity that the Concurrent DOS implementation would not. But if growth and connectivity are not needed, then this little-known system would be ideal. If you are interested in a system using Digital Research's Concurrent DOS, inquire about operating an MS-DOS-based system under this with the system's vendor. Even if not mentioned in configuration specifications, it should be possible for most MS-DOS software to run under Concurrent DOS since they are quite compatible. A competitor to MS-DOS/Microsoft Windows combination of single-user, multitasking system is IBM's OS/2. This system will run MS-DOS programs in a compatible window as does Microsoft Windows. IBM is attempting to popularize OS/2 by pre-installing it on many IBM PS/2 microchannel-equipped models, but this does not guarantee that OS/2 will ever equal Microsoft's Windows and related products in number of installed systems. Microsoft is also offering its Windows for Workgroups v.3.11 program that allows peer-to-peer networking, similar to the Artisoft LANTastic network. With the lower costs and rapidly increasing popularity of Ethernet in its twisted-pair form, called 10Base-T, this LAN topology and structure is growing at a much faster rate than IBM's Token Ring. LANTastic is a much more mature and stable product, enabling better and larger growth currently than Windows for Workgroups. However, this could change in the future depending on what Microsoft is able to do with this new product. Windows and Windows for Workgroup are still 16-bit-mode systems.

The system could be a 32-bit OS/2 from IBM as an outgrowth of its alliance with Talagent and Apple. However, such a system might be UNIX based if NeXT, Inc., and Steve Jobs were successful in their May, 1993 introduction of their NeXTStep operating system on Intel and other chip systems. It should be noted that NeXT has stopped all hardware manufacture and sold its hardware manufacturing facility to Canon. Canon recently announced Intel 80486 systems specially optimized to run NeXTStep. Silicon Graphics has licensed NeXTStep's interface for incorporation into its MIPS-based systems. More likely will be the emergence of Microsoft's Windows NT (New Technology) as the dominant operating system for the Intel chip-based desktop/LAN. This is a full 32-bit-mode system and, like NeXTStep, is offered on Intel and Alpha processors, with other ports in the works. Another factor complicating our knowledge of what will occur in the marketplace as to future microcomputer operating system directions and thus likely moves by application developers is the release of Novell's Advanced Netware v.4.0.

Actually, it is UNIX based and incorporates support for mixed LANs where UNIX servers would coexist with traditional Novell Netware servers. Like Advanced Netware 3.12, it provides enhanced support for Apple Macintosh connectivity. Novell has bought UNIX Systems Laboratories, the company that AT&T spun off to develop, support and market UNIX System V. UNIXware is another related product that Novell has released. This product attempts to make UNIX a more attractive desktop system. Some of the programs in this chapter are available for the Apple II family systems. There are other systems no longer considered competitive mainstream products.

The Apple Macintosh is a current mainstream system that keeps getting better all the time. Apple recently introduced quite powerful models incorporating the new PowerPC chip at very competitive prices. This makes them very attractive user-oriented systems. MAC System 7 is multitasking and also provides good support via the SuperDrive on current Macs for data transfer between Macs and MS-DOS-based systems. SuperDrive will write out an MS-DOS-formatted 3.5 inch, 1.44-MB floppy and also read it so that data can be imported between these platforms with increased ease even without the benefit of having a mixed-platform network and electronic transmission. Macs have built-in AppleTalk or Ethernet network connectivity.

Single-user MS-DOS systems cannot really provide adequate retrieval capability since even the smallest library needs to allow for simultaneous access by a librarian and a patron. Therefore, any library must consider that it will need a system able to be accessed by at least two users simultaneously if the system is to perform the most basic tasks associated with an online, integrated library system, e.g., access to an online public catalog and circulation control.

PC/MS-DOS and family products

These systems form the mainstream of our desktop microcomputers used in business, education and government today. With competition providing a continual decrease in price relative to performance, the average desktop system today can be acquired for around $2500 or even less depending on the actual components specified. These systems can perform more interactive computing in integrated library systems than mainframe computers were able to do until the early 1980's.

The ever-improving price/performance ratio, the continual rise in labor costs and the need to provide better access and retrieval to growing numbers of library users mean that no library today can remain totally noncomputerized. The market will see new companies introducing new software in an attempt to acquire some market share.

The University of Guelph, replaced its GEAC GLS system, an 835,000-title database and 150-workstation system, with a SEARCHME CD-ROM catalog and integrated library system. Other sites use this product to back up their GEAC GLS systems. The INCOLSA library network in Indiana is a large U.S. customer. This system can operate as a stand-alone MS-DOS product or as a UNIX-based system and within a TCP/IP network.

The SEARCHME catalog can be a CD-ROM or hard disk-based system. It can be kept up to date via a supplementary file on hard disk when a CD-ROM catalog is used. Searching this medium is transparent to the user. The library can define many different system parameters, display screens, fields to be indexed, look and feel of the user interface and multilingual operation. With its network-linking capability, users can have access to multiple resources on an institution network from the microcomputer workstations in the library.

The circulation subsystem can serve remote locations through this network. SEARCHME uses a UNIX file server. Searches of the online catalog can be saved to disk. The cataloging system can run stand-alone or networked via its client software. There is an online coding manual for MARC, context-sensitive help, interactive error checking during editing with a central database on any UNIX server to which the MS-DOS-based workstations are connected via TCP/IP protocol. Multiple library databases are supported, including loading of LC or National Library of Canada MARC tapes. This is the platform for producing a CD-ROM catalog or operating the online catalog from a central bibliographic database.

The circulation system and other SEARCHME functions use a fourth-generation database management system. Fully customizable reports may be generated from this system. Similarly, the acquisitions subsystem is a client/ server implementation or can be implemented on a single workstation if that is all that is needed.

The online catalog can optionally index by media or material type so that searches can be made by these criteria. Keyword access to the entire record and full-text indexing are also options. Field labels on display screens can be changed by the library. This system uses programmed function keys on the workstation keyboard to perform specific commands such as "Find by title" or 'Display results. Two keystrokes and a user's search term retrieve most records. When using the PF key mode special keycaps provide labels on the keys.

A library does not have to use this mode but can instead choose to use a menu-based interface where the user chooses items by cursor keys and the Enter key. The user search interface is provided in two forms: a novice mode-where author, title, subject and call number are used most commonly for known item searches-and an expert mode. This latter mode implements full Boolean searching either via PF key or menu. AND, OR, NOT, ET CETERA operators are used. The user creates the search one term at a time as index displays are retrieved to assist.

These Boolean searches can be qualified by location, material type, and publication date if the imprint field has been indexed in the ALL Keyword Index. An UNDO key permits removal of search conditions. The system uses implied truncation when typing a character string. The ETC ET CETERA operator is a special SEARCHME feature to have the system automatically process a Boolean OR on successive terms in an index list. Once a record is retrieved, the user can browse the items surrounding that record. The system is excellent at handling compound personal names. For example, the name "De La Roche, Maria," can be located by any of the following, "Maria de", "La Roche, Maria De "Roche, Maria De La, or "De La Roche, Maria. " Diacritical marks are translated to the IBM character set on the workstations to display on screen.

If a CD-ROM catalog is used at individual workstations, these can have their hard disks updated with new additions either through loading from a floppy or a portable magnetic tape unit. Or, the system can operate from a central server. Bibliofile, various sources of MARC tapes and other MARC record sources can be integrated to provide local catalogers with MARC data records on which to base their work. This integrated library system offers excellent functionality coupled with some cost-lowering options such as the CD-ROM catalog, designed to minimize the server storage needed. Very large databases can be accommodated either on the UNIX server or in a CD-ROM approach.

An Ethernet TCP/IP LAN provides sufficient transaction capability to support relatively large circulation loads-certainly those found within academic libraries and even larger public libraries. This system represents a good growth capability for the smaller library also as they can start with a small CD-ROM based system. The fact that SEARCHME has been used to replace these larger and older GEAC GLS online catalog and/or circulation systems is a key indication that this system has the performance necessary for current and future institutional demands for interactive networked services. The IMPACT system is a CD-ROM catalog with a separate but integrated module for interlibrary loan.

AGILE Ill is Auto-Graphics' host-based central online cataloging system and network in which shared file users can use all other shared files while private users are restricted to their own files. IMPACT/SLIMS is the Small Library Management System which incorporates an online catalog, cataloging, circulation, reporting and system administration. It can link to the IMPACT CD-ROM catalog or to other CD-ROM data. Both IMPACT systems can be customized to the library's data needs, descriptions and search provisions, record downloading and screen time out.

Databases have complete union list-of-serials capabilities and can be for a single or multiple institution or location. OCLC, RLIN and other MARC record sources can be used. Auto-Graphics provides central cataloging database support for libraries under contracts via the AGILE 111 system. This includes database preparation, CD-ROM mastering, and authority control. Auto-Graphics also offers many other services such as smart bar code generation, ions from one system to another competing system and special database cleanup to isolate records not meeting LC MARC standards, one customer of this IMPACT CD-ROM system is Arrowhead Cooperative Library System in Minnesota.

The CD-ROM catalog uses the standard 10-function-key IBM PC keyboard, with brief and full record displays using labelled fields. The library can decide which fields will be shown to the library user. One can have selected stations switch between MARC record-type displays and full labelled displays by doing an ALT-M keystoke combination.

The ALA MARC character set diacriticals display over or under letters as appropriate. Author, title, subject or a combination of the above feature browsing access. Browsing by Dewey or LC call number is optional. There is a separate keyword search of author, title and subject using an implied AND. All-word indexing searches keywords in all indexed fields, with AND implied. An all-word index is required to support the research-level software module. This expert level supports additional searching of standard control numbers, location-based searching, the use of OR and NOT operators plus other search qualifiers such as LANguage, publication date and wildcard characters. This system is programmed in the C LANguage and a variant known as Vitamin C. The IMPACT interlibrary loan module produces printed forms or will forward electronic requests via a file server when installed in a LAN environment. Novell Netware LANs or LANTastic also can be used for the LAN.

Any IBM-compatible personal computer with at least 1 MB RAM can be used with MS-DOS 3.3 or above on the individual PC. In the LAN interlibrary loan, the server can dial each branch's interlibrary loan station each evening and collect the outbound requests for next-day processing. The system assigns a serial number and acknowledges that the request is in process.

Requests are forwarded through a referral list to each lender until the request is filled. The system automatically flags overdue items, time-expired requests, renewal requests, and any other request needing action. It also maintains statistics and generates a transaction log which can be printed. Auto-Graphics will sell hardware and software for this system or the software and CD-ROM for installation on the library's own hardware.

The IMPACT/SLIMS system is designed for libraries under 45,000 titles. Auto-Graphics will custom quote prices to create the database for this system. Bar code scanners can be used optionally for recording circulation transactions. This system is currently in version 3.0 and is appropriate for school, special, public and academic libraries. It can operate as a single-user, stand-alone MS-DOS system or in a LAN using LANTastic or Novell Netware 2.11 at minimum. It probably would work with Novell Lite, although 1 have not actually tested it ,in such a configuration. It is programmed in the C LANguage and uses Btrieve for its indexing. One can operate IMPACT/SLIMS along with IMPACT, where the local library database is in the SLIMS system and the IMPACT CD-ROM system is a union database. This system can also be used to generate a hard- disk update to the CD-ROM, which can be installed on the hard disk on each workstation to keep the CD-ROM current between its remastering. The library can import MicroLIF records as supplied by various dealers. Although searches between IMPACT/SLIMS and IMPACT on CD-ROM are not transparent, it takes only a couple of keystrokes to toggle back and forth. This is an attractive system for consortia or individual smaller libraries and can be operated quite economically according to the extent of the LAN used and the frequency of remastering the CD-ROM catalog. Since standard CD-ROM drives can be internally incorporated into the main chassis of the microcomputer, these stations can be attractively packaged but use relatively inexpensive hard disk-equipped Intel 80386SX systems.

Auto-Graphics' central system uses several host platforms to provide its various services. A Sperry 90/80 superminicomputer together with a Data General Aviion workstation having two 16-MB central processors operating at 20 MHz, two 1600/6250-bpi tape drives, two 2-GB cartridge tapes, one 150-MB cartridge tape and 16 GB of direct access storage devices and a printer provide these services. In addition a Meridian Data CD-ROM publisher is used to produce the CD-ROM catalogs. The Aviion is connected via Ethernet to a Xyvision XFPS 55-typesetting system with four Xyview workstations, a Linotronic L300 typesetter with 250 type faces, two Linotronic laser proofing devices and a Linotronic 202 typesetter. In addition there are microfilm processors to produce microfiche products. Auto-Graphics has a good history of providing service to its library clients. It has provided the IMPACT computer systems since 1987. Morrow and Lee have written about this product in some detail.

Balboa Software: This product is a bibliographic and textual database manager. The current version is release 2.0 which has added over 100 new features to an already abundantly featured product at its introduction. This software is available either as an MS-DOS Single-user license or as a LAN multiple-user license. Prices are very competitive with competing products such as Pro-Cite, BRS/Search, INMAGIC and Zyindex. The network version will operate under Novell or any Netbios-compatible network.

This software will run under MS-DOS v.2.0 and above and on systems with 512 kB RAM available after loading MS-DOS. For small databases, even a dual 720-kB floppy system could be used, but a hard disk is really necessary for serious, continued production use. In the network version each user can save her or his own default settings. Public read-only databases can be put up, personal databases in private sub directories and shared databases for workgroup projects are all supported. Multiple users on the LAN can search simultaneously in a database. Automatic record locking ensures data integrity as individuals update databases. One of the strengths of this product is its ability to produce bibliographies in many styles. A catalog of books and an index to periodical literature cross-indexed by authors, subject and journals are other products from this system. Titles can be italicized or underlined. This program supports Post-Script output and interfaces to WordPerfect v.5.1 or above in MS-DOS or Windows versions. Suffixes such as "Jr." or "III" also may be treated several ways. Letter case conversion to capitalize all words or just the beginning of the field or each word and an option to keep capitalization for foreign LANguages where capitalization rules differ, such as German or French, are another slick feature.

The Format File options also allow centered lines, joined lines, records indexed and grouped under any field, special treatment of records with empty fields and special processing if a field is the same as or different from the previous record. Records can be imported into a Library Master database from MELVYL, NOTIS, GEAC, University of Toronto Online Library Catalog, Chemical Abstracts STN, Compact Cambridge MEDLINE v.4, EPIC, RLIN short title catalog, ABI/INFORM, AGRICOLA, religious and Theological Abstracts CD-ROM. Notebook II and NB Citation data formats can also be handled. The optional, separately priced Data Magician program can import and export MARC records. After a search, records are displayed in a browse-mode, brief-view display presenting seven records at a time. The fields displayed can be chosen. A single record can be formatted and printed as well as a whole listing. One can edit a record without leaving browse or search modes. It is possible to search a subset retrieved by a prior search, and search strategies can be named and saved for reuse. One can spell out Boolean search operators AND, OR and NOT in the search. Record number and record type searching is supported. For color monitor or laptop gray-scale monitor use; the system has complete color customization.

Dates can contain non-English month spellings. There is a utility to repair a damaged database and an option to retain original record numbers. A PIF file is supplied for running Library Master in a DOS Window under Microsoft Windows v.3.1 This is a very price competitive product for its features. It has an improved manual and a basic tutorial that will help the user get up to speed quickly. Balboa's upgrade prices are also reasonable and based on the version being upgraded. Library Master is well named.

LePac is a CD-ROM online catalog introduced in 1985. It also serves as the online catalog for the Precision One (P1) Integrated System. P1 is a retrospective conversion and cataloging system for school and public libraries that use a CD-ROM MARC database. The P1 Integrated System is implemented using the LANTastic LAN to provide circulation, public access to the LePac catalog, cataloging and database maintenance, interlibrary loan, local authority control, holdings maintenance, bibliographies and an interface to the Precision One MARC record database.

Collection Development and Acquisitions support was under development at the time of my inquiry to Brodart, so prospective users of this system should be confident that this module will be released to round out this system's capabilities. LePac can store up to one million tides on a single CD-ROM disk using a proprietary data compression scheme. The system has a nice browse feature done by scrolling alphabetic lists of authors, titles or subjects.

An express access by typing in an author name, subject or tide brings the user quite quickly to the desired records. A single library or a union catalog database can be constructed as a location field is provided. Searching uses the implied "AND" when multiple terms are entered. To implement the OR operator, one merely encloses terms in parentheses, while a tilde before a term implements the operator NOT. Cross-references produce the actual bibliographic record when the enter key is pressed.

The LePac CD-ROM can be supplemented without the expense of remastering the whole CD-ROM via either a supplemental CD-ROM disk or downloading current records to the workstation's hard disk. Using the P1 Integrated System, these supplements can be fully integrated. An add-on to LePac is the QuILL interlibrary loan software. It will produce printed ILL forms, download records to disk and enable a centralized processing center to form an ILL network using an MS-DOS microcomputer.

Modem connections over telephone lines can be used to communicate with ILL software-equipped systems in the individual network libraries. This system can operate unattended, making its calls each evening on a predetermined schedule, then transferring requests and replies. It can make 2040 calls per hour and store up to 30,000 ILL requests. The downloading to disk-type operation is used by systems that use an electronic bulletin board system for request and reply distribution. Precision One features over 1.2 million MARC records on CD-ROM and has particularly high hit rates on audio/visual records. Libraries can subscribe to monthly current cataloging with LC MARC and audio/visual records created by Brodart. These are cumulative so only two disks are ever searched.

The P1 Integrated System complements the above systems to form a well-integrated application suite. Using this system to create local supplements to the LePac CD-ROM database allows a currency of records just as with a fully hard disk-stored database system. The P1 system will generate spine and pocket labels as well as shelf list cards or complete card sets. Records with added holdings or other modifications are stored on the system's hard disk and replace the CD-ROM record in a catalog search.

The Collection Development and Acquisition module under development will be a separately priced subsystem with a database built on Brodart's Books' file of tides in print. It will supply MARC record, title information, in-print status, age level and review source. Then, in the acquisition phase, a new program called PC Rose Plus from Brodart's Books is going to be integrated. A BISAC format disk will be used to transfer electronic orders to Brodart or other vendors. An interface to the circulation system will support bar code label production and building item records. In addition to these systems, Brodart provides vendor conversion services using its over 12 million cataloging record database, mainly for school and public library customers. For this service and as a separate service to libraries it also uses its central Interactive Access System to store each customer's database at a fixed monthly cost.

This system features full-screen editing with author and title searching for the cataloger. The personal computer interface software can download records to the workstation, where the record is processed with considerable flexibility. Brodart has a long record of service to libraries and certainly has systems installed in sufficient numbers to prove its worth in the marketplace. This system is designed to provide museum collections with support for bibliographic and artifact databases. It is equally at home in an archive and manuscript setting, slide collection, art works collection, or photography library. It uses a MARC II record structure and locally defined fields to extend MARC to cover these specialized materials. The user can specify which fields will be indexed for faster retrieval. It supports all seven MARC formats, including the Authority Format and the new Integrated Format.

Record transport features allow the conversion of non-MARC databases to MARC and the MARC database to other, non-MARC formats. These are dBase dbf format, R:Base, SQL and word-processing formats. Records may be up to 65,000 bytes each in this system. The system will print inventory reports, collection guides, catalog cards, and folder and slide labels. Searchers use browsable indexes, wildcards and keyword searches in any field. Browsable indexes in pop-up windows make the user interface appealing and easy to use. The accessioning support is quite full, printing deed-of-gift forms and other outputs customary to museum and archive collection administration.

The authority system is fully invoked to provide search terms and record-building terms to the cataloger. Various receipt and record transfer forms can be generated. The accessions screen actually incorporates the cataloging information on further record pages which can be built later in brief or full form. The system can also mimic RLIN or OCLC record displays for users already familiar with these. The National Archives of the Episcopal Church is one of some 200 clients using this software. Donald Firsching has written of his experiences with Minaret. (3) The other package that implements the Archives and Manuscripts Control (AMC) MARC format is the MicroMARC:amc system developed by Michigan State University, which is presented later.

Firsching is particularly impressed with the authority file features of Minaret, the addition of keyboard macro capabilities and the use of record layouts that can be copied, then modified to generate new MARC formats not supplied with the system. For example, he created an OCLC books format by modifying the AMC format copy. The system is conceived around the use of a construct known as an "environment," which brings together groups of records with the forms they will use. The records in a particular group will be of the same structure, i.e., with the same database field definitions or layout. Some 30 forms are already defined in the system as provided. The F9 key activates a menu bar at the top of the screen, but this bar is not of the pull-down type, so multiple menus must be paged through when performing some tasks. He also described Minaret's searching power as "somewhat primitive" compared with a standard database management system.

Queries can be entered in three ways. The first is "EZ," which uses any bLANk fill-in-the field screen template. The second is Boolean, which offers operators that work only within fields. The third is "free form," which uses a Query LANguage. The searching in this system, while adequate, probably could be improved through some user interface and index-building changes. This system is available as a Single-user MS-DOS system, as a Netbios-compatible LAN version and as a UNIX System V, release 3 program. Thus multiple-user systems of some considerable size can be implemented or very small systems supported with the same functionality in the software. Minaret is an interesting system, with a specialized market niche for museum and archive organizations. It is priced competitively, has excellent growth potential, and a good design foundation, and should continue to receive enhancements to keep it competitive in its specialized market. The Columbia

Library System is a product whose main market is in schools, with only 20% of its sales going to types libraries. These others are mainly public and college libraries. This system can handle up to 300,000 catalog records either as an MS-DOS-based Single-user system or as a multiuser system running under a Novell LAN.

Each of the modules is separately price but fully integrated. Cataloging and online catalog, circulation, MARC record interface, acquisitions and serials constitute the currently offered modules. The LAN version is in use by 67% of customers. The average collection size for these customers is 14,000 tides, although the largest site has close to 200,000 titles. Columbia uses pull-down menus and is a system that will appeal to most users. Columbia originated in Regina, Saskatchewan, Canada and was originally developed by ABALL Software, which licensed it under the name Ocelot Library System.

In Australia it is still licensed under the Ocelot name. Dr. ALAN Ball was its principal designer. Further development of the software had been underwritten by the Canadian network UTLAS. In 1986 ABALL sold it to Columbia Computing. In 1989 this system was completely rewritten. It should be noted that a form of this earlier software is still supported by UTLAS and is called the M/Series 10 product, but it has only online catalog and circulation modules. This system offers some menu customization to integrate MARC record source products such as Bibliofile or Mitinet/MARC. One can provide a gateway to a LAN electronic mail facility, a neighbouring library's online catalog or a union catalog via an asynchronous modem-type connection. With an Internet gateway connection, a shared CD-ROM resource on the network can be accessed from the library's workstations.

The system's browse and Boolean searching are very

flexible and easy to learn. Pressing the F1 function key on the PC keyboard brings up context-sensitive help. The system uses its menu colors on a colored screen very pleasingly. The main menu offers the following choices: catalog, circulation, MARC, acquisitions, serials, utilities, files/DOS and quit. Catalog searches are displayed in a card format.

For libraries that still use cards, the system will print card sets or shelf list cards and spine/pocket labels. The circulation system has some features that will appeal to schools. For example, one can generate lists of overdues by homeroom instead of merely generating individual student overdue notices. The sample reports from the system are nicely laid out, clear and can be generated on differing frequencies.

The system exports its records in MicroLIF and a similar format called NearLIF. Records can be imported into this system from LaserQuest, OCLC, UTLAS, WLN, MARCive, Bibliofile, and different book vendors. The serial check-in uses a familiar metaphor-the Kardex-as its interface. It can predict expected issues using a start date coupled with the MARC standard frequencies from daily to triennial to establish its prediction calendar.

Columbia customers are sent Libra News, a newsletter covering Columbia news. They also have an 800 number for support if they have purchased an annual support agreement which costs roughly 10% of the original license fee for each module. There is also an electronic bulletin board. This system is competitive in its features with other MS-DOS-based products and in some cases really offers special features that will appeal to the school market. But other types of libraries within its database size range are advised to examine this system before jumping to the conclusion that it is only for school libraries.

CALICO has provided library automation software to small libraries, mainly schools, since 1981. In the spring of 1993 the Macintosh version of LION was introduced. CALICO did not have a demonstration system to send me but invited me to come to St. Louis, Missouri to see the system in action in Principia Upper School where LION has been in use for six years. LION is an online catalog and circulation system designed for school libraries. It has had well-satisfied customers since its introduction in 1985. Data Trek was founded in 1981, making it one of the pioneer companies to produce microcomputer software for the library market. Its original product, the MANAGER Series, is a MARC-compatible, menu-driven system.

The new ULS Professional Series is a fully integrated MARC-standard product for libraries requiring full-MARC compliance. GoPAC is a Microsoft Windows-based online-catalog-search front end for all Data Trek software. Both MANAGER and ULS Professional run on MS-DOS-based computers as Single-user systems or on Novell LANs for multiple-user versions. The MANAGER is also available on the Apple Macintosh and as a mini-computer product as mentioned MANAGER is functionally equivalent across its three platforms. The MANAGER Series, implemented in dBase Ill and C LANguage, is composed of separate but integrated modules: cataloging, online catalog, circulation, serials, acquisitions, DataBridge, report generator, audio/visual handler, and corporate documents.

Hard disk storage estimates for this system are 2 MB per thousand titles, with hard disk capacity as the only limit in either single user or LAN versions. A full-screen editor is used for creating and changing records. The cataloging module will print catalog card sets or can be used in conjunction with the online catalog. It will generate new acquisitions fists. Spine and pocket labels are also a feature. The online catalog features both browsing and a power search facility that uses Boolean operators plus right and left-hand truncation. Search results can be sent to the screen, the printer or to a disk file.

A Hypersearch is possible through highlighting a word on a search result screen and then retrieving all other items containing that highlighted word. The circulation module also supports loans by the minute for college reserve book room use. Bar code labels and wand readers or scanners can be used or transactions keyed in for low-volume situations. The serials module features single-keystroke cheek-in, issue routing, and table of contents routing slip generation. It prompts the operator when items are ready for binding and predicts next expected issue. There are optional online vendor interfaces and claiming.

A full subscription history is maintained and there is support for bindery preparation, including printing binding tickets and packing slips. The acquisitions module also has optional online vendor interfaces. Fund accounting, invoice tracking/processing, order file maintenance and order creation are all nicely implemented. Boolean searches on the order file can be sorted by up to three keys. The system generates order letters, claims and cancellations for all ordering situations. The DataBridge subsystem performs MARC import for LC MARC, OCLC, MARCive, NLM, WIN, MicroLIF and quite a few other MARC sources. There is a CD-ROM and an online interface. Transferrable local MARC tags can be specified. Field selection is user defined. The report generator has over 150 user-customizable reports. It features full editing, repositioning and elimination of fields, margin controls, page length and compressed print controls.

Reports can be sent to any printer or to an ASCII text file for later printing or transfer to a word processor. The audio/visual handler supports media collections, while the corporate documents module provides special record definitions and features for these collections to be integrated into an automated system. The MANAGER Series uses a non-tagged form record into which MARC data is loaded. It is complete enough for most libraries to use for their operational and public service needs. Multiple fixed-length standard fields are used in MANAGER Series modules. MANAGER Series also uses multiple dBase-compatible bibliographic record files for its respective modules.

The ULS (Ultimate Library System) Professional Series uses a full-MARC record for storage, downloading, editing and output. It is programmed in the C LANguage. The EasyMARC feature lets a user edit MARC data without being intimate with each MARC record tag, subfield or indicator. The system then creates a correctly tagged MARC record. In the displays a user can switch between a MARC format and an attractively labelled display with no data loss. It has true variable length and repeating fields, with variable length records.

Zoomable fields, pull-down browse lists and pick lists make this an attractive stem from the user's view. This product uses a single integrated bibliographic database, with all modules accessed from a single menu. The Power Search capability is integral to the system, and there is an optional add-on called USM. The GoPAC graphical user interface for the online catalog for either of the above systems is really well designed. It, too, is a C LANguage implementation. The point-and-click searching makes catalog searching easy and invites one not to rush through an interaction with the system as it really appears fun!

An EasySearch browse by author, title or subject will probably locate most known item-type searches. An Expert search using Boolean operators is easy to do. A user can send comments to the librarian or library staff. The output from searches can be in ascending or descending order by publication date or in alphabetic order by title. One can turn on and off automatic truncation. GoPAC is an excellent example of a Windows implementation of an online catalog user interface. Libraries using this system should pLAN to implement GoPAC on their public workstations as a minimum and preferably on all workstations within the LAN where the online catalog can be searched. There are some 2000 customer libraries around the world that use these products, with some modules available in French, Spanish and Italian.

Data Trek has distributors in New York, Ohio, Canada, France, EngLANd, Spain, Australia, PoLANd and Turkey. Special libraries are the main customer, but other types of libraries are represented in the customer base as well. If you are considering an MS-DOS-based system or one that you will run on a Novell LAN, then you will need to examine this product very seriously and make comparisons with its competitors' systems. Data Trek has had the longest history of continuously enhancing its MANAGER Series, and with the introduction of the ULS product in 1989 and the GoPAC in 1992, it is continuing the production of very competitive, feature-laden systems using the latest in software technology and current platforms. Open Access Strategic Information System (OASIS) consists of interlibrary loan (AIM), serials management system (SMS), acquisitions, circulation and online catalog designed to operate on Intel microprocessor systems in a Novell network.

The AIM module was jointly developed with Leicester Polytechnic and it provides electronic access to the British Library Document Supply Centre or to any other lending source. Another nice feature of this system is the file reformatter and automatic text editor, also jointly developed. It will handle diverse database downloaded records, extracting records from full-text retrievals. The serials module provides check-in, routing of issues with reader ranking and integration with the acquisitions module for subscription and payment details.

Acquisitions handle the full spectrum of possible order types and information needed for accounting, invoice payment and claiming. The online catalog provides the expected author, title, subject and Boolean access. The system supports the main European LANguages. The catalog is authority based and provides cross-referencing and global control through its authority system. This is a user-friendly system with pop-up windows, fill in the bLANks forms, and scrolling windows to pick choices to fill in fields.

The integrated workstation (IWS) used in this system is an IBM or clone computer with client software for access, manipulation and formatting output from this system. Special libraries, public libraries and college libraries are the major users. A relatively small server with a 200-MB hard disk will handle a 40,000-60,000 record database. Dawson encourages schools and colleges as customers by offering this software at a discount. The system is available in separate yet integrated modules for either Single-user MS-DOS operation or on a network license, priced depending on the number of PCs in the network. The prices quoted in pounds sterling do not include Britain's 17.5 % value-added tax. This system is competitive in its features and design to similar U.S.-developed software but does not appear to be marketed outside Europe. This system has gone through several major revisions. It was formerly called MELVIL. It is a MARC record-based inventory, circulation and online catalog/cataloging system designed for the school library market. Some 80% of SURPASS/2 customers are schools. This system is very easy to use, so easy that young children can be taught to look for topics and items in the online catalog quite quickly. There are eight security levels built in which should be sufficient to provide protected access to its staff-and patron-oriented functions on a LAN.

Given a school-implemented Novell LAN, access to this online catalog can be brought from the media center to each classroom. The system will import both full-MARC and MicroLIF records from any known CD-ROM or commercial service source. The circulation system can be set up with parameters controlled by grade level as well as patron type. Defining your MARC database uses a scrolling MARC tag list and windows with the subfields shown where you fill in the subfield name or label as it will appear on your OPAC and data entry screens. Even support for nonfiling indicator values is provided. The user can control alert tones from workstations for caution or warning messages on overdues or fines. If the library still wishes to provide a card catalog, it can generate card sets and book label sets from this system. At year's end it is very easy to purge graduating students and to advance students to their next grade level. The system comes with some utilities such as printer. exe, which one uses to define the printer(s) available to the system. An editor called smenu.exe and a menu maker called menu.exe are two others provided. The use of color, pull-down menus, flexible system setup, allowance for full or abbreviated amounts of bibliographic data in the records, scrolling windows and comfortable and familiar catalog card image that OPAC displays make this a good system to install where students and staff have been long accustomed to a card catalog.

The online catalog uses either scrolling windows for selecting search terms or a direct entry of author, title or subject. Searches can be saved for later reuse or printed out. Search results can be in MARC or MicroLIF format. The Boolean operators AND, OR and NOT are supported. Keyword searches are done by capitalizing the word instead of entering it in lower case.

Another slick feature is that one can access from the catalog screen published reviews and bulletins authored by users, and users can choose to submit reviews for this published review collection. This file can also be complemented with tables-of-content of the collection for patron view. The circulation system uses bar-coded labels and stores its item records as Tag 901 in the bibliographic record. It is flexible enough to handle any school circulation need. The report writer permits custom reports definition and is easy to use. While some users have operated this system in a peer-to-peer-type LAN such as LANTastic, the less problematic way to provide multiple user access to this Clipper-programmed system is to use a server type network with the preferred LAN software, Novell Advanced Netware v.3.12. The system can be packaged as a turnkey hardware and software solution or, if the customer already has the necessary equipment and Novell LAN in place, as software only. Adding workstations is quite economical, with inexpensive license fees. This system will have strong appeal to school students, make teaching library skills to young students a pleasure and yet be a good price/ performance value to the school system. System support for those customers purchasing it is provided through a toll free telephone number.

A separate system for media center management, called The Eloquent Media Manager, is a sister system to the integrated online library system, called The Eloquent Librarian. This latter system is discussed here. The

Eloquent Librarian is programmed in Revelation. The license fee is based on the number of titles in the catalog. The base system provides cataloging and online catalog, spine and pocket labels or printed catalogs.

A research-only system can be licensed to provide search-only capabilities on a workstation. There are further modules for circulation, media management, acquisitions, serials, MARC import and MARC export. All of the above systems run on stand-alone MS-DOS PC/AT class systems or Novell LANs. The Eloquent Librarian's base module can come as a predefined configuration for school library, media resource center or special library. The developer recommends working with a small test database if one decides to customize these setups as once the database is built, it is more difficult to make field changes to it. One can add or delete fields, change field names, add user codes and modify code names.

After a database is built, one can still add fields, but not delete certain fields if these are titles in the database, nor can one select a new standard configuration. The system uses operator levels of trainee, search, research, data entry, all and system to control security. There is a French LANguage module for libraries requiring French and English. The basic configuration has the first comment field used for storing the edition, place, publisher, physical description and general note. To differentiate these data elements, a two-character code is used. For those used to MARC-tagged work forms, setting up this system may appear a bit cryptic since the workforms do not contain any MARC tagging labels, indicators or subfield designations.

A nice feature of this system is its global synonym authority file capability. British and American spelling forms such as "Centre" and "Center" can be indexed under a common form, yet still be located if the nonpreferred form is entered. Global stopwords have been defined, but these can be changed from their "the," .0 an," and "a" form. There is a spelling assist feature that can be turned on or off.

Both MARC and MicroLIF formats can be imported or exported from this system. Each title record is limited to 64,000 characters but can contain repeating and variable length fields. If one needs to print catalog card sets and book label sets, this module will produce these to the quality of the printer used. Searching in this system is flexible and powerful. There are four different search screens used, three of which are basic templates, with the fourth providing expert search.

Keyword searching looks for words in the title, variant title, summary, all authorities and comment fields that have been chosen for indexing. The second search screen permits basic author, title and subject searching, while the third provides multiple keyword, title and subject combinations. The expert search screen provides one or multiple access points with Boolean logic operators, including nested bracketed, parentheses or braces evaluation notation. The AND, OR and NOT operators can be written also as symbol codes and both right and left truncation are features. A search can also have a "must contain" value by enclosing the value in brackets like this: [steam]. Search results Can be saved as lists and also the search strategy saved for later reuse.

Feld technologies: DATA route

Through the years there have been quite a few microcomputer programs written to provide periodical issue routing labels, but DATARoute appears to me to be the best of this genre. It can run on a hard disk or floppy-only system. It is an MS-DOS program with dBase 111 file structures. The three files it creates are READERS.DBF, PUBS.DBF and LIST.DBF. Each reader has a three-character code-usually the reader's initials. Each serial title/copy has a five-character code. The reader record also includes a department (4-character abbreviation), telephone number, location (4 characters) and status (4 characters). This last field shows the reader's status or seniority within the pecking order of routing. Routing slip assignment can use this seniority code, to determine what readers will be on which routing slips for a particular copy of a publication and their order on the slip. Operation of this system is quite smooth. If you press PF3 in the Change Readers menu Edit function, a menu of reader names pops up and you can select a reader. Soundex codes are also used to index readers so "sounds like" searches can be performed where the inexact spelling of names will still produce valid hits, For browsing through a list, the Zoom feature displays the first entry that matches a string in an exact-match mode search.

The manual accompanying this program is quite complete except for no mention of the exact size of label stock needed for the regular or oversized label option printing. The samples appear to use half of an 81/2" by 11" sheet for oversized and 2" by 5", for regular. The form length can be set for 15" with one-eighth inch line spacing and 3" for oversized with that same spacing.

This program allows you to choose its menu colors to suit you and your monitor's preferences. Regular sized labels will hold up to 12 names and the oversized up to 32 for routing. Data entry is rapid, operation is bulletproof and reliable for both novice and experienced computer users. If all you need is routing slip production because your present automated system does not adequately provide it or you have a manual serials operation, this routing program will be an invaluable work saver.

Follett Corporation is composed of six companies serving the education market through wholesaling textbooks, operating college bookstores, and providing software to elementary and secondary schools and public libraries. Over 20,000 customers use this software. Follett's approach to automating these libraries is the "crawl, then walk, then run" technique in which small steps are taken before large and complex multifunctional solutions are approached. Therefore, the products range from single-function programs such as the CardMaster Plus to the Circulation Plus and Catalog Plus systems. CardMaster Plus is a MARC-based database for producing catalog cards and label sets. It can interface to Mitinet/MARC for current cataloging source data.

The Union CD Plus is a CD-ROM union catalog. MAC Search Plus station is an add-on to the Circulation/Catalog Plus products which uses an Apple Macintosh as a user station on a Novell LAN. For libraries still equipped only with an Apple II, there is Circulation Plus, which allows bar code-reading devices to be used, just as with systems based on more powerful computers. For retrospective conversion, Follett has Alliance Plus, a CD-ROM file of MARC recon records. Follett also offers retrospective conversion services to libraries. The Circulation Plus and Catalog Plus have features comparable to minicomputer and main-frame-hosted systems with these functions but operate in a Novell LAN or as Single-user MS-DOS programs. They also feature a hand-held scanning device called PHD+ to perform inventory control in the stacks and then transfer this data to the Circulation Plus system. There is no comparable inventory software or scanner provided with the NOTIS mainframe-based system which is directed at large libraries. Could it be that large libraries are thought not to need such a feature or that they can just develop this capability themselves with a bit of Turbo Pascal and any commercially available portable scanning device? The Follett software is competitively priced, particularly its LAN versions of Catalog Plus and Circulation Plus, which most client libraries operate as an integrated pair. Follett's systems can be a solution for a single school or a school district, given the LAN configuration, use of asynchronous gateways and the Union CD Plus catalog. Customers have a firm with a long history of financial stability, bringing products to the education market and providing good support service. This product is reviewed by Saffady.

If you want to experience a real gem in software distributed as shareware, you need to get BIBL, the creation of Clyde W. Grotophorst. This program licenses for $39 for a single user, and its LAN version, called BIBL/NET, licenses for a mere $150 per server no matter how many simultaneous users access the server. BIBL is a full-featured catalog program for an individual's personal library or for a corporate a project library. It features multiple database, full-text retrieval, mouse support, Boolean searching, keyword validation and over 13 reports. One can import ASCII files and with the numerous utility programs that GMUtant has, it is possible to import records from CD-ROM sources, ERIC, PsychInfo, Medline, ABI/Inform, AGRICOLA and others. BIBL gets regular updates and has been distributed from Grotophorst's bulletin boards (BBs) at George Mason University Library, through shareware distributors such as Public Brand Software and various other BBs such as the University of Minnesota Libraries BBs.

Moreover, it is easy to learn, the documentation is in the archive file distribution and there should be little need to have much help in using this software. The beauty of shareware is that you get to try it before licensing it so you need not have a problem with returning and getting a refund if the program does not fit your needs as you would with regular commercially distributed programs. FidoNet-connected BBs should also be able to get copies of this program and its ever-increasing number of utility programs via a File Request to the George Mason University Library BBs.

Access is via LC card no and title. Once a search produces a record, the record can be modified and saved to diskette. Records can be uploaded to an online system via modem, used to produce catalog cards, sent to GRC for creation and maintenance of the library's database or uploaded to GRC's sister product, an online CD-ROM-based catalog called LaserGuide. LaserQuest will operate on an MS-DOS system having at least 512 kB addressable memory available or it can work in a Novell LAN, with multiple workstations sharing the CD-ROM database in a tower CD-ROM server. One to six CD-ROM drives can be used in a stand-alone workstation or the Pioneer 6 disk changer used to hold the six disks constituting the database. The LaserGuide online catalog uses the MS-DOS CD-ROM extensions. Its LaserMerge facility allows updated records stored on the workstion's hard disk to update the CD-ROM transparently between re-mastering of the CD-ROM. Staff can display records in a MARC-tagged display and can modify the local screen colors. Searching is through keyword in author, title and subject indexes. Bibliographies can be printed from selected records. A library map feature can show a flashing arrow for book location. By placing hyphens to connect words or quote marks around words, one can perform a phrase search.

An asterisk is used for a truncation character, fill in the appropriate area on a searches. Boolean AND, OR and NOT are implemented through a "fill in the appropriate area" on a search screen. There is a shelf list browse available, too. This system has easy-to-understand screens, is simple for the library user to learn and will perform the standard kinds of searches expected of an online catalog. This online catalog can be operated on stand-alone workstations or on a Novell LAN. LaserGuide was one of the early CD-ROM catalogs. Both LaserGuide and LaserQuest have been marketed since 1987, so they have proven themselves in the field. They are suitable for any type of library.

Information Transform was founded by Hank Espstein. Some years previously, he was the Director of the Ballots Project at Stanford University. Ballots later became the software on which the RLG/RLIN network offered its members interactive mainframe cataloging, acquisitions and other services. It is evident that not only excellent programming but a thorough knowledge of MARC and cataloging standards form the underpinning to MITINET/MARC.

While its initial customer base was mainly school libraries, it is now used by hundreds of libraries of all types. It can be the MARC record source for over 60 different commercially available library automation systems. This cataloging system is available on Apple II, Macintosh and MS-DOS microcomputers. It is programmed in the C LANguage. It was originally developed in 1986 by Information Transform and the Wisconsin Department of Public Instruction as a joint undertaking.

The beauty of this system is that it conforms to the AACR2 and ISBD rules, implementing 118 punctuation rules to make cataloging much easier for the novice. One can use this in conjunction with a MARC source such as Bibliofile or another CD-ROM MARC database to catalog all non-MARC record match titles. All MARC formats are supported, and the General Materials Designation (GMD) is assigned automatically after all cataloging data is entered. The operator can have screens prompted in plain English, in a terse form or in MARC-tagged form the nonfiling indicator is set correctly for the English "a," "an," "and," "the" and 96 other foreign LANguage leading articles.

There are versions set up to feed records to specific systems. For example, the MS-DOS versions include Follett, MOLLI, Dynix, Bibliofile, and Winnebago in addition to the regular version. Be sure to check with this company on your specific automated library system as additional versions have been issued and will undoubtedly continue to be produced.

New versions of this software have been regularly released, and it is now in its third major release. These variant versions implement different local holdings field tags depending on the system. For example, the regular version uses the MARC tag 852 for local holdings, while the Dynix version uses MARC tag 949 and a different subfielding. The manual is very well organized, clearly written and replete with numerous cataloging examples. Using this system makes cataloging a pleasure for both novice and experienced librarians as well as permitting easy training of nonprofessionals to do cataloging work. If one were to award marks as for an Olympic gymnastic performance, this product would score a perfect 10 for every routine-and it even keeps getting better with each new software release.

The Macintosh version is Mac all the way and yet implements the same capabilities as in the MS-DOS version. The MS-DOS version is programmed in C LANguage, while the Mac version is done in object-oriented C. The latest in programming techniques and a superb understanding of a very complex operation make these implementations rock-solid performers.

Certainly, no software is a substitute for the professional expertise of the cataloger as to choice of entry, proper classification, descriptive treatment and subject analysis, but a tool such as MITINET/MARC surely makes a cataloger's work so much easier and leaves the cataloger more time to be concerned with professional content instead of with learning lots of the arcane punctuation and form that is a part of both AACR2 and ISBD. Information Transform's service and support are also excellent. This system has matured over a decade of versions and migration from its original Datapoint minicomputer implementation. 'It is oriented toward special libraries and operates as a Novell Advanced Netware LAN product.

It is MS-DOS-based in its Single-user version. A Digital Equipment VAX version is also available. The VAX version implements media booking, interlibrary loan and reserve book room modules, which are not a part of the microcomputer version at least at the time 1 was able to examine this product. Special libraries, schools and colleges are the major customers of these versions. The SYDNEY PLUS system starts with a base module which provides cataloging, queries, thesaurus and system management. There is an unlimited number of copy records, and the system has excellent cross-referencing support via its thesaurus. Any bar code reader and label code standard can be used for circulation.

The MARC record interface supports Bibliofile, DOBIS, MARCive, OCLC, RLIN and UTLAS. Records can be exported in MARC using the output format generator program and export conversion program. The acquisitions module has full fund accounting and also permits billing user departments for materials and services. One can prepare online abstracts of items and incorporate these in the online catalog. There is an imaging module that supports optical scanning of documents, viewing and cataloging them, and incorporating image data in the online searchable database.

The circulation system is flexible enough to handle many special and academic settings. The serials module allows operators to easily modify expected issue arrivals and perform the complex operation associated With maintaining large serial collections. There is a remote public access catalog module also. This is a nicely color implemented, menu-driven system with considerable customization features.

Security is handled by module and by function, with 99 levels possible. The online catalog has a public check-out capability so that routine self-charging can be done by users. The report generator produces customized reports and the syntax of commands is much like INMAGIC or DataEase. A SYDNEY PLUS database uses approximately 4 MB for each thousand catalog records. The programs comprising all the modules require about 22 MB of hard disk space. So a relatively modest 340 MB hard disk system could easily service a 50,000-item collection. Of course, if the imaging module were to be used, disk requirements would go up considerably. However, one can obtain SCSI-2 hard disks that have 2.1 GB capacity for around $2100. Therefore, a very large database system could be implemented, particularly within a LAN environment. SYDNEY PLUS is one of those products that has proven itself in the long-term market, and it just keeps getting better. Special libraries acquiring automation software should consider this product-in either the MS-DOS/Novell version or the DEC VAX version. New competitive capabilities are being added by ILS, and system prices are competitive

This system is installed mainly in special libraries. It was formerly a product of Library Automation Technologies, Inc., which was acquired by Inlex. This is a polished, menu-driven system with acquisitions, cataloging, online catalog, circulation and serials modules. It is MARC based, and the online catalog is able to display MARC-tagged records and catalog card format in addition to its regular labelled catalog display. Pull-down menus and selection lists make this system a pleasure to use. Unlimited notes can be added to records. The authority file provides cross-references and powerful global change facilities.

All file maintenance operations are easy to understand and to perform in this system. Security is quite flexible and can be tailored to the particular staff member's needs. Key entry and bar-coded labels scanned for circulation transaction entry are both permitted. Circulation has good calendar control and features to handle any loan periods and as many patron and material types as needed in any library situation.

Library users can inquire of their own record of books checked out, overdue items and fine amounts. MARC records can be imported from many external sources such as OCLC or Bibliofile. The serials module is particularly strong as would be expected for a special library-oriented system. The issue routing has good flexibility and uses the patron record as does circulation. One can position a user on a routing slip in any order for a given copy of a journal. A patron can be added to multiple title routing slips in one operation through a selection of system is competitively priced to encourage LAN licensing. This software has been used by numerous special and academic libraries as well as nonlibrary clients for over a decade.

The original INMAGIC was implemented on Digital Equipment minicomputers. When MS-DOS systems became the desktop standard, INMAGIC became available for them and for LAN installation. There is a version for Digital Equipment VAX series computers, and INMAGIC for MS-DOS systems will also run on a Macintosh using DOS emulation software.

The beauty of INMAGIC is its completely variable length fields and records, its repeating fields at a keystroke and its indexing options. There is no maximum record size and any record can have up to 75 defined fields and up to 100 indexes. The number of INMAGIC databases that can be set up is limited only by hard disk storage capacity on one's system or LAN server.

Geared to handling text, this software is popular for customization not only for library operations and bibliographic search support but also for such applications as litigation support, documentation tracking, personnel/human resource systems and numerous other applications that can take advantage of its variable fielding and indexing strengths. A nice feature of this software is its relative independence from the hardware on which it runs. For example, except for the text editor which was intimate with the IBM system architecture in versions prior to this completely new release of INMAGIC Plus v. 1.0, release 1.0, 1 could run this software on a non-IBM compatible system such as the Victor 9000 under its customized MS-DOS. These files were then completely transportable over to the later MS/PC-DOS versions running on conventional IBM and clone computers.

Traditional relational and flat file database software is oriented toward fixed length data and manipulation of numeric data. Text retrieval systems, on the other hand, are set up to treat text as a single large field or a group of related paragraphs. INMAGIC is engineered to handle both text and numeric data. Any field in any record can be any length. Any field can be indexed or globally changed.

Unlimited repeating fields can be added any time during record editing without rebuilding the database.

Searching can be by word, word stem, phrase or proximity to another term. Ranges of data values and Boolean operators are part of the search provisions. Performance of this software is superb. Even very complex searches on very large databases can be executed in a few seconds.

The search screens are fill-in-the-bLANks with clear, unbroken labels. Each of these screens can contain up to 10 prompts and each prom can search up to 20 fields at once. One can browse through a field and paste a term of choice into a prompt. Validation look-up tables, format criteria range values are techniques used to maintain data accuracy and consistency. The Report Writer can produce products ranging from labels to full-blown reports with added custom text, columns, page numbers, headings and arithmetic operations on rows and columns. INMAGIC Plus has added menus and pop-up windows to the traditional command line interface which is maintained as an optional interface. Phrase and proximity searching and the prompted search mode are further enhancements. These give power and improve ease of use for both novice and expert user.

Another strong plus of INMAGIC is its very well done system documentation, with a booklet covering its installation and another covering upgrading from an earlier version of INMAGIC. The installation guide covers both a stand-alone MS-DOS system and installation on a Novell LAN. A command reference, user's manual and the library guide are the other portions of the documentation.

A companion product called SearchMAGIC is a search-only run-time engine for INMAGIC databases. Using a SearchMAGIC license at lower cost and packaging any INMAGIC created database could enable distribution of the database as a self-contained application to remote sites not equipped with LAN access. A small library could put up a user searching station on a separate computer at lower cost than a LAN and run the full INMAGIC Plus on the librarian's microcomputer and distribute database copies to remote users periodically. The numeric date fields and the @ DATE command are controlled by the country statement in the CONFIG.SYS file. One must have 500 kB of DOS addressable RAM to install this software for full operation. INMAGIC will take about 1.2 MB of hard disk space for its program files.

With 485 kB, one can run INMAGIC but not run its utilities from within the program or shell out to MS-DOS. Below that RAM, the program may not function or load. With MS-DOS 5.x or 6.x memory management or use of a memory manager such as QuarterDeck's QEMM to load high drivers, files, buffers and DOS itself, one should easily be able to get 500 kB from any 386/486 class system that is equipped with at least 2 MB RAM. Even on 286 systems equipped with QRAM from QuarterDeck and with at least 1 MB RAM, some loading high drivers will produce at least 500 kB, As an example, my 386120, with 8 MB RAM and QEMM running MS-DOS 5.0, has been optimized to produce 623 kB of addressable RAM. The Library Guide features database structures and report formats on diskette with an extensive manual covering the setting up of INMAGIC systems for library automation operations. It is quite easy once one has learned the Report Writer and system to customize these to any individual situation, but many users may not even need to do such customizations. The previous versions of INMAGIC had a companion called the Biblio Guide that is now re placed by this Library Guide. Print formats are provided for both laser and matrix printers.

European LANguage support is via the extended ASCII characters entered by holding down the ALT key and typing the ASCII value from a table provided on the numeric keypad. With an MS-DOS version price of $1250, this is a solid value, and INMAGIC has always provided reasonable prices for its major version upgrades.

Various dealers also sell and support this software as well as provide customer training and consulting. If you want excellent flexibility and fast search performance and have needs that may even stretch beyond the traditional online catalog and processing support, then this software will definitely show a strong capability to fully meet your present and future needs. This system is a database management system geared toward special, school, church and small public libraries where several systems on a small LAN are all that is needed.

The current software (v.4.01) does not presently provide a full-blown online catalog but does allow string searching, which should be ample for smaller collections. It also prints out catalog card sets. The software is implemented in BorLANd's C+ + and uses function keys to do basic commands. The system uses a dBase file format and dot commands like dBase. One can save records in ASCII, USMARC and MicroLIF. One can also save file records in list, card, bibliography, display and labelled formats. LEXIFILE supports circulation of items via the CIRC command.

The program has a nice customization for printer, help messages, programmable keys, use of password security, and colors. The online manual is well done. The card printing and label printing is worked out quite well in this software for those needing these features. This program has a sound design and numerous installations, mainly in Canada although it has been marketed in the United States.

Our expectation is that subsequent versions of this software will provide improvements and further functional support beyond the database and circulation subsystems. One of the strong points of this software is its pricing, which is done on the size of the database for Single-user systems, with a LAN license adding only 30% to the cost. Add another 50% for the circulation program. This pricing definitely encourages LAN installation. The search and circulation programs are separately priced modules. An example of such pricing is to imagine a library wishing catalog support and circulation for its 10,000-title library collection. The search program would license at $695 ($995 for an unlimited size database). The circulation program would license at 50% the cost of the search program, i.e., $347.50 and a network license would be 30% of the search program, or $199.50. This totals to $1242 for the software.

The library corporation (TLC): bibliofile and total library computer system

The Library Corporation was founded in 1975 and was the first library-oriented company to use CD-ROM data storage technology in its Bibliofile product, a database of USMARC cataloging records and a cataloging system. TLC is also among the top 100 PC-based network integrators in North America according to LAN Magazine's LAN 100. Over 4,000 libraries operating 10,000 stand-alone and networked PCs use TLC products. Through the years TLC has had an excellent record of customer service and support together with good product evolution.

The Total Library Computer System revolves around modules that are implemented on a Novell Lite or Novell Advanced Netware LAN, depending on the size of the installation. The online catalog is CD-ROM based and can be accompanied by circulation, acquisitions, the Bibliofile cataloging system, and MARC record import/export. TLC also has developed PACLink, a means for linking a Bibliofile online catalog to an existing circulation system. The first of these installations is at Queens Borough Public Library (New York) where the Bibliofile online catalog is linked to the Data Research Associates (DRA) minicomputer-based circulation system.

TLC is working on other PACLink systems and is trying to enlist support from a number of library system vendors. The Bibliofile database and cataloging system does have direct online interfaces to both NOTIS and CLSI systems and bridging software for Dynix, DRA, GEAC and Innovative Interfaces. Operating the Total Library Computer System on a LAN is improved through the use of Server Down circulation software which allows any workstation on the LAN to continue to spool circulation transactions until the server is restored and then to update the server.

The circulation system is a robust, large-system-featured application. There is a Mark Reshelving Carts function that can help stack staff presort checked-in items by a shelf destination and a reshelving cart number. The cart numbers are set up in the system setup. One can also define a lag period to cover the number of days after cheek-in for an item to get back on the shelves. If the circulation system is accompanied by the Intelligent Catalog, the item will not display as available until after the lag period is up. A reshelving message is the status shown on the online catalog when this lag period is in effect. This system is function key driven and is firmly integrated with the Intelligent Catalog.

The public access catalogs for this system are ColorCat, AutoCat, Generic Catalog, BibCat and the Intelligent Catalog. These products use a different user interface. The Intelligent Catalog and Generic Catalog offer additional advisory features to suggest recommended fiction and incorporates dictionary or Boolean searching, KWIC and divided catalog searches.

Type a single letter to begin a search and the right side of the screen fills with a word list that narrows as each added letter is typed. Then select words from that list to incorporate into the search. The labelled display asks "What would you like to find in the catalog?" The Generic Catalog offers the same capability as the Intelligent Catalog except that it does not use the special custom keyboard of the Intelligent Catalog. ColorCat is a color screen version of the Generic Catalog. There is a remote DiaLCat facility that can be licensed for a LAN system to allow remote users to search the catalog on a modem connection. The Intelligent Catalog also simulates artificial intelligence features with its AI expert system, hypertext, syntax analysis and thesaurus substitution techniques to prevent search failures.

These catalogs provide a choice of card image, fully labelled or MARC record displays. The LAN server stores updates to the CD-ROM catalog to provide real-time currency between CD-ROM remastering completely transparently to the user. The acquisitions system can import items into its consideration file from the Bibliofile cataloging CD-ROM databases. There is a publisher database of over 20,000 publishers on CD-ROM that can be used with this module. The system supports printing on any Epson-compatible printer.

Further enhancements to the circulation and catalog are anticipated since this writing. Also upgrades to multibranch systems features and a release of serials control, interlibrary loan and media booking modules will soon flesh out this already strong, well-integrated and cost-effective system.

When using the Bibliofile cataloging system, noted that the system expected to find MS-DOS 3.30, so 1 had to use the SETVER.EXE facility within MS-DOS 5.0 on a test system. When I did this and set Files= 100, had no problem installing and running this software. Those interested in some further information on Bibliofile products should consult the review by William Saffady. Besides offering this MS-DOS and LAN-based integrated library system called BIB-BASE, Library Technologies, Inc., has offered retrospective conversion services to libraries for a decade and has prepared databases for most commerically available automated library systems from OCLC tapes and its own USMARC source records.

Library Technologies, Inc., is a privately held company and has a number of service distributors in the multitype library network area such as Bibliographical Center for Research (BCR), SOLINET, NELINET, PALINET and WILS. There are over 350 U.S. and Canadian libraries that have installed modules of this system. In the network version of this system Novell, PC Network and LANTastic are all supported, so one can select depending on the size and physical layer network desired. The system starts with the Core module comprising a text editor, search-and-retrieval and the database management system required for all other modules. The Cat module provides catalog card and book label printing.

The Public module provides patron search by author, title, subject, series, call number, ISSN, ISBN, OCLC/RLIN control number and a library-defined field. The Acq module is a full acquisitions, fund accounting, order tracking and purchase order production system. The Multiuser module adds LAN support for serving multiple simultaneous users, while the MARC module enables loading OCLC MARC records into BIB-BASE and exporting MARC records to other systems. There is a BISAC module that supports electronic ordering in the BISAC format and licenses for $395.

Libraries have 180 days of free customer support and then can subscribe to annual support for 10% of the purchase price of the BIB-BASE modules they are using. At the time of my examination, the Core and Public modules were priced at $795, Multiuser was $995, and Acq, Cat and MARC were each $595. These are reasonable and competitive prices for the functionality of this product. The performance of this system is excellent and its ease-of-use features are very well conceived. It uses clear menu-driven screens. Its MARC display is easy to work if one has some familiarity with MARC tags. While the online catalog uses simple searching, without Boolean operators, if more than one record is retrieved, a brief list is presented for browsing and selection of the specific entry. The record displays are clearly labelled. The system can store a full or partial MARC record.

The system's major lack is the omission of keyword indexes so the search must be entered in the exact word order. If a search fails to produce any hits, a rather arcane message to the effect that "Search Request is not in the—Index" is displayed. Just a simple misspelling or typing could produce such a result. It would be better if the system put the user in the proximity of the search in the index entries.

Documentation for the system is well organized but does not have a glossary or any section tabs separating the numerous chapters. This system focuses on creating and maintaining quality bibliographic records. It is suitable for academic, public and special libraries, particularly those able to implement this on a LAN since the real utility of any of these microcomputer-based systems is their ability to be simultaneously accessed by both library staff and library users. This system was introduced in 1987 and was one of the early MS-DOS-based integrated library systems.

The current version is v.2.52. MANDARIN has a full MARC database at its heart. It is programmed in the C LANguage to assure accommodation of the field structures suitable to MARC record processing and good portability to future operating system and hardware platforms. The user may define up to 100 different databases.

Libraries decide what fields to index or map to related fields for simultaneous searching. Parallel fields permit creation of synonym fields which can be mapped to the subject index for cross-reference support. All records are stored as MARC records and can be exported in USMARC to another system. One can mix MARC records such as USMARC, OCLC, UTLAS, UKMARC, MicroLIF or CD-MARC. This system on a LAN can coexist with a MARC or other CD-ROM database on a CD-ROM server. Apple Macintosh users can access a MANDARIN database from Mac Attach interface software released in October, 1992. All commands and menus can be displayed in up to 10 LANguages, with English and French currently available. This system serves multi-cultural needs well and stores diacritics, correctly displaying them on the PC screen. The online catalog opens with a bulletin board where library announcements can be placed and changed at Will. Searching uses Boolean operators AND, OR, NOT, XOR, <, and >. For simple searching, a screen with lines for entering author, title or subject is presented, and the above operators can be typed in on this screen to invoke the Boolean features in a search.

A function key press brings up an Advanced Search screen that looks quite like one from Dialog. It allows saving search sets and searching any indexed field, including the Boolean operators between and within fields. There are summary and expanded display formats that can be defined by the library. Patrons can print out selected search results up to a maximum number determined by the library. When the circulation system is in operation, the item status is shown for each cataloged item. The circulation system allows library definition of fields in the borrower database and 20 different borrower categories, each having its own set of privileges. Self-service check-out can be set up when the system operates on a LAN.

An inventory module allows the use of a hand-held bar code reader to perform data collection in the stacks. Code 39 is the preferred bar code scheme but the module will also accommodate CODABAR codes. Items found missing can be marked in the online catalog. Eradication of missing items can be done via a global delete after a period of time.

The Data Spindler data transfer utility will permit loading of records from OCLC, UTLAS, USMARC, MicroLIF, OCLC Screen Save, dBase, ASCII, GEAC, DOBIS, EBSCO, Bibliofile, LaserQuest and many others. Records can be manually entered and edited in any MANDARIN database. The system also features a diagnostic and repair utility to handle corrupted indexes and databases. The report generator has many standard reports and outputs specified, even catalog cards and book/spine labels. There is a toll -free customer support line for U.S. and Canadian customers.

MANDARIN is also implementing other external databases such as the SELECT Annual Database, which cites curriculum-related material in print and other formats favourably reviewed in Booklist, School Library Journal and other school material review sources. The newest feature is an interlibrary loan subsystem with a graphical user interface, implemented in the C + + LANguage. If your system is on a LAN, you can receive direct dial-in customer service to your system via modem connection if your server has an asynchronous gateway. For full-MARC record storage estimates, it is recommended that you multiply the number of titles in the library by 3000 characters for each record and its index overhead.

The pricing for this system is competitive and encourages LAN implementation among its predominantly school and public library customer base. There is a price discount on license fees for schools. Even some college libraries, such as St. Lawrence College in Ontario, Canada, use this system. This college has 3000-4000 full-time students, 8000 part-time students and a 60,000-item library collection. MeLChior Management Systems, Inc., of Montreal, Canada is the developer of MANDARIN, and Media Flex is its U.S. Distributor.

In Canada, Bibliofiche of Montreal and United Library services in Calgary handle customer licensing and support. This system has considerable power and features but occasionally appears somewhat cryptic to the user, such as in its short mnemonics for some of its function keys. Despite that, the system is relatively easy to learn, and once learned, it should not present any major problem. This system was developed at the University Archives of Michigan State University and is backed up by a solid understanding of the MARC archives and manuscripts record and the other MARC record formats. It is composed of an editor module to create and modify records, and a search module to search the first word or all words in a string when searching names, corporations or subjects.

Accompanying these base capabilities are modules for MARC record input and output that create a standard MARC: amc formatted file that can be transmitted to systems such as OCLC or RLIN. A report module allows access to any field in the database and generation of custom reports. There are predefined reports for accessions, processing status, future action, index terms and several other miscelLANeous reports.

The AUXINDX module allows the archivist to define any leader or fixed or variable-length field as an index to search. This system was the first to implement the MARC amc record in a microcomputer system. The work was funded in part by a grant from the National Historical Publications and Records Commission. Licensing of this system supports its current enhancement and support. Version 2.0 was released in early summer of 1988.

In 1989 there were some 60 users of this software. The system does not yet use color displays. A greater drawback is that the Single-user MS-DOS program apparently has no LAN capability or license provision to enable multiple simultaneous users. Otherwise the system is well documented and has positive views from its users. LANdis (9) and Honhart (10) each give a good view of their experiences using this software. There is a user support group within the Society of American Archivists. MicroMARC:amc remains a very good program for providing a basic level of collection access support to an archive.

Midwest library services: MATSS

This is an excellent MS-DOS or Novell LAN-based acquisitions system with menu-driven interface. Specific functions can be password protected. Ordeing, fund accounting, claims, cancellations and standing orders are all handled effectively. Bibliographic records can be selected from bibliographic utilities or from CD-ROM cataloging sources such as Bibliofile. Book orders can printed either in 3″ by 5″ or 8.5″ by 11″ formats. The BISAC fixed-length format is supported for electronic ordering. The screens are uncluttered a quite consistent in overall appearance and position of fields. There are few noticeable delays in moving between functions and in the menu and data entry screens.

In-context help screens really do make this system relatively easy learn. The very large manual in 85' by 11 "format is quite complete but do lack troubleshooting and tutorial sections. While this software licenses a rather premium price, it is a premium product that also effectively utilizes color screen capabilities of current microcomputers. Security is quite good, with three levels of users: master supervisor, supervisor and user. Each user has the menu items specified to which he/she may have access. Users can also be up for inquiry only. When this system is installed on a LAN, the PCAnywhere program an modem are used to provide support. The online help files contain over 35, words of documentation. Midwest Library Service provides invoices diskette. Baker and Taylor, Blackwell NA, Academic Book Center, Ambassador Books, Yankee Book Peddler and Coutts Library Service are examples dealers accepting MATSS electronic orders using the BISAC format. If you are doing an order for a title with multiple ISBNs, a window d plays each ISBN and its binding and price. Paperback and price fields then v reflect the chosen ISBN. This system was obviously designed by people who know the book-ordering business. If you order the low-cost demonstration di its cost will be applied to the system license if you decide to license this product.

This system is designed for the school library but does have about 10% of its customer base with public libraries. MOLLI appears to be the easiest library system I have seen. It handles full-MARC records and does keyword searching. The system is modular, with circulation, searching (OPAC), cataloging, inventory and reporting. Separate acquisitions, serials, borrower conversion and custom label printing programs are also available. Help is always a keystroke away with an F1 key press. The consistent menus and good use of color screens are another bonus.

For a stand-alone configuration, an Itel 80386SX is required at minimum. Circulation supports bar code readers of either light pen or laser scanner type. For multiple users either a Novell or LAN Tastic-based LAN using either Ethernet or Token Ring physical hardware can be used. A 486 server with 386DX or 386SX workstations with at least 2 MB RAM is needed. A 70,000-item collection would require a 210-MB hard disk on the server at minimum. This is a pretty good disk utilization for MOLLI records, the LAN software and the MOLLI application programs. MOLLI requires at least 515 kB addressable RAM in your computer under MS-DOS. MOLLI has a demo/tutorial disk available with an accompanying booklet that is a marvel of clarity in showing this system's catalog searching and circulation functions. This system uses passwords to protect system functions. The master password allows the system administrator or librarian access to all MOLLI functions. Menu passwords allow control of who sees which menus and their commands.

The circulation password allows eligible personnel to perform circulation functions. The current release of MOLLI (v.5.0) allows backup and restore functions to be carried out from within the program. The restore function is password protected to assure that only trained staff perform this critical operation and ensure that files are not overwritten with old backup data. Even the printer usage can be restricted by requiring a printer password. In the event that the master password is somehow forgotten, there is a utility provided through a password recovery program.

Workstations can be made "search only" or "quick search only" and separate collections can have separate passwords. The quick search is used for searching on simple single keyword. For example one could type "science fiction" and see a list of the search results in a short, long or MARC format screen.

On the short display up to seven items are presented with title, author and call number. Pressing the number on the short display of the item will bring up the long display, which shows the circulation status in addition to full descriptive and tracing information. Commands such as Next, Previous, Left, Right, Display, Holdings, Print and Exit appear at screen bottom. The Left and Right commands show the item that should be on the shelf to the left or right of the selected item. The Display command allows the choice of a different display format, including the MARC display. The full search allows up to three search terms to be combined using AND, OR and NOT Boolean operators.

On full search there is a bibliography menu to permit printing the search results as a bibliography, changing its sort order, limiting a search by material format and adding a search to an existing bibliography. Bibliographies can be printed in short, long or MARC format. Call number and accession number searches are supported also. The beauty of this system is that it provides the necessary functionality to the school library, having incorporated customer suggestions in subsequent revisions, while maintaining an ease of searching that enables users of all ages and reading levels to perform searches and interpret results on the screens.

A newsletter offers helpful hints on using MOLLI, typical problems that users have encountered and their solutions, and various technical tips and news of staff and product development at Nichols Advanced Technologies, Inc. This is a competitively priced system with over a thousand installed sites. William Saffady has reviewed this software. Novara's system is an integrated library system that gives the appearance of a Microsoft Windows graphical user interface even though it is an MS-DOS or LAN-based program.

The catalog is authority based to provide cross-referencing. Searching uses a fill-in-the-forms type screen, and if the search does not produce a result, the system will perform a soundex code-type search and try to produce a result that way. Boolean searches are supported using the AND, OR, NOT operators.

Various listings can be produced from the "Files" command on the main menu screen. These include bibliographies and card/label sets. The catalog display uses a card format analog, which can depict a multiple display of results as a row of file cards. Hitting Enter blows up a catalog card in the foreground. The next version of this software will support full-MARC records, but the current version allows import of MARC records into the BIBLIOTRAC data format. The circulation system provides the features expected in a product aimed at the school library market. This system's customer base has been mainly Canadian school libraries, but the system is now being actively marketed in the United States. BIBLIOTRAC was originally developed for the Inverness County District School Board in Nova Scotia. It shows excellent ease-of-use features, and the next version will be able to compete better with those MS-DOS and LAN systems that are able to support full MARC.

The system is programmed in ZIM from Zanthe Information, Inc., to achieve its good graphical user interface. This system can also operate under the QNX multiple-terminal operating system from Quantum Software for a small multiple-terminal installation which probably can be put together more cheaply than a LAN. Saffady has reviewed this software in Library Computer

Systems and Equipment Review. Around eight years ago, Victor Rosenberg, founder of Personal Bibliographic Software, Inc., envisioned software able to produce quality bibliographies according to the prevailing standard styles and adapt to any new bibliography citation standards that might emerge.

From a modest beginning using the UCSDP native Pascal operating environment, this software has evolved as MS-DOS and then Apple Macintosh versions. Formerly this program was called the Professional Bibliographic System; several years ago it was renamed Pro-Cite 2.0. Pro-Cite has become a market leader in software for managing references and producing bibliographies in numerous styles.

The program is nicely customizable to recognize default directories, database settings of various sorts, quick search fields, authority lists, punctuation files, stop lists and foreign LANguage character sets. You can design your own customized workforms in addition to those supplied. In fact, you can tailor this program to produce just what you want as to the format of any bibliography so that if you write papers for many different journals that each use different styles, you can select the appropriate citations from the database and produce them in the style you need. You can determine the record number interval to be used and determine the first record number to be assigned to a citation. This permits an alphabetic order accessed via the record number.

This system has authority lists for art and chemistry journals, author names, composers, drama and film journals, MLA journals, Index Medicus journals, general journals, music journals and playwrights. The user can easily establish new authorities, and existing authorities can be modified by adding, changing and deleting entries. These authorities are stored in LST files in either their own subdirectory or in the Pro-Cite subdirectory.

A clever feature of the authority file is the alternative text feature. With this, one could use a very shorthand journal abbreviation to have the authority list supply the correct fully descriptive title. Punctuation files control the bibliography format and 29 of these have been predefined. You can define other custom punctuation files to produce totally customized bibliographies to meet a new, previously undefined style. The utilities menu selection allows copying selected records and workforms or workforms only. Here you also can perform import and export of records and repair a corrupted Pro-Cite database. This repair creates a new uncorrupted database under a new name. The program comes with printer drivers for Epson-compatible printers and for Hewlett-Packard LaserJet or compatible laser printers, but if you have your printer manual with its printer codes, you can define your own custom printer driver. If you routinely create bibliographies that you would like to make available to others on a LAN or their own workstation there is a Pro-Cite read-only program for both platforms to allow distribution of Pro-Cite databases in a public access setting.

Pro-Cite for MS-DOS requires at minimum a 640-kB RAM, Intel 8088 or above microcomputer with MS-DOS v.3 or above, hard disk and printer for output. The software in this version ships on either a single 3.5-inch double-density (720kB) or two 5.25-inch 360-kB disks. After its installation from its compressed state, it requires 1.7 MB of hard disk space for the basic program and its small sample database. A read.me file on the distribution disk updates the excellent manual with any last-minute changes or pertinent installation information. Pro-Cite is a comprehensive and flexible bibliography generator. It is relatively easy to learn to use the program from the well-organized and presented manual as you proceed on your first bibliographic project.

Each aspect of the program is thoroughly covered in the manual. "Creating Character Sets," discusses how Pro-Cite sorts records by its default character set and that any character not included in this default set is ignored. So a custom character set can be selected that includes those characters not in the default. The chapter walks the user through altering these characters in their sort order and defining a new character set. There is no limit to any Pro-Cite database except your physical hard disk space. Each record can have up to 32,000 characters of information.

In short, Pro-Cite is truly a classic piece of software for its intended purpose that only keeps getting better with age! This program runs well in a DOS window under Microsoft Windows. Perhaps the future might bring a Windows-compliant version of this program. Pro-Cite retails at $395 for the full program and $195 for the read-only version. A demonstration disk is $75 and the price of these latter two products can be applied to licensing the full program, so you cannot go wrong by getting the demonstration disk.

This company also has a suite of accompanying programs to Pro-Cite that are called Biblio-Links. These are programs that allow the import of records from numerous other online services into a Pro-Cite database. There is a Biblio-Links Library Package that covers DOBIS, DROLS, MUMS, NOTIS, OCLC, SCORPIO and USMARC for $295.

The IBM Biblio-Links packages are $195 each and in addition to the above databases offer DIALOG, MEDLARS, SilverPlatter, STN and DGIS. There is an online Biblio-Links package for the IBM system that allows user access to BRS, DIALOG, MEDLARS, SilverPlatter and STN.

The Macintosh Biblio-Links package will import records from BRS, DIALOG and MEDLARS into the Macintosh Pro-Cite version. It is priced at $295. On April 19, 1993 Biblio-Link 11 for the Macintosh was released for a license fee of $195. This is a single program that can transfer downloaded files from DIALOG, MEDLARS and SilverPlatter databases. It needs no customizing to read any of these files. Users can change the settings in Biblio-Link 11 to place information into different Pro-Cite workforms and fields. System administrators can create custom configuration files that will permit the transfer of downloaded information from any other database or local in-house system. Personal Bibliographic Software also has a product called Pro-Search, which is a specialized front-end program that will simplify the DIALOG databases search sessions. This program uses a menu interface and puts Dialog's blue sheet data on disk. One can construct and store search strategies offline to reduce online connect time and charges. There is a built-in accounting feature to track online charges.

An optional quarterly subscription service includes free program upgrades and keeps the bluesheet disk upto-date. The MS-DOS version is $495 and the optional subscription service is $150. The Macintosh version is $295. Customers are supported well by this company and their software upgrade prices are quite reasonable. Personal Bibliographic Software is known worldwide for its reliability and flexibility, and the good ease of use of its programs. RLibrary/Cards is a Macintosh program licensing at $144, which does level 2 cataloging, including GMD, edition, details, series, ISBN, ISSN and LCCN. Ten subjects or added entries can be assigned and five lines used for call numbers.

Again, the catalog cards printed by this program on an Apple printer are high quality. It also prints book spine and pocket labels. The RLibrary/Cards 11 program is a $274 Macintosh program with Apple Laser printer support and network compatibility for libraries whose Macintosh is connected to a network or that have a laser printer. This program also prints book spine and pocket labels or spine labels by themselves, and it offers a choice of fonts and point sizes. The Apple Library User's Group Newsletter of January, 1990 includes an article discussing the problems of printing catalog cards, the Rachel's program for the Macintosh and how most of these problems are addressed by the Rachel's programs. These are basic programs and are a great value for the library needing to find a good, low-cost way to print catalog cards and label sets. Reference Manager is a database program for managing citations to materials of many different formats. It has an optional slide manager to enable a separate 35-mm slide database to provide lecture support. The program comes in both MS-DOS (version 5) and Macintosh (version 2) forms.

It uses compatible database formats for complete record exchange compatibility. It is available in a special version for NEC 9801 microcomputers which are Japan's leading desktop system. Another optional program is the Splicer TSR that allows the full retrieval power of Reference Manager from within your word processor and the ability to paste a retrieved reference identification number in a manuscript within delimiters for later bibliography generation.

Reference Manager uses a lookup menu to show lists of names. One can mark words in titles to use as keywords with @ and connect multiple words in phrases with an underscore. Text formatting supports underline, bold and italicized fonts. Search and retrieval uses Boolean AND, OR, NOT and also browsable windows in each parameter type or field, or keyword search.

If you have any of the following word processors

you can load Reference Manager citations into these manuscripts: MASS 11; Multimate; WordPerfect 4.2, 5.0 and 5.1; Visiword; Volkswriter; Microsoft Word v.4.0 and 5.0; WordStar v.6.0; WordStar 2000; and XyWrite. You can also load into an ASCII text file written with a text editor. There is an optional capture module for importing records from more than 50 different databases-some online, some CD-ROM.

The user can edit records during the import to add keywords. There is a duplicate record check made at the time of loading. This program will appeal to those who publish numerous scholarly papers. There is a special student edition of this program available for $79 that makes it attractive to the college student. Depending on the options above, Reference Manager licenses from $299 to $499. This program also is a potential competitor with Pro-Cite and Balboa's Library Master, and one is advised to compare all three. Reference Update is available for the same computer platforms as Reference Manager. It is a microcomputer-based current awareness service that provides a weekly diskette containing table of contents information for over 1200 scientific journals in biology and medicine.

The search software comes with the initial subscription, and searches can be saved for later reuse with each subsequent weekly disk. The user may print lists of references or request cards and export selected references to Reference Manager or down-load them to another disk file. Optionally in this subscription one can have article abstracts on disk, by modem or fax, or use the Abstract Express Unlimited service to down-load abstracts from this company's central system for a fixed annual fee. The central service bills per downloaded abstract and either the customer calls a toll-free number and pays connect charges or a toll number and does not pay connect charges.

Abstract Express will also generate reprint requests to authors, allow use of document delivery services for the article from the Information Store, Inc., in San Francisco or print a generic document order form for use with another document delivery service. This company is the largest producer of micro-based software for libraries plus some hospital, medical, law and veterinary support programs. Some of its over 35 programs have LAN versions for MS-DOS-type LANs. These are Super Circulation Control, Circulation Control, Online Catalog Plus, Online Catalog Enlarged, Periodical Manager, Subscription Manager, Magazine Article Filer, Acquisitions Manager and Complete Inventory Control. Over 18,000 libraries worldwide have ordered programs from this company. Prices for these programs range from $479 for Super Circulation Control to $129 for Magazine Article Filer. Right On Programs sells bar code readers to use with its system to complete your circulation system needs. Super Circulation Control combines Circulation Control and Online Catalog and is an easy-to-learn program as are the others offered in the catalog. These programs are available in MS-DOS and Apple 11 versions in their stand-alone forms. Right On Programs offers a step up to the next level of automation for the smaller library and the school library from single function programs that print catalog cards or perform some other similar task. Its programs make automating routine library housekeeping and patron services easy and quite affordable when one considers the amount of staff time saved and improved service resulting from their use.

Librarian's Helper is a product that has been on the market since 1985. It prints catalog cards and book spine and pocket labels. It will handle any material types but does not store the material type in its record. There is even a more basic version of this program that does not offer any data storage feature. The program prints cards to AACR2 standards. It is menu driven but does not have a full screen editor, only a line editor. The enhanced version allows data storage and reprinting of cards and labels from the saved datasets. The enhanced version permits data transfer to other programs but the data is not saved or output to a MARC format. In the basic version, 32 fields can be entered, with up to 10 subjects and 10 added entries. Call numbers can be up to five lines on cards and labels, with a sixth line on the label for volume number. For multiple volume works, multiple label sets are generated. The enhanced version will allow up to 78 fields, with a total record size of 3000 characters. The enhanced version for MS-DOS systems is licensed at $250 and the CP/M version to run on an Apple 11 equipped with a CP/M card is $350.

The basic version is $175 for either MS-DOS or Apple CP/M version. This product could be improved by a full-screen editor and the use of the PC keyboard's arrow keys and insert/delete keys. Otherwise, for the library merely needing basic card printing and label preparation this is still an excellent program in its output, albeit somewhat dated by its user interface and lack of MARC record format for data storage. Librarian's Helper Online (LH Online) is an online catalog and cataloging system that is designed for the small library or for a special collection within a larger library. It displays its records in a card catalog format. Users can produce reports sorted by author, title, publisher or call number. Also, author and title authority reports can be produced. It can run as a stand-alone MS-DOS program licensed at $600 or on a Novell or LAN BIOS-compatible LAN.

For a $900 license a LAN version with up to five users can be purchased. For a $1200 license a LAN with 6 or more users can access this program. Upgrading the single-user license to a LAN license is $300 for the up to five user system. To run this product you need Intel

80286 or above computers. The record storage is a variable-length record instead of the fixed-length record used in the above Librarian's Helper Enhanced program. Simple and complex searches using Boolean operators are featured of author, title, subject, publisher or keyword. Records can be entered from the keyboard, from Librarian's Helper Enhanced and MicroLIF format. Although this program is relatively easy to use and does permit a satisfactory amount of cataloging information to be stored, it does not appear to store MARC records nor export or import full MARC. The librarian works from a special expanded version of the program which includes all patron features plus maintenance and administrative functions. If you need a simple online catalog for a small collection and do not need to transport full MARC records into the catalog, then this program may do the job for you.

Western library network (WLN)

The Western Library Network (formerly the Washington Library Network) serves over 750 subscribing libraries for cataloging and acquisitions support in Washington, Oregon, Idaho, Montana, Alaska, California, Arizona, British Columbia, and other states and Canadian provinces. It originally operated as a division of the Washington State Library, but in 1988, WLN was established as a private not-for-profit corporation. There are two categories of member libraries: those that add records to the database and those that do not. Contributing online members use microcomputers to contribute original cataloging and holdings information while contributing offline members send their records in magnetic tape or other batch methods.

Many of these libraries use WLN's LaserCat, CD-ROM catalog. The offline libraries do not have online access to the WLN database. Union list members add original cataloging and serials holdings for the purpose of participation in a union list. Search-only members can access the WLN database for reference, bibliographic verification, interlibrary loan or other purposes but are not obligated to contribute. Some 8 million catalog records, 8.2 million authority records and 17.4 million holdings statements were reflected in the WLN database at the end of 1992. The central system offers members an acquisitions system and interlibrary loan system in addition to the union catalog and cataloging system. The LC Name and Subject Authority files and the WLN Authority file are searchable as are the bibliographic and holdings data. The WLN LaserCat system was introduced in 1987. It currently provides some 4 million records and associated indexes in 4 CD-ROM disks and several years of current MARC records to use in cataloging. GPO, CATLINE and NLC records not held by WLN members are also included. Searching is very flexible as exact match, browse and keyword searching on multiple access points is provided. LaserCat subscribers also get the Ultracard/MARC program from Small Library Computing. This program permits MARC record creation, editing, catalog card printing and spine/pocket labels.

In 1988, WLN introduced LaserBridge. This program converts downloaded Lasercat records into comma-delimited ASCII text that can be imported by dBase 11 or 111, Lotus 123, PC-File 111 and many other micro-computer software packages. LaserCat subscribers receive quarterly updates. LaserCat requires an MS-DOS 3.1 version on a computer with at least 640 kB RAM, two disk drives or one floppy and one hard disk. Either color or monochrome monitors are supported. The MS-DOS CD-ROM extensions must be loaded and at least two CD-ROM drives need to be attached to a single interface card. As of December, 1992, 540 libraries subscribed to LaserCat.

A new graphical user interface for LaserCat was released in December, 1993, and both MS-DOS/Windows and Macintosh versions of LaserCat have been developed. Libraries or groups of libraries can procure their own records on a CD-ROM basis in a product called LaserPac. It uses the same search software and interface. LaserPac can be updated on a frequency selected by the library, with additions being entered on a hard disk to supplement the LaserPac CD-ROM. The CD-ROM LaserCat and LaserPac products have a very powerful search engine. Searches can be limited by particular file, library, date, type, LANguage, government publication, juvenile work and large print classifications. Exact searches can be done on record identification number, LCCN, ISBN, ISSN, author, title, subject and all fields. Keyword performs searches on author, tide, subject, contents and all of these fields. Browsing can be done in the author, tide, subject or all of the above.

In addition, other record identifiers such as GPO and CANMARC numbers can be searched. The index displays include cross-references and codes to tell if the heading is authorized, authorized without any records, unauthorized or a children's heading. The brief record display screen lists up to four records resulting from a search. The title, author and publication information in the imprint fields is shown. The full display uses labelled fields, or the user can display a MARC format display. The holdings screen display is also nicely formatted for clarity. The MARC display labels each tagged field with a field name. The WLN mainframe system's software has been licensed to numerous national libraries abroad. Biblio-Techniques, Inc., now no longer in business, based its BLIS system on the WLN host software, which uses ADABAS as its dbms.

In 1986, when Biblio-Techniques ceased business, its

five customer sites-Indiana University, Columbia University, Brown University, University of Cincinnati, and the Metropolitan Toronto Library-formed a consortium and became a WLN licensee. Also, the University of Missouri and the University of Illinois had used WLN software to create an online catalog. WLN products are high quality and will meet continuing long-range needs of members as is witnessed by the growth of this network despite the dominance of OCLC among the bibliographic utilities generally and the popularity or RLG/RLIN in the research library community. WLN has grown from a small regional network to a major network spanning Western North America. Winnebago was founded in 1982 and has shipped thousands of programs to school libraries since that time. Public libraries also constitute a significant customer base for Winnebago software. Winnebago packages a thoroughly professional product. The documentation is in ring binders that are slip cased just like the older, expensive microcomputer programs that we grew used to such as Lotus and WordPerfect. In addition to the programs previewed here, Winnebago offers numerous other programs to perform specific library tasks.

CIRC/CAT is a circulation and online catalog that work together as an integrated public services system for the school library. Saffady has written a review of this program in Library Computer Systems and Equipment Review. Separate LAN licenses are also available so that a school or school district LAN can operate this software for access at numerous locations.

The circulation system handles up to 300,000 items and 100,000 patrons. There are 300 different material categories that can be assigned their distinct circulation set of circulation parameters. There are 99 different patron categories possible. One can attach up to five messages to any patron or material record. Bar code labels for both books and patrons can be printed on 3.5 or 2-5-inch label stock if one obtains the add-on bar code program. This program will print Code 39, Label Code 4 or Codabar on laser and Epson-compatible dot matrix printers. If one wants to maintain text book issuance and control, material types 200300 are reserved for this purpose and do not display in the online catalog or circulation system. These also do not count on a patron's limit for number of materials checked out. The database is a MARC record and records can be exported in MARC or MicroLIF. This MARC import and export feature is provided by another add-on program called the MARC Compatibility Module.

Import from CD-ROM cataloging sources such as Bibliofile or from diskette is supported through this module. Another optional capability is a CD-ROM interface so that a CD-ROM-based database can be used in conjunction with the online catalog. A shell out from the main menu and then a return to the catalog is how this is done. The online catalog uses a fill-in-the-bLANk or browsable window search. On a retrieved record, one sees the catalog card type display but pressing the M key will change the display to a MARC-tagged record display. The MARC-tagged display also has English labels on each tag for the beginning MARC user to understand easily. The circulation system prints all the needed notices and reports to manage the collection and its usage. Over 30 reports can be generated by CIRC/CAT. One can assign bar code ranges to denote specific libraries in a multi-library system such as a school district.

The system will recognize materials belonging to another location on any library location for a system-wide circulation approach. There is a separate input module that lets one build patron and material data on floppies for loading into CIRC/CAT. In the online catalog, searches can be limited by reading level, interest level and material type. The library can choose the tags that will be used to provide keywords. One can browse through the list of keywords shown and activate or deactivate specific keywords. If one deactivates a keyword and later wants to reactivate it, there is a Keyword Rebuild feature that will rebuild its record pointers.

The online catalog is searched via character string match or keyword. Search results can be sorted into a call number sequence. Keyword searching permits up to three words to be entered, linked by AND, OR and NOT Boolean operators. Adding, editing and deleting MARC records is provided with three screen formats: condensed, easy entry and full entry. The whole MARC record including leader and fixed fields can be edited. This system uses its menus effectively. However, it is the use of the pop-up scrolling windows that makes this program a joy to use.

But the circulation system, with its initial bLANk screen and "Ready" prompt, which is ,expecting either a patron bar code or patron name entry, could have been made a bit clearer and more friendly by an appropriate label or text box. This system should be a strong contender for school libraries, particularly those with LANs or district wide automation using a LAN. Customer support is free the first year and then is available for a competitive fixed charge each subsequent year.

As an example of how one high school has provided some wide access on its system, the Farmington, Missouri High School has linked its CIRC/CAT system to the local Farmington Public Library, using PC Anywhere. The high school students can access the public library's database by typing a command to call a predetermined phone number, entering a password and performing a search just as if they were at the public library. The public library patrons can do the same from their system to the school system.

An area community college is also pLANning on using the Winnebago software and PC Anywhere to link into this arrangement as are some other schools in the area. Winnebago's UNION CAT is a district-level online catalog for the MS-DOS operating system and provides all of the features of the CAT program above with provision to handle an unlimited number of locations and hundreds of thousands of bibliographic records in MARC format. The version current at the time of examination was v.3.0, which superseded version 2.62-which we have also examined. UNION CAT v.3.0 now includes the MARC Tag 852 for local holdings and the user-defined field is now tied to tag 961, subfield u. Several new reports have been added since the earlier version.

In the card image display format the note field now displays up to 765 characters. The card image displays are in AACR2 format. One can choose whether to allow two or three keyword fields to be entered during keyword searching. There is a new keyword update utility that builds keywords for added records and it performed quite fast on our test 386 20-MHz microcomputer.

CAT and UNION CAT would be strengthened if they were authority based as they do not provide cross-references. LAMP, the Library Acquisitions and Management Program is a dBaselll/ Clipper application also using some Turbo Pascal and assembler routines. It has a consideration for purchase file, prepares purchase orders, maintains book fund accounting and performs invoice and account reconciliation.

Old records can be archived to floppy according to rules the user sets up. It is possible to send orders to a vendor by modem. This is a simple system to learn and should fill the needs of most small libraries. It requires an MS-DOS system and if the modem transmission for orders is used with a book supplier, then an appropriate speed modem would be needed. An Epson-compatible or laser printer can be used to print the outputs from this system. Winnebago users have both national and local/regional users' groups.

A quarterly newsletter, which has excellent layout and is full of news, tips and such, is sent to licensed users of the software. This is a strong company with a good record of customer service and continuing evolution of its programs. Zyindex for MS-DOS systems has been an established text retrieval package for almost a decade. In June, 1992, the Microsoft Windows version of Zyindex became available. Both versions will also operate on Novell-, Banyan, 3COM-and Netbios-compatible LANs when licensed for LAN use. *Infoworld* said, "Zyindex for Windows is easily the best program for general text retrieval in Windows." Version 5.0 added features to the current MS-DOS product. It builds indexes twice as fast, with a 30% overhead for its indexes. You can launch an application program from within Zyindex, with a quick return to Zyindex when finished with the other application. You can archive multiple versions of a file after a search and view any and all versions at will.

Bookmarks can be inserted to mark your place to return at any time. Link points of interest in or between files and traverse the link at any time. Another neat feature is being able to add your own notes-which can be indexed and searched and not compromise the original file integrity. Links and notes can be personal or public. If graphics are embedded in the file or linked, they can be displayed on the screen.

TIFF, PCX, BMP and EPS graphics formats are displayed. If you have dBase format files, even with memo fields, these can be searched by Zyindex for Windows. Zyindex will search WordPerfect, WordPerfect for Windows, Microsoft Word, Microsoft Word for Windows, MSWrite, WordStar, AmiPro, Displaywrite, Xywrite, Mtiltimate, Volkswriter, Total Word, ASCII, and ANSI file formats using the IBM PC character set. There is a runtime version of the search engine available for those who want to distribute a published text database application. Searches in Zyindex take from one to five seconds on an Intel 80386 at 33 MHz, while building indexes on such a machine takes an hour for 10-12 MB-sized files. Zyindex searching is really sophisticated, with words, phrases, Boolean operators and wildcards all used. Unordered proximity searches are possible where word A is within *n* words of word B. Ordered proximity searches also are implemented where word, A is up to n words before word B.

Many other advanced search features to either narrow or widen a search among documents or defined fields are provided. This is a full indexing and retrieval package in a class with BRS Search on the search engine side but able to handle a variety of common text formats. The noise word or exclusion list can be modified as well as the default character set. The Windows version of Zyindex implements the Windows standard interface of dialog boxes, buttons and pull-down menus.

For index building particularly, this program will perform much better with the faster microprocessor systems. The same is true for search speed, although typical searches are already sufficiently speedy to satisfy even the speed demon user.

The conventional microcomputer software ring-bound documentation is well organized and clearly written. Zyindex for Windows licenses for $395 for a single-user and $995 for a three-user LAN license. If you have the MS-DOS version, you can update to the Windows version for $149. There is a companion program called Zyimage, which is a complete electronic document filing system that unites Zyindex search and retrieval with scanned text documents produced by Calera's Wordscan OCR software. It preserves both text and image files of the document. This program is available in LAN license at $2459 for a five-user license, $3995 for a ten-user license and $5495 for a twenty-user license. A single-user license is $895. This program is optimized to handle from 1 MB to 10 GB of text in a single index. The Zyindex Developer's Toolkit High Level Programming Interface (HAPI) provides direct program access to the index building and search engine to enable a developer's application to perform essential text retrieval functions. Create, add or remove documents in an index; search an index; obtain a list of retrieved files with number of hits and comments and text with hits from retrieved files. The HAPI add-on is $3995 and is available for MS-DOS, Windows and UNIX on 386/486 systems.

Macintosh systems

There are quite a few specific library function programs that are available for the Macintosh. The previous section examined software that is thought of mainly as MS-DOS platform products but which some developers have also implemented on the Macintosh. We have not attempted to cover programs that perform a single task such as writing overdue notices, Hypercard-implemented applications such as bibliographic instruction or collection guides.

We chose to separate these Macintosh systems because they are all integrated, online, multifunctional library management systems designed to compete with similar offerings on an MS-DOS or LAN platform in many cases. For the library or institution with Macintosh systems and Mac networking, these programs offer some competitive choices that should be examined before determining whether it would be advisable to move to an MS-DOS or other platform to implement online library computing support. At the Caspr Library Center, Caspr, Inc, has computer labs, CD-ROM production, training facilities and a multimedia demonstration library to show its library automation products: Library Works", Library Browser', and LibraryDisc. Library Works" is an online catalog, cataloging, acquisitions, serials and circulation system which is designed specifically for the Apple Macintosh family systems. MARC records can be imported and exported. AACR2 cards and label sets can be printed.

The system provides Boolean searching and left and right truncation. With the Expand feature one can scroll through author, title, subject and keyword indexes. The serials module supports routing but does not provide any bindery preparation support. For a multiuser system one can use an Appleshare server, a Novell Advanced Netware server or a Digital Equipment VAX-server. This system handles up to a million records, with special versions available to handle even larger databases. School libraries are the main target for this system, although it has been installed in many other types of libraries.

Library Browser is the client software for public access to the above online catalog. It uses a card drawer metaphor in presenting search results on the Macinstosh. Records can be displayed in card, short, medium or long formats. There are client versions of this program for the Macintosh, MS-DOS/Windows systems and Apple lle and lIgs systems. Any of these systems attached to a LAN running this software is able to perform searches.

The search sets can be saved to disk or printed.

LibraryDisc uses the Library Browser interface to search CD-ROM databases. Currently these are the MARC School Edition, which is produced by the Catalog Card Company with Dewey Classification and Sears subject headings; ERIC Journals", which is the CIJE section of the ERIC database; Magazine Article Summaries'", which contains indexes and abstracts to magazine articles from EBSCO Publishing; and National Newspaper Abstracts from University Microfilms, Inc. Caspr's products are well laid out and the documentation has a tutorial included. The Macintosh user interface is well implemented and therefore this software will be easy to use for users of all levels. Caspr also has a catalog card and label-printing program called MACCARDS for the Macintosh. If you are looking for a system that uses the Macintosh platform, this system should be included in your serious examination.

These systems from Canada are a part of a series of software directed at school systems. The larger system is called the MacSchool System. Its other modules are Student Information System (SIS), District Student Management (DSM), Fund Accounting and CSL Precis. This last program is a simplified administration system for smaller schools with up to 750 students, with demographics, discipline, daily attendance, report cards and teacher gradebook. MacSchool Library is the integrated library system module of this larger system. Advanced Booking is another module aimed at media center support. MacSchool Library and its sister modules will run on a single Macintosh or on a LocalTalk', PhoneNet, or Ethernet network using MacTOPS', Appleshare or Novell Advanced Netware.

This library system supports cataloging, an online catalog and circulation using the typical Mac interface of pull-down and pop-up menus, dialog boxes, radio buttons, scrolling windows, and other familiar Mac interface features. Up to 65,000 bibliographic records and 5000 user records can be handled by this system. There is an optional MARC record import module that is separately licensed and can handle records from many different CD-ROM or book jobber sources.

An unusual feature is that the online catalog displays bibliographic records in a spreadsheet-like tabular format for browsing. A vertical scrollbar is used as with many other Mac programs. Using this type of display eliminates the need for horizontal scrolling on the Mac screen. The user can double-click on a title for a full bibliographic display in a catalog card image format. When a question mark icon within a title column is clicked, an annotation will come up in a pop-up window. Searching can be based on any bibliographic field. Keyword searches can be on titles, subjects and annotations.

Boolean AND, OR and NOT operators are supported. This system will also print catalog cards, individually or in sets, and spine and pocket labels. The separate advanced booking module, probably most useful for media and equipment items, permits advance reservations for specific items. It generates pick lists for reservation dates and will check out items on those lists, and it can print shipping labels to route materials to borrowers. The circulation portion of this system integrates with the MacSchool Student Information System, or borrower records can be key entered if that program is not being used. This is a competitive product with good appeal for school district implementation as well as for an individual school. There are a variety of single and multiple licensing arrangements with prices competitive with other Mac software products. For a LAN installation the server should be at least a Mac lLCi, IIvx or one of the Quadra models.

7

ELECTRONIC SERVICE DELIVERY

Information as a commodity has always been vital to our service and with the growing demands of students and others, it is unlikely to diminish in the near future. We should not, therefore, undervalue systems which can provide access to large, up-to-date databases which are user friendly in ways which old manual systems could never be. If the face of public libraries is to change radically during the next ten years it is probably in the area of electronic information delivery that we will make it happen. These technologies have literally the potential to give the power of information searching to the customer rather than through the librarian to the customer. That does not mean we are an endangered species if such a situation comes about—the systems will need to be managed, exploited and the customers trained. It does mean that our roles may change. That is the real challenge of electronic information delivery. In the last survey hyperbole was necessary to describe the impact that the CD ROM had made on public libraries. Like the compact disc in the audio market, the CD ROM has been the high flier of the late 1980s and will continue to change the way that we operate as librarians (and listeners) well into the 90s. Just to remind you, before looking more closely at the data from the present survey, in 1987 two libraries indicated that they were considering using CD ROM while in 1989, 49 were actually in the thick of it. A variety of databases were being used, but all were using Bookbank which was the catalyst for most libraries. In four years the number has gone up 50 times, since 1989 it has more than doubled. Any way you look at it, CD ROM is a popular delivery system for information and is likely to continue its sweep through public libraries. The data are pretty self-evident, there are increases everywhere.

Northern Ireland scores a full house while all other authorities show a rapid take-up. Only Scotland and the Non-Mets lag behind the 60% and over which is seen elsewhere. The size of these two exceptions might create barriers to buying the system and that still seems to be the case; although the relative cheapness of the hardware and the real savings and benefits of using Bookbank, for example, continue to raise question marks about these discrepancies. There are in the end only two possibilities. Either the scale of operations in these two types of authority is such that resources cannot be found for what elsewhere is spreading like wild-fire or, the nature of demand means that other priorities must take precedence. Looking closely it is not clear that all authorities are using Bookbank, although the vast majority are.

Indeed it may well be that those who did not report its use felt that it was not worth mentioning! The data also show, however, that a wide range of databases are now in use, ranging from those of local relevance, such as the Northern Echo (affectionately known as Panda), to national newspapers, official publications, British Standards and the odd encyclopedia. Selection tools remain a popular sue for the CD ROM equipment and alongside Bookbank we now find Bookfind (from Bookdata), American Books in Print, BNB and the British Library Catalogue. Respondents were asked to indicate whether the systems were staff only or made available directlv to the public, without staff intervention. Of the 101 total, 66 indicated that their systems were staff only while nine report direct use by the public. That leaves 26 who said nothing about access. From the databases the 26 'question marks' are using pretty sure that they are not providing public access, which means that only about one tenth of CD ROMers are allowing customers to get their hands on the technology.

Of the nine allowing public access, a fair smattering (five actually) are providing it to the Northern Echo, evidently a strong catalyst to encourage public access. This balance of 10% public access to 90% of authorities using staff as intermediaries is in marked constrast to the developments taking place in university and polytechnic libraries where CD ROM networks (clusters of terminals linked to a jukebox of CD ROMS) are seen as an essential means of giving the customers what they want. For a whole variety of reasons we in public libraries are taking a different approach.

The case for CD ROMs as selection/bibliographic aids is won, the case for purchasing databases to support reference and information services looks set to be a victory, but, perhaps because of the diversity and differing levels of customer ability in public libraries, direct access is not yet seen as the highest priority. We certainly hope that we are not, since it is costly to provide one PC and CD ROM drive per database and, if there are fewer PCs than databases, switching disks in and out all the time is a pain.

The evidence from the academic sector is that the task is labour intensive and leads to disks 'disappearing'.

With the jukebox well out of harm's way and a menu of databases to choose from at the terminal the process is much simplified. We are confident that the benefits of direct public access and the provision of networks will appear in the returns when this survey is undertaken again. The breakthrough will come when three criteria can be met. First, that jukeboxes can be readily connected to the big networks supported by library management systems so that the richness of CD ROM databases can be exploited at terminals far and wide.

Experiments have hit a number of problems of software compatibility and lack of intelligence on the networks and these problems have kept the breakthrough from coming, but come it must. Second, search software can provide a standard query language which is applicable to all CD ROM databases so that the user once trained can sue any system, and finally, that reasonable pricing structures can be negotiated with CD ROM publishers for networking agreements. Online access to remote database hosts has been around for a long time. It must have been in use outside esoteric research labs for twenty years and many public libraries have been providing online access for upwards of ten.

In some ways the potential of online access is not unlike that of CD ROM—providing the ability to search very large stores of data—with the added advantage that the information can be as up to date as today. The risks of incurring high costs through long searches has damped any enthusiasm for providing direct public access to hosts, but online access remains an important tool to those librarians involved in the provision of information services.

Pricing structures which do not discourage the occasional user and the wide availability of micro-computers have seen a steady increase in use over recent years. What used to be a hit-and-miss affair using dedicated terminals and devices called acoustic couplers has become a simple and reliable matter of hitting a few keys. However, we suspect that a continuing subjective feeling that searching online is expensive and complicated has created some barriers and the growing availability of databases on CD ROM which incur no cost at point of use has influenced decisions on whether or not to use online searching.

There is no conclusive evidence that the two methods overlap significantly, however subjective evidence suggests that an important use of CD ROM is the formulation of search strategies which can then be used during an online search. Also, it would appear from a recent report on the 1991 International Online Information Meeting that demand for online hosts continues to grow despite the popularity of CD ROM databases. Turning to the data from this current survey, there are now 107 authorities using online searching. That is a 10% increase over the figure in 1989, which was 97. Looking at the percentage changes since 1985, we can see that there has been a slowing down in the increase—the change between 1985 and 1987 was 30% up, and 1987 to 1989, 13%. This suggests that the majority of those libraries who see online searching as an asset to their services have already begun using the technique and that the increases seen in the past are tending to plateau.

Whether the remaining 60 authorities suffer a financial barrier, a psychological one or simply do not believe that online searching is relevant to their services cannot be evinced from the data available. However, as we shall see below, the nature of the databases most used implies use by libraries who prioritise bibliographic and business information as important. Perhaps the non-users have set other priorities for their services.

The fact that only 25% of Scottish authorities use the technique influences significantly the overall total. Non-mets are also at 25% but they are only four in number, yet Scotland, with the largest number of authorities, lags far behind. We cannot claim an in-depth knowledge of Scottish library services, however elsewhere in this review we will see that they tend to plough a separate furrow in their use of IT. The other data show manly steady increases and no decreases, from which we may conclude that once adopted, online searching has lasting value to service delivery. A trend which previously proved of interest is the method of access used to search online hosts. Trend is an important word in this context since, on occasion, the replies received from the questionnaire needed some interpretation.

When compared with 1985, the data from the current survey reinforce patterns which were noted in 1989. The fairly even mix of dedicated terminal, Prestel and microcomputer which existed in 1985 has been routed by the micro which now stands head, shoulders and keyboard above all other access methods. Not really very surprising when you come to think about it since the micro has been widely adopted as the access medium for those who operate outside our world. Modem boards can be fitted into machines and there is bags of cheap software around to be played with.

Insofar as online searching can be a suer-friendly business, the micro can facilitate it since it is possible to set up dialling and log-in codes for rapid access, and the micro can still be used for so many other things. The other significant feature of the data iis the steady increase in the number of authorities using the circulation system as the medium of access. While five is a very small figure when compared with the micros, there are some interesting implications in the decision to use the library management system for online searching. First, most of the new systems allow you to do so, and have done for some time.

There is nothing particularly fancy about it, but for very good reasons most libraries have shied away from doing so. While in principle it should be a good thing to provide online access in a variety of locations, where the information is really needed, it requires trained staff to use the systems effectively and untrained staff can run up some hefty bills in no time at all. Use can be limited to defined terminals, but the strategy which has been to focus online searching to key locations where specialist staff, capable of knowing for certain when online should be used, are on hand.

Without doubt, the use of the library management system as a delivery medium holds great potential and we will be very surprised if more libraries do not take the plunge (or the risk?). Certainly if the complexities which remain in host interfaces can be reduced so that infrequent users have a chance of getting in and out more quickly, there is every incentive to widen the network, and that is precisely the value of the library management system, it has a wide network of terminals.

The truth of these comments becomes more clear when the total terminal population is considered, rather than the use of the medium alone. What we have been looking at so far is the number of authorities using each method, rather than the number of terminals used by each.

	1989	1991
Dedicated terminal	45	68
Circulation system	35	61
Microcomputer	121	263
Prestel, etc.	4	2

The above table provides a comparison only between 1989 and 1991 since the information is not available for 1985 or 1987. Of course, there can be no certainty about the freedom which is allowed for all of the library management system terminals to be used for on line searching, but the potential is clear.

Other points to note from these data are that although the number of dedicated terminal users has risen by only one in two years, there has been a 50% increase in the terminals in use; suggesting that while this route may not be the one chosen now by new entries, for those already using the method, it is of sufficient value to encourage wider availability. Finally on hardware, there are now a great many micros being used for online searching; the total more than doubling while the number of authorities has only increased by 14%. Next we must look at the purposes for which online searching is being used—the hosts being accessed. Just as with the CD ROM world, we are facing more diversity all the time.

While 'umbrella' hosts can give access to a wide range of databases, sometimes duplicating other hosts, there are also individual database providers who are being used by public libraries. The two obvious examples are laser's Viscount interlending service and Volnet, which is a database of importance to the voluntary sector. In reality, rather than this diversity being reflected in the data from libraries, the range reported is very similar to 1989. This tends to suggest that the markets being served by online searching are quite clearly defined and are common to most users. If these data are considered in conjunction with the 'other' category, the trend in the use of online searching is quite apparent. Blaise is still an important source of bibliographic information, but with a growing range of CD ROM-based products it may become less used.

The major use for online searching is clearly business information. Added together these business-orientated databases dominate Blaise by a factor of more than three to one. The only joker to be found is Acompline, which is unique in providing current information on local authority affairs and which is still quite popular. The fact that access to this database, which is provided by the London Research Centre, is free may have something to do with this continuing popularity. The last two aspects of online searching which can be considered here relate not to the technology or the range of services available, but how they are delivered to users.

The first factor is the costs which are passed on to users and the second is the management of the service—staff skilled in the techniques and how it has changed traditional provision. Charging policies ought to tell us a great deal about the priorities of libraries and their responses to changes especially those outside their control, whether from competition or from the comments of the Minister for the Arts! Back in 1989 made some observations about the reasons for the high level of certain replies. Discretion, for example, could be an excuse for saying one thing and doing another—telling everyone that certain categories of user are charged, or charges are levied when a search is requested, while not bothering because of the hassle of recovering the money. No comment, on the other hand could be an excuse for doing almost anything; anything that is except charge.

The use of online searching has grown up in a tradition where it is the exception to levy a fee for a service at point of use. The whole point of public goods is that they are funded from individual contributions (rates, taxes) which bear no relation to level of use made by that individual.

The management of the service includes the

organisation of specialist staff and the changes which have resulted from the development of online searching. There is just as much need to have highly trained staff undertaking searches as there has ever been. Despite developments in the design of user-friendly interfaces, online searching remains a special skill, both in the knowledge of command languages and in the formulation of suitable search strategies. It is likely to be a long time before access is provided to customers without the need for a trained intermediary, since cost rises and effectiveness falls if the searcher is not properly trained.

Libraries were asked to indicate numbers of locations of trained staff and 86 provided replies, as opposed to 78 in 1989. As with all questions demanding more than a yes or no reply, we must be cautious about making too many assumptions from the data. The evidence provided in the replies shows that all but a very few authorities focus their online services (and staff) in key locations—usually reference libraries, business information centres and the like. The average number of trained staff in each authority is something over four, a slight increase on 1989, but remains fairly stable. It seems that whatever changes may face public libraries in the next few years, this is at least one service which will continue to require 'gatekeepers' to make it fully effective.

Changes in the form of other services resulting from the use of online searching was the last question asked on this subject. Again, since the data re textual rather than precise responses, only general conclusions may be drawn. Despite that, the replies add some detail to the overall picture of online searching in public libraries. Fifty seven authorities commented, compared with the 39 who did so in 1989. Of those 28 implied in their reply that online searching had enriched the range of services available.

Eight libraries reported that printed sources had been cancelled and ten that there had been no significant change; either because online had been used for so long that no-one could remember what life was like before, or online was such a new acquisition that there had not been time to see any impact. On the other hand, two authorities reported dramatic changes to the scope and method of service delivery. While online searching involves only a few staff and demands small amounts of the budget, it is an important and emotive topic. The trend which has emerged over the past four or five years is for the databases to form part of services to business and now, for those services to be viewed in many places as 'suitable cases for charging'.

The CD ROM/online searching duopoly should be a key focus for our attention over the next few years and will be the subject of further research. Indeed, a recent report from the Centre for Communication and Information Studies at the Polytechnic of Central London reports research which looked in much more detail at the actual pattern of database use by analyzing bills from a range of authorities, and interviewing a sample of users in great detail. The general trends reported above are echoed in the research results and the report is well worth reading to gain a clearer picture of what the future may hold.

Videotext/teletext

By and large, through this survey until now we have seen a mixture of steady growth in some applications, dramatic growth in others. Turning now to videotex and teletext we are in the realm of technologies which have been around for some years, have become well established, to the point where we are beginning to see them superseded. We can remember a time when there was much talk about Prestel (videotex) as a major medium of information delivery. Organisations were clamouring to be a part of a readily accessible and widely spread public network. Today Prestel is still around, but many new systems have arrived which are Prestel-like in their utility, but have much more power to exploit data resources. Such systems are now used in private viewdata networks, closed user group systems providing information using the format of Prestel, but managed by some local information provider.

Teletext, an information system available on broadcast television networks such as Ceefax and Oracle has never been a critical element in publicly provided information services since the data cannot be manipulated locally and is usually of momentary interest—news, racing results, etc. Moreover, it is common for home use television sets to be sold with Ceefax and Oracle decoders as standard. The trends for teletext and videotex show a situation which has matured to the point where use has levelled off and appears at present to be falling slightly. We have already indicated possible reasons for this above. Private viewdata, on the other hand, is growing steadily in popularity as a medium for the delivery of information tailored to the local community.

In six years there has been an almost threefold increase in the systems in use and we may expect this to continue since often these systems are developed as corporate information systems, sometimes managed by the library service, sometimes not and while libraries may find themselves low down on the corporate IT programme private viewdata systems may not.

Analysing use at the level of the authority provides only a general picture of developments and that to establish more clearly the impact made it is necessary to consider the penetration of systems within individual authorities. Respondents were asked to report the numbers of terminals used on each of these systems and, in addition, to show whether their use was seldom, steady or constant. These data support earlier points about the fall in the popularity of videotex and teletext as information systems in libraries.

Not only has there been a fall in the number of authorities using the systems, but the number of terminals provided has also dropped—videotex almost to the level of 1985, teletext below it. Of course, mean numbers are just that, and the actual distribution shows that in a few authorities there are relatively large populations of terminals. Wiltshire, for example, reports 38 for videotex. In contrast, not only has the total number of authorities using private viewdata risen, but the mean number of terminals shows a 23.5% rise. Not surprising since if private viewdata is the means of delivering community information, as it usually is, then terminals should be as widely available as possible.

Having descended from the level of total use, to penetration within a library system, we can finally consider how much the systems are used. The questionnaire invited comment on whether the use of each of the three system was seldom, steady or constant. We must exercise some caution. One person's steady is another's constant and we can only draw limited information from these data. Also, use is likely to vary from terminal to terminal so the single comment may not reflect reality where more than one is in use. Steady is the most frequently cited option, except for videotex where seldom is top.

We do not think there is much value in a detailed analysis of these data since their objectivity is questionable, but we can give a personal opinion. Videotex is not used much since alternative sources of information may provide speedier access (and you have to pay to use Prestel). The cost of teletext is unaffected by use since it is broadcast with the TV signals. Leaving terminals lying about for people to play with, therefore carries no risk of large bills. Safe for the customer to come in and tinker with.

Many customers will now know more about the resources available on teletext than the managers providing it—they will have it at home. We see in private viewdata systems a locally tailored system more likely to meet customer information needs and it should be no surprise that respondents reported many more steady and constants (83% of the total) than its cousin videotex (45% of the total), and even more than teletext (75% of the total) which is free of use cost [private viewdata has a cost in use since remote terminals will be connected by a telephone line or wide area network].

The automation of community information highlights one of the paradoxes of information technology. It is very easy to start—just buy a micro and printer, some database software and off you go—but it can be very hard to keep the data comprehensive and up to date. Anyone who has had much to do with computers knows that the data are the most valuable commodity, much more valuable than the hardware or software that can be replaced at the corner shop. Creating any database takes time, maintaining it takes time, and time is money.

Community information has always been an attractive product to automate since so much of it is in the form that can readily be fitted into database software products. Clubs, societies, business organisations and the like are the lifeblood of the community information database and are maintained in some form or other by the vast majority of libraries. Indeed, comprehensive community systems are something unique to libraries; you certainly can't buy them at Smiths. Not surprisingly then the number of libraries automating community information continues to grow. 1987 and 1989 has been matched in the past two years by a total increase of just over 19%. the rend which was apparent between 1985 and 1987, use of the micro and wordprocessor, has now changed. This time the micro, still the most popular medium, remains unchanged at 38 while use of the library management system shows the most significant growth, up by 75%.

It is also not unexpected that private viewdata continues to increase since we have already noted in this chapter that the number of authorities providing the medium continues to rise. One question which comes immediately to mind, however, is if 40 authorities reported use of the system under the videotex/teletext section above, but only 18 report using it for community information, what are the other 22 doing? Just the same question had to be asked in the last survey and suggested that the problem was one of interpretation—that the authorities might not be managing the private viewdata system and therefore thought that it should not be reported under the community information banner. Whether that is true one cannot say.

Certainly the prime purpose of private viewdata networks is to deliver information of relevance to the community. Finally, while considering the method of processing, it should be noted that a further five libraries indicated that they were actively investigating the automation on their community information files, and by now they may have done just that. That gives a potential total of 102 authorities who use IT for community information or 60% of the 167 country wide.

Micros and wordprocessors have been around for so many years, have at least 40% of the libraries in the country not started to automate the community information files which they certainly must have. With common sense, transferring manual files to a micro can save time and make the product much more useful. Mail merge makes remainders easier and with multiple indexing possible, more variety of presentation is not a problem.

A micro/printer set up is not pricey and there are so many examples of applications that not to try seems swimming against the stream. To see whether there was any pattern to this reticence we looked a bit more closely at the 66 libraries without automated community information. An interesting fact emerged—that nearly half of the 66 were authorities of the same type. Twenty seven of the 41 Scottish authorities (66%) have yet to do anything about automating their community information; only one of the four Welsh Non-Mets has done so and none of the Northern Ireland libraries has started. Elsewhere, the most likely authority type to find automated systems is the English county where 85% have automated their community information. London, the Mets and the Welsh counties range from 74% uptake down to 63%. You will remember that Scottish authorities were also behind on the library management system front and one can only repeat that perhaps they have set different priorities or lack of resources places severe restrictions on the acquisition of technology.

Conversely, English counties are large organisations with disparate service points and the benefits of using IT for community information has clearly been recognised. Lastly, the questionnaire sought details of how the information is actually made available to customers. There are three possibilities—online, hardcopy and a mixture of both—online in some places, or for staff use, hardcopy elsewhere, or for the customers. The trend which was reported in 1989 was towards more data to be presented online rather than in printed format and the 1991 data confirm that this trend has continued during the intervening two years. Online as the only means of delivery has increased by more than a third and online/ hardcopy has also edged up. On the other hand hardcopy has fallen by something over 10%, having remained unchanged for the two years before. It is a pity that ten libraries did not give any indication of dissemination format since, had they, the data might have looked different.

Nevertheless, from what we have it seems hat progress towards direct public access for customers continues. Hardcopy should not be dismissed as an anachronism just yet since there are many occasions when it is useful to send the customer away with a list to browse through—doing that online in the library has implications for the number of terminals provided. The benefits of online access include the freedom of the customer to search in their own way without an intermediary and sometimes the opportunity to search the database from the comfort of the office or the front room. This chapter has considered a number of IT applications all of which are linked by their role as deliverers of information to customers. The options available to library managers deciding what applications to use are not limitless.

8

PUBLIC SERVICE NETWORKING

This chapter deals with the areas of information networking within the community context, ranging from voluntary community networks aiming to provide the citizen with general information for everyday life, to sophisticated systems for urban management and health care. Each of these areas has seen a growth in activity in recent years, as access to information becomes a more important factor in daily decision-making, whether at the individual or organizational level.

Recently, the ubiquitous spread of network access and microcomputers have encouraged the development of more pro-active forms, under the aegis of local governments or local voluntary not-for-profit groups (particularly in the United States), which aim to provide the framework for community action which supports two-way networking, rather than the simple one-way passive consumption of display only systems.

Viewdata systems have been installed in public libraries since the early 1980s, following the emergence of the British Telecom Prestel public information system. This is now a rather outdated and unsophisticated system, and is not amenable towards tailoring for local community information. The late 1980s saw the growing use by public libraries of private viewdata systems which are developed and sometimes managed by commercial enterprises on behalf of their clients; these can be customized for individual applications and managed as a closed user group facility, offering specific information targeted at a well-defined user group. A recent survey showed that 40 public library authorities use a private viewdata system, and that this use is replacing that of Prestel (and broadcast teletext services such as Ceefax and Oracle) both in terms of numbers of systems and in overall usage by the public.

Added to the local focus in information content, there is also the advantage that some local authorities adopt private viewdata as an internal corporate information system, allowing the library to make use of any spare capacity. The Electronic Public Information Network (previously the Local Authority Videotex Association) acts as a forum for channelling ideas and advice in videotex, investigating hardware and software issues, and developing applications for community information needs. This has some 46 local authority members and a number of other public sector and private organizations.

In the context of local government authorities rather than just public libraries, a survey by the Society of Information Technology Managers in 1992 revealed that 19% of UK local authorities already have public access terminals installed, and that a further 14% planned to do so in the near future. These were installed in venues as diverse as libraries, council buildings, and shopping precincts, containing information on:

— local organizations and events;
— details of general practitioners;
— transport information;

— tourist information, including accommodation listings;

— information services aimed at local economic development, for example EC information on legislation, calls for tender, potential European business partners;

— one-stop enquiry shops, staffed by assistants able to make use of the local authority computer network to answer information enquiries on council services and activities.

Since community information needs do not exactly match local authority boundaries, there is a growing tendency to combine together localized services to form geographically wider-ranging information systems. Doncaster Metropolitan Borough in South Yorkshire, for example, has developed a successful viewdata service known as DONFACTS, giving details of employment vacancies, and local events and activities; in 1989 the South Yorkshire Libraries Viewdata Information Service was formed to create a regional service from this and other participants in the area.

An alternative to Integrated library system module is the use of a purpose-designed module within an integrated library system such as GEAC. This has the advantage of allowing the information to be directly controlled by the library authority itself, and to integrate it with the other activities and information services offered by the public library.

Community information, for instance, may appear as one option on an Online Public Access Catalogue terminal, along with information relating to library holdings, updated and maintained in the same way. An example of this approach is the CINDEX system, the Camden Community Information Network Directory and Exchange, developed from the GEAC Local Information

System. The use of an integrated system gave the possibility of direct access to the information, rather than requiring the user to traverse the 'tree' structure of menus typical of viewdata systems, with the use of various access points; and offered the functionality to manipulate and print subsets of the information base as specialized products. Once again, maintenance of this system requires co-operation with neighbouring areas, since urban information requirements are not constrained by administrative borders.

A recent development in the provision of community information has been the growth in co-operative host systems which, instead of building up a centralized bank of information for dissemination to users at terminal access points, concentrate rather on building a facilitating infrastructure which offers a framework for diverse groups to build and maintain their own information systems and services. Host systems offer general facilities for creating local information files, the exchange of information between specific small user groups, and the creation of developmental projects and workshops, as well as more traditional services such as access to external databases.

The Manchester Host system uses an internationally available communications software system more widely known as Geo-net, which is installed in some 40 countries around the world; Manchester Host is directly linked to several of these other Hosts in Europe (including Eastern and Central Europe), Russia and the USA through the international telecommunications networks.

The Host is accessible to its subscribers through use of a phone line, PC and modem. Services include:

— *electronic mail* to other Host subscribers internationally, and to telex and facsimile services, and X.400 mail, as well as gateways to other e-mail systems, such as BT Gold, MCI Mail and Telemail;

— *data facilities* for the creation of bulletin boards, computer conferencing, and file exchange, and for the uploading of data to create new local online database services;

— *online database access* through a common searching language to external databases in both the commercial and voluntary sectors, for example to FT Profile, and the Amnesty International bibliographic database on human rights, together with an integrated billing mechanism which removes the need for each user to have individual subscription to specific database hosts;

— *network access* to other systems, such as Easynet, the Internet, GreenNet, and APC GreenNet.

The Host approach assumes that users are potential information providers as well as consumers of information, encouraging an active participation in creating new applications and making contributions to existing ones. This led the Host initiative to borrow the idea of electronic village halls from the telecottages movement, and establish these in localized areas of Manchester, offering new technology facilities and training for particular groups, organized and managed by these groups themselves: for example electronic village halls have been established by women's groups, for small local business, and for the local Bangladeshi community.

As well as supporting greater participation for the individual in the information age through a philosophy of low-cost access and distributed processing, the Host approach has been to promote private and public sector partnership for the development of specific project initiatives for closed user groups. This involves cooperation between local government, employers and businesses, higher education institutes, trade unions, and non-governmental organizations, working on projects to extend the ISDN network and the consequent development of broadband information services, the extension of electronic data interchange (EDI) to smaller enterprises, and the development of a communications park for business. A number of closed user groups built around specific cooperative needs have evolved including:

— the Manchester Chinese Information Centre, supporting document exchange in Chinese script to the local ethnic community;

— the Manchester Business School, which uses the system to communicate with similar institutions on an international footing;

— the Manchester Asian Trading Network to improve trading links between local Asian business and suppliers in Bangladesh;

— the Manchester Design Community, in which smaller enter prises co-operate on bidding for larger contracts as a consortium.

On a wider geographic level, links with other European cities allow for greater co-operation in trans-regional development initiatives. GeoNet systems are existing in Berlin, Athens, Moscow, Seville, Sofia, Siberia, Cyprus, Crete, Poland, and Finland among others. The European and international linkages are likely to develop more strongly in the longer term, encouraged by the recent bid by Manchester to host the Olympic Games.

The Host system brings together a diversity of community issues and related information activities focused on a locality. A range of networks have also sprung up to link together groups and organizations working in similar Areas, though geographically dispersed. The 'networking' term is sometimes used rather freely in this context; some examples of these are closer to centralized database systems which offer remote access to users. Volnet, for example, is a central database host, providing a route to information for workers in the voluntary and community sectors at low-cost. The database offers online access to a bibliographic database, backed up by a photocopy-based document supply service, and to information on research projects and the details of UK parliamentary candidates.

GreenNet provides a similar service for non-governmentai organizations and individuals working with ecological and environmental issues, giving access to a range of computer conferences and resources, with a common structure to the location of information files in the network. APC GreenNet links together progressive organizations with an interest in the development of information communication for social change, such as Amnesty International. A range of similar networking initiatives exist, some short- and some longer lived. These can operate at a purely national level, or work on an international scale, for example the *TUDIC* network which supports co-operation and the sharing of information between trade unions in Sweden, Denmark, and the UK.

While many of the existing community networks in the USA have evolved from local initiatives, stemming either from citizen groups or public authority organizations, recent years have seen the emergence of commercial organizations piloting or operating information networks directed at local users on a for-profit basis. These organizations make information produced by, others available whilst profiting from advertising through the network facilities. *American CitiNet* operates this service bureau arrangement, with particular customer bases in Omaha and Boston. The *regional Bell operating companies,* the US regional telecommunication suppliers, are beginning to offer gateway facilities to information providers who are then able to recover their costs from information users through the normal billing arrangements of the Bell companies. A number of local government agencies are providing information and services in this way.

As well as communicating with clients of their services, local government authorities have used information networking as a means of co-ordinating and delivering the services for which they are responsible. There is an increasing recognition for the need to integrate and consolidate the single-focus information sets that are incomplete and incompatible, or fragmented across departmental and administrative boundaries, in order to deliver services effectively and support local development.

The networking of databases and administrative systems increases access to information and forms a platform for the development of more powerful and sophisticated integrated systems. Local access to council services and information is effected by networking local branch offices and the creation of information points at which the public can find out about a range of council services, such as housing, employment, transport, and trading standards, together in one place; and can make specific enquiries about their individual progress, in areas such as payment of council tax or council house repairs.

Information access points such as these can be queried by telephone, and in some areas have taken the form of mobile services linked to a central computer system. This growth in the integration of information systems is linked to the development of new forms of service based on emerging information technology. Geographical information systems are a prime example of this, since much of the work of local authorities is spatially related.

Different information bases, for example, may contain mapping data on the location of gas, electricity, and water utility pipes, property ownership and land use, and demographic information for strategic planning. Although these may be distributed over different locations and agencies, their integration across a network offers the opportunity for more advanced services: for example, transport information management systems which link traffic flows with highway maintenance and emergency services; or demographic planning with library development and community analysis to determine information needs.

Local authorities are increasingly providing information services linked to local economic development. While the Manchester Host is one important example of a far-reaching approach to this, more traditional information services include access to European databases for information on European Commission tenders and contracts, EC legislation, and searching for business partners in other EC countries. Staffordshire County Council, for example, is one of 25 areas connected to a European network for the communication of this type of information.

A similar requirement encourages the integration of information access between different service delivery agencies. Recent changes in UK legislation have reinforced this trend, particularly with regard to the delivery of personal social services; this is one area in which the local authority is presented with a lead role as an enabler for their delivery.

The Child Protection Register maintained by social service departments, for example, is in some cases available to accident and emergency departments of local hospitals in electronic form. The recent Care in the Community Act presupposes the exchange of information between social service departments and community health authorities.

The National Disability Information Project, formed under the auspices of the Department of Health, is a further influence developing this role for public service agencies. One of the pilot projects is the GUiDe system under development in Gloucestershire between the Gloucester and Cheltenham Health Authorities and the County Social Services Department. This deals with information for elderly and disabled people, and gives networked access to health professionals in hospitals, voluntary organizations, health centres, and social services offices. Another project is based at Gateshead Libraries and Arts Service, well known for its innovative viewdata-based home shopping experiment.

The Gateshead Disability Information project aims to make information from the council on disability available in various complementary forms—sound, text and video—of the user's own choosing, and through a variety of delivery mechanisms.

There is a similar requirement for local government and local agencies to interwork with central government in an online networked environment, dealing with electronic information, often driven by central government directly. The Department for Education, for instance, uses electronic data interchange (EDI) to communicate with school educators on statistics and teachers' pensions matters, and similar arrangements for transport and trading standards are likely to emerge.

Quasi-governmental organizations also have information exchange requirements with local areas, and as these bodies automate their information resources and archives they are developing online access arrangements to replace manual administration for remote users. Increasingly, these applications demand more sophisticated information exchange facilities and broadband network links to accommodate heavy data transfer loads and multimedia information types. A recent example is the MONARCH system developed by the Royal Commission on Historical Monuments of England, an electronic version of the National Monuments Record. The online version of this gives remote access for about 200 users to some 6 million items of information on ancient monuments, including graphic images with hypertext linkages as well as text-based searching.

The information is used by local government for planning purposes, by English Nature for conservation decisions, and by the National Trust for property management, and will in the future be linked to geographical information systems for map-based searching and retrieval.

Local authorities have traditionally been involved in the direct provision of services, including information services and information related to other activities. As information becomes more and more important as a basic commodity for daily life, many see local government as having a role in the planning and development of a local information infrastructure, aimed at facilitating the integration and sharing of information from many sources and encouraging a policy of common access and citizen participation as well as enabling local economic and community development.

The growing interest in teleworking and the establishment of service centres for telecommunications seem to call naturally on the support of local government, and this approach has found heavy investment in Japan, for example, where telecommuting has formed a major plank in the development of regional information systems; although in the UK, there has not been the same display of interest.

As changes in society, and in the structure and nature of organizations create changes in work patterns and habits for those who work in them or use their products and services, the change towards client-focused rather than organization-focused services may offer opportunities for a new role for local government in this area.

Perhaps the first developments in this area can be seen in the recent creation of 'One stop shops' providing information, counselling, and advice support services for local businesses, established under the auspices of the Department for Trade and Industry. These are mostly based on joint arrangements between Training and Enterprise Councils, chambers of commerce and local authorities, taking different forms in different areas. Six main areas have been selected as the first pilots. These include urban areas such as Birmingham, where the Birmingham Libraries business information service is involved, to larger rural areas such as Hertfordshire, where the Hertis Information and Research consultancy and Hertfordshire Libraries are involved in the feasibility study.

Several of the development programmes started by the Commission for the European Community programmes are aimed at the development of networking as a supportive means for social and community development. The STAR programme, aimed at the less developed areas of the EC, has been used to develop the telecommunications infrastructure for rural areas to stimulate the use of information networking for employment and skills development.

The ACE-HI scheme, administered by the Association of Community Enterprises in the Highland and Islands of Scotland is an example of this type of activity (with additional funding from BT), resulting in a £16 million investment in ISDN networks, and their successful use for the delivering of training and the development of enterprises which conduct their business through such networks, in remote islands and isolated parts of the mainland. Other EC social programmes have made extensive use of networking and telecommunications. The COMETT programme has used networking to promote trans-national co-operation between commercial enterprises and universities for the delivery of training in technical skills.

The HORIZON programme is establishing a disabled people's network through Europe, while the New Opportunities for Women programme is funding the partnership of Athens, Manchester, and Seville in building a telematics development network for the exchange of skills, information, and experience on women's training, employment, and enterprise.

The European Community established the ROME (Reseau Observatoires Metropolitains en Europe) network in 1989 to advise the Commission on research and information development activities for urban areas. A three-year project known as the European Urban Observatory was initiated in 1992 linking ten European cities (Amsterdam, Athens, Barcelona, Birmingham, Berlin, Genoa, Glasgow, Lille, Lisbon, and Naples) in a European-wide network to support strategic decision-making and the common interpretation of information on a European-wide basis. The aim of this project is to monitor urban trends through the sharing of urban management information, the transfer of experience and comparative evaluation of policy.

Information is structured into three levels, dealing with basic indicators for policy decision-making, with quantitative comparative data, and with individual city data stored locally; these levels are linked together through the use of X. 25 private networks, and the BT Tymnet wide area network employed to form a closed user group. This networking of public management information contributes to the development of pan-European urban policy issues, and gives a comparative background resource at the local level.

Information networking in the health service sector in the United Kingdom has become a vital activity in recent years, stimulated by a growing movement for the improvement of health information services, following the work of the Korner Group on information systems, and stimulated by the radical organizational changes creating an 'internal market' for purchasers and providers of health services. These tendencies have created a pressure for the harmonization and integration of all forms of information within the sector, and a demand for wider accessibility and sharing through computer networks and other applications of information technology.

The distinction between traditional bibliographic information services and other information sources has lessened with 'information' and 'intelligence' being taken to include, sometimes primarily, statistical and demographical information. Within this context, networks are used to link the office automation and service environment with information providers across many administrative levels.

Management information in this framework would include:

— literature in the form of written or audiovisual material: published books and journals, etc., as well as unpublished material in the form of correspondence, internal reports, and committee minutes;

— quantitative information, in the form of data relating to the activities and context of the organization; statistical returns, demographic analysis, performance indicators, trends analysis.

Within the health sector, an integrated delivery of information services more often requires sharing and exchange between fragmented units, now within a more competitive context. Library units, for example, may include within the same region headquarters libraries, departmental libraries, small service points in branch hospitals, postgraduate medical centre and research information points, and nursing libraries; each with varying degrees of autonomy.

With a growing amount of information available in electronic form, user requirements are likely to involve the retrieval of information from remote sources across a network, as much or more than from a local collection, and to varying forms and types of data. A medical researcher, for example, could require not only bibliographic references, and full text source material, but also images and the ability to process images, datasets of published social and epidemiological statistics, and so on. At the international level, medical information services are developing strengthened links through the use of networks.

The HealthNet system, for example, provides access for health professionals in developing countries to medical literature and databases and to colleagues elsewhere, through the use of low-cost packet satellite technology. HealthNet is initially targeted at Africa, and includes access to British and North American gateways which allow medical libraries and information units in these areas to 'twin' with similar organizations in Africa.

Generic facilities such as electronic mail and file transfer through computer networks open up the possibility of more extensive contact between health professionals in the context of an electronic community.

The increasing depth of special knowledge possessed by a widening spectrum of health professionals, located geographically separate from each other, and the interdisciplinary nature of health science, point towards a need for networked and integrated solutions to information needs. At the same time as information management has assumed a higher profile within the health sector, there is a growing interaction with external agencies fuelled by information interchange. Some instances of co-operative networking with local authorities have been mentioned earlier—a common interest in demographic analysis for strategic planning is another obvious example—and the same trend emerges in health service relations with other public service organizations.

The range and volume of data involved can be quite significant: a medium-sized hospital can send some 300-400 pathology and radiology reports per day to several dozen local general practitioner centres, and up to 100 discharge letters; a large general medical practice may make some 40 referrals per day to hospitals, and perhaps 7000 registrations per year to Family Health Service Authorities. Each of these activities involves the transmission of information and storage within the receiving systems, with the desirability of enabling the direct capture by the receiving application, and avoiding a need to re-key data which is already in electronic format.

The data needs to be exchanged between autonomous sites, loosely coupled in systems with a local focus. Externally, information flows will move from the National Health Service to product suppliers, service providers, government agencies, local authorities,

European and international organizations, the insurance and banking sectors, private health care agencies, and other national health services. To achieve an electronic data integration across the whole health service delivery chain, and with organizations in its environment, the development and application of standard forms of information interchange is required.

The United Nations standard for electronic data interchange EDIFACT has been adopted by the Information Management Executive of the UK National Health Service as a widely used and comprehensible standard. The EDIFACT standard requires the use of structured information formats primarily intended for autonomous computer processing, and transferral across telecommunication links.

The standard provides for the definition of data elements, syntax rules, and the structure of messages built from these data elements in a way that can be adapted for various applications; EDIFACT is managed by the United Nations as a cross-sector global communications standard, and is also defined within GOSIP, the UK Government Open System Profile. The NHS Information Management Executive has initiated many projects intended to contribute towards the development of a common infrastructure through the use of information systems strategy.

A major plank within this strategy is the desire to create a unique NHS number for individual patients, enabling the creation of a population register designed for sharing across the sector, and forming a natural integration of basic administrative activities. This will underpin NHS-wide electronic networking, and together with agreed standards for information interchange, lead towards a shared language for health care throughout the sector.

A number of these projects are aimed at general practitioners, and their links with other health agencies, involving the identification of a basic information structure common to all GP practices, and the development of compatible systems. Some examples of these development initiatives are:

— the electronic linking of GPs to hospitals for the exchange of pathology and waiting list information via the RACAL Healthlink system and local regional networks, in the Oxford Region GP/Hospital Information Exchange Project;

— linking general practitioners with Family Health Service authorities (FHSA) to enable the direct registration and update of FHSA databases by local practices, and vice versa, and the linked updating of payments to doctors through FHSA systems;

— the update of FHSA databases to the NHS Central Register (NHSCR) as the most reliable measure of movement of the population between Health Authority areas;

— an information collection project to network GPs together to facilitate the continuous collection of morbidity data as the basis for a national agreed set of morbidity data.

More broadly, projects are developing standards which apply across the sector, for:

— the development of a common basic specification as an extension of the NHS Data Model, to cover data exchange standards, minimum datasets, clinical information for resource management; and the information demands of hospital and regional decision support systems;

— the development of an NHS Administrative Register to act as a shared register of basic administrative details meeting the requirements of District Health authorities, Family Health Service authorities, general practitioners, and hospitals;

— a Community Information Systems Project to facilitate the exchange of information to support contracting, and the development of datasets for ambulatory care in hospital and community settings, for use by community health services.

The National Health Service in the United Kingdom has seen a vast increase in the importance of information management, with information networking forming a vital part of this. It is certain that the importance of networking activities will continue to grow as a strategic element in the construction of integrated information and intelligence.

In the past, telecommunications has largely been regarded as a natural monopoly in the same way as gas and electricity. The long-term nature of the investment needed to create a national infrastructure, and the massive amounts of capital involved, have discouraged private initiative and relied upon governmental support and backing.

During the 1980s, in many countries around the world, this arrangement began to be perceived as too parochial and inflexible; liberalization of telecommunications regulation was seen as a means of stimulating innovation, by encouraging the development of market forces through the introduction of new service suppliers.

The liberalization of telecommunication has taken two main forms. they are the following:

— *Privatization*: In which the monopoly authority is established as a private corporation, which competes on the same terms as any other business;

— *Deregulation*: In which allows new service operators

to offer competitive services, by the removal of restrictive practices which legislate against this.

Many countries have opted for a mixture of these two forms, often with a transition period setting special conditions which alternative services must adhere to. The extent of deregulation has also differed considerably; since the telecommunications infrastructure is seen as so essential to economic development, the total abolition of all regulatory mechanisms is not considered desirable. For this reason, many people speak of re-regulation, stressing a change in the conditions of government control rather than their complete removal.

The United States has historically been different from most countries, in that telecommunications have always been controlled by a private corporation, licensed under government monopoly. The AT&T corporation which provided the telephone systems prior to liberalization was forbidden in a 1956 ruling from entering the computer or information business, in which it would be considered to have an unfair advantage. In this period, two major corporations, AT&T and IBM, dominated the telecommunications and computing industries respectively, but did not directly compete with each other. A Federal Court ruling of 1982 ended this arrangement by requiring the divestiture of AT&T under the corporate anti-trust laws. This resulted in the creation of seven independent regional Bell operating companies out of the former AT&T conglomerate, each of which provided the public telecommunications service in a separate geographical area of the United States.

AT&T itself remained to compete for the traffic between these regions with other long haul private network operators, such as MCI and US Sprint. AT&T was also permitted to enter the computer and information business in its own right which, as the original developer and licensor of the Unix operating system through Bell Laboratories, was an attractive new direction for its corporate development. This 1982 judgment did not, however, end all regulation over the sector. The divested AT&T was prevented from entering 'electronic publishing'—the provision of information services on their networks—for a period of seven years while competitor network suppliers developed their strengths. This restriction was removed in 1989. The regional Bell operating companies (RBOCs) are now permitted to offer:

— electronic messaging;

— audiotex;

— electronic gateways to other information services;

— integrated billing for online information through these gateways;

The AT&T corporation, however, acting as the carrier of inter-exchange traffic, is increasingly interested in developing information services through co-operation with the regional operating companies; for example by using national customer databases of names and addresses for credit card and target marketing schemes.

The exact relationship between monopoly and non-monopoly services has been the subject of debate and conflict between the Federal Court and the Federal Communications Commission throughout this period, with the former championing a more restrictive approach. Realizing that the computer industry which telecommunications serves has global interests, both AT&T and the RBOCs are also diversifying into foreign markets, both as telecommunications carriers and as providers of online services, following the creation of new opportunities through liberalization abroad. Although the trend has had an uneven develo-pment, there has been a steady blurring of the distinction between information provider, information vendor, and telecommunications carrier which will continue in the present decade.

The same global trends have affected the structure and development of the telecommunications and information industries in Europe, but here the influence of the large multinational corporations has been diluted by a more robust government policy concerned to afford some protection to national and regional interests.

Within the European Community (EC) public data networks evolved independently in separate countries, resulting in a smaller overall market for each and a relatively higher cost of equipment than in the United States. This concentration on a national scope has led to the development of somewhat different technology, in particular the installation of different digital switching systems, which reduces the potential for European connectivity as a whole. The European Commission has taken an active interest in the development of the telecommunications facilities within the member countries, where the role of the PTTs has been crucial in the growth from fledgling services to sophisticated international networking. A major project sponsored by the EC which helped to fuel this growth was the Euronet service developed in the late 1970s.

The EC commissioned the national PTTs to create a packet switching network capable of supporting access from all the member countries, and itself mounted a variety of information services on the network under its own auspices as well as encouraging the development of others. This initiative gave a boost to the developing information industries in Europe, helping to create a market sector in which information vendors could establish themselves, while the PTTs were engaged in building up their own national packet switching networks to an adequate standard for a reliable international service. Once these had begun operation, Euronet was discontinued in 1984. This period saw the development of Packet SwitchStream in the United Kingdom, and similar ventures in France, the Netherlands, and Germany. These developments were driven through at the national level, with little detailed co-ordination between network suppliers who increasingly came to view each other as business competitors. This has resulted in the duplication of services and multiple international links to the United States and the Far East, with the network suppliers effectively competing to capture the market for data traffic entering and leaving Europe. The European Commission has been concerned to develop international research and development programmes, and has used the liberalization programme to stimulate innovation and corporate investment, in order to build a compatible European communication infrastructure capable of supporting the open internal market from 1993.

The creation of a European Telecommunications Standards Institute and the progressive reform of the PTT authorities have been explicit actions taken to support the declared EC objectives of:

— opening all network services, except the basic phone and data transmission services, to full competition;
— opening the terminal market to competition, within accepted operating standards;
— establishing uniform telecommunications charging across the EC;
— creating European standards for equipment to increase compatibility and remove trade barriers.

To support research and development, the Commission has embarked on programmes intended to develop the economic power of the region through advanced telecommunications technology. The RACE programme is a ten year effort, begun in 1985, to develop the standards and technology for integrated broadband communication through EC funded project teams drawn from industry and the academic world. The less favoured regions of the EC are supported by the STAR programme, which funds in part the development costs of upgrading commu-nications infrastructures in the more rural areas of Greece, Ireland, Portugal, Spain, France and the United Kingdom.

The development of narrowband ISDN, however, has not progressed as fast as considered desirable by the EC, which set itself a target of 5% market penetration by 1993 a decade earlier; in early 1992 there were only five commercial ISDN networks in operation in the EC and it was forecast that only 1% would be achieved, failing to impact small and medium sized enterprises and the residential sector. This slow progress is due to a lack of standardization in ISDN technology, a consequent lack of cheap equipment available for the mass market, and an unwillingness on the part of network operators to take committed action in the face of this uncertainty. Within the EC, individual countries have taken a path of deregulation; rather than of complete privatization. Many former publicly owned PTTs have been transformed into private companies, but often with a majority share-holding still held by the State; and although these compete with private corporations in some areas, most still retain a degree of monopolistic privilege and control which in some cases can be quite substantial.

In the United Kingdom, changes in tele-communications occurred within a more general perspective of a Conservative government free-market philosophy committed to reversal of state monopoly industries in general. The successive Telecommunications Acts of 1981 and 1984 separated telecommunications from the postal authority, establishing British Telecom (now BT) as a private corporation.

At the same time, licences to offer similar services were granted to other companies, with the intention of creating a competitive market which would encourage innovation and efficiency. The principal competitor was Mercury Communications, founded for this purpose by Cable and Wireless; two other licences have also been granted for the establishment of cellular radiophone services. A curiosity of the British situation was the third licensed operator, the city of Kingston upon Hull, which for historical reasons already ran its own local phone system; so successfully, that it was able to provide free local phone calls. This was privatized in 1987 as Kingston Communications, eventually becoming part of a larger corporation. The 1984 Act also created OfTel, the Office of Telecommunications, charged with administering the regulatory structure and overseeing the implementation of the licensing conditions imposed on operators, to protect the public interest and ensure fair trading. These included, for instance, a requirement for Mercury to develop a commitment to geographical coverage of the United Kingdom as well as more specialist business services.

Mercury Communications was originally targeted at large corporations, but since obtaining the right to interconnect with the BT network, and thenceforth the ability to provide complete end-to-end services has extended beyond its limited geographic base to provide data services to medium and smaller businesses. As well as digital phone services, Mercury now provides a packet switched data network under the name of Mercury 5000, and an ISDN service called Premier 2100. In this way, it is now competing with BT in all major areas, and is actively co-operating with foreign companies such as AT&T to provide advanced satellite network services.

While Mercury has built an all-digital network from the start but has limited geographic coverage, BT has a completely national service but is only just becoming fully digital in operation. At the same time as upgrading its national network, however, BT has developed international networking capabilities, for instance by the acquisition of the US-based value added network Tymnet, and has developed a range of value added services for delivery on these networks. There are two levels of integrated digital services, ISDN-2 and ISDN-30, with connections to ISDN networks in many other countries. In conjunction with this, BT provides video-conferencing and 'narrowcast' television services for intra-corporate communications. There is no restriction in the UK on the development of information services by the carrier operators, and BT in particular has developed many such services. The Prestel system was an early venture in videotex or viewdata, but has had little long lasting success despite being one of the first examples in this field.

Although successful in niche areas such as travel and insurance, after ten years of operation Prestel had only 95,000 terminals in use, and had failed to fulfil its original objectives of serving a mainly residential domestic market. Business oriented information services have proved more successful in areas such as financial, currency, market, and company information. Despite deriving some benefit from a loose regulatory structure which in practice has shielded BT from some of the effects of direct competition, the lack of a unifying structure under which services are offered, and a general philosophy of 'let the market decide' has retarded the development of a strong direction for telecommunications in the UK.

The relatively low cost of leased lines, for example, favours the building of private networks and encourages third-party suppliers of value added services, while discouraging the take-up of national services such as ISDN. BT must therefore compete on the same terms as these third party suppliers, and increasingly on an international basis. A further round of liberalization has opened up the possibility of other interested organisations applying for a licence to offer telecommunications services. These potentially may include:

— cable TV franchises, which have extensive links to customer premises, but no national infrastructure,
— cellular phone services, which are now allowed to build trunk networks, and could offer a packet switched radio-based network;
— recently de-regulated satellite services, able to both receive and transmit from small and cheap terminal devices;
— other national industries, such as British Rail, which have extensive rights of way for laying cable.

The cost of entering the telecommunications market in a competitive age is likely to mean that any of these options would be likely to seek an alliance with a foreign network provider, with particular interest expressed from United States Bell companies.

The relationship between the telecommunications authority and the State has been markedly different in France. The national PTT was established as France Telecom in 1986, a private corporation owned by the State. The organisation largely retained control over equipment approvals policy and operating conditions, able, for instance, to levy a 30% surcharge on leased lines used for value added services by competitors and to prevent certain kinds of services altogether. The Transpac X.25 public packet switching network is claimed to be the largest in the world, and has extended its value added services across Europe, including the recent acquisition of the London Regional Transport network in the United Kingdom. Transpac is already used by some United Kingdom companies for facilities such as electronic data interchange, in preference to leased lines from BT or Mercury, and is expected to be a major competitor in the European open market for telecommunications services.

The best known success of the French PTT has been the Minitel service. This videotex service, in contrast to the British Prestel, is now the dominant videotex system in Europe and has been sold to many other network operators, including NTT in Japan, the Italian PTT, and the Bell company US West.

From its first operation in 1983, Minitel grew to 4 million connected terminals in its first five years, and nearly 6 million in 1992, of which at least half are business users. Videotex is generally seen as providing access to large databases of information, presented through an easy to use interface which is accessible without special knowledge or instruction.

The system was originally developed by telecommunications interests as a suitable information service for linking the telephone with a domestic television set, but is now often supplemented by an intelligent terminal or personal computer.

A major reason for the initial success of Minitel lay in the policy of freely loaning the specially designed Minitel terminals to telephone subscribers, at the same time as replacing the printed telephone directory with an electronic version accessible only by videotex.

The Electronic Directory, provides access to a national database of phone subscribers through a simple enquiry language, as well as Yellow Pages information. The great success of this service very quickly created a substantial user base for Minitel, which encouraged other information suppliers to participate by offering other information services. These other services now cover a wide range, aimed at both the business and domestic markets, and including:

1. Electronic messaging; professional services; business and financial information; domestic shopping and banking services; and chat lines.
2. The Pancatalogue comprising the online catalogue of the Bibliotheque Nationale and of the SIBIL user group of 22 universities is accessible via Minitel; the new French national library, due to open in 1995, plans a Minitel link which will enable the user to reserve materials from home, and book a reading place for a particular arrival time,
3. Newspaper publishers offer a package of services including news bulletins; information on sport, entertainment and leisure; classified advertisements and games.
4. Professional level services include access to a range of online databases with sophisticated search interfaces. Services are organized in a kiosque system, in which the user has the available services displayed, but pays only for actual use with no fixed subscription fee. There are seven different levels of charging for information used, priced per hour of usage regardless of distance, ranging from almost nominal fees to typical online database searching rates. The vendor is responsible for mounting the information, and chooses the applicable charging rate. Teletel, the service umbrella under which Minitel is managed, provides access through the Transpac network, and includes the user charge in the normal telephone bill on behalf of the vendor. An international service is being introduced which interlinks with other national videotex services, and with Teletel hosts abroad.

France Telecom opened its Numeris ISDN network in Brittany in 1987, and established a national network by 1990. The development of suitable applications was encouraged by a partnership scheme in which France Telecom sponsored pilot projects with commercial and client organisations, paying half of the research and development costs.

Many of these applications involved the transmission of high definition images, such as the transfer of X-ray and ultra-sound images between medical sites in emergency cases, the transmission of satellite weather images, and the distribution of high definition house pictures around a network-of estate agents.

In Germany the PTT authority was turned into a private corporation, owned by the State, in 1989. Prior to this, the Deutsches Bundespost had resisted the encroachment of competitor services by keeping prices high for leased lines, charging by volume rather than by fixed rental, and by refusing equipment approval.

The 1989 reform following re-unification created a Bundespost subsidiary Telekom, and allowed private companies to compete in establishing value added services, although it has been reluctant to change this policy. The Deutsches Bundespost established a basic rate ISDN in eight major German cities in 1989, and expanded this to a broader national network, using the promotion of applications as a development device in a more limited way than the French experience. Telekom currently offers the following services:

— a videotex system, called BTX, similar to Prestel;
— an electronic mail system, called Telebox;
— a facility for remote monitoring of industrial plant and processes.

The development of the telecommunications infrastructure has stimulated the growth of the information industry, creating a larger potential market for information suppliers by bringing many more people into the communications web, building a more reliable and higher quality service.

The European informatics organisation, Eusidic, organizes an annual monitoring exercise on the reliability of international packet switching services by asking its members to record a typical week of use. This has recorded a steady increase in reliability, showing a 25% failure rate in calls in 1988 compared with a 14% failure rate in 1991; a large proportion of these faults are believed to occur when a dial-up connection through the PSTN telephone line is used as a local link to the packet switching exchange. An increase in, the total number of packet, switching exchanges in many European countries has reduced the importance of this link, and simplified the installation of new network connections. More dependable communications together with a network infrastructure which is capable of offering a connection to all potential customers has led to a substantial growth in the number of databases produced in both Europe and the United States, and in the number of host systems which offer access to them.

By 1990, there were estimated to be 1048 databases produced in EC countries and 2214 produced in the United States, excluding those only available in videotex model; this represented an 11% growth rate per annum in EC countries and a 7% growth rate in the United States. Within the EC the same report counted 227 hosts offering access to a total of 1256 databases, and 299 online hosts giving access to 3348 databases in the United States, although this is counting some databases more than once when they are accessible from several different hosts.

Compared with earlier surveys, this figure indicates

that the number of hosts in Europe is growing while those in the United States are remaining stable. A similar growth has taken place in the professional and business database usage sector of the videotex market in Europe, although the trends here are not so marked.

The French Minitel system dominates the area, with just over 85% of the total number of installed terminals across Europe (6.6 million) in that country; some 50% of the estimated 5 million or so Minitel customers are professional users compared to about 80% of the 100,000 Prestel users in the United Kingdom.

Overall the European Commission estimated that there were 15,000 information providers on European videotex in 19912, although once again most of these are mounted on the Minitel system which provides the predominant means of access to professional information services in France.

The distribution of the online market is uneven, with the United Kingdom, France, and Germany accounting for about 70% of the market share, the majority of which is held by the United Kingdom. The large number of potential databases, of which many can often be consulted through competing hosts at varying charging rates and using different command languages as the search interface, is a source of confusion and uncertainty for the end-user.

The diversity of choice has led to a growth in the use of gateways, links through from one system to another. Gateways in telecommunications networks can take one of three main forms:

1. Conversion facilities which link dissimilar systems and information types by translating back and forth between the two, typically used for the forwarding of electronic mail between systems.

2. Hosts which have a link through to other relevant hosts in their own area of interest, so that the second can be contacted directly through the first: the user can drop out to the second host, consult the services available, and then return to the first host on completion.
3. Value added services, which provide a 'front end' to a range of databases on different hosts, to ease and enhance user access by masking detailed differences between hosts in a common presentation and interface.

The use of value added networks has been an established part of the online scene for many years, especially attractive in situations where the reliability of the public telecommunications network cannot be guaranteed. The Dialnet value added network used by Dialog Information Services is an example. This offers regular users a local network connection point with billing for telecommunications costs integrated with that for database usage, as an alternative to dealing separately with international telecommunications vendors.

A third-party gateway service takes this a step further by offering integrated access to many different hosts through one connection.

A well-known example is the Easynet service, which allows users to access more than 900 databases on various hosts; the user may select a database directly or enter the relevant criteria for the service to select automatically the most appropriate one itself. The service offers one command language (the Common Command Language) to all the host systems made available, so that the user is not required to learn new search languages and unfamiliar systems are made more accessible. The Common Command Language reduces the degree of sophistication possible in search statements by imposing commonality, so there are facilities for the experienced user to express the search in the native host language. The Easynet gateway also provides management facilities for monitoring the most effective database usage, and for controlling the costs of use throughout the process. This growth in the online information market in both provision and usage is predicted to continue at increasing rates, with market research forecasts continually revised upwards.

The expanding availability of information services and the almost ubiquitous presence of tele-communications networks is beginning to have a substantial impact not only on the way in which traditional information consumers such as libraries and information units are conducting their activities, but also on the development of new information-related occupations which can take advantage of these new communications features.

The practice of teleworking—the conduct of work-related business and interactions over a distance and through the telecommunications networks: with the employer, with colleagues, with customers and contractors—is one of these areas.

The development of information networking, in both the informal and personal sense as well as a formal substitution of electronically-mediated work relations, is fundamental to the growth of distance working. A major plank, in the telecommunications development programme of the European Community has been the encouragement of teleworking through funding of the necessary infrastructure, as a means of economic development in rural and less-favoured regions of Europe. An example of this is the development initiative conducted in conjunction with BT to provide digital exchanges and line plant for the installation of integrated digital services in the Highlands and Islands region of Scotland in the Hi-ISDN project.

A complementary project, called Hi-VANS, provides an easy to use interface to national and international services and to the public data network, as well as local information services for the development of tourism and community enterprises. An example of one such enterprise is the use of the network to transmit scanned images of articles which require abstracting from the Elsevier journal publisher in the Netherlands to distance workers in the Highlands. The articles are scanned in the Netherlands from the print version and sent to abstracters in Scotland; the completed abstracts are then returned for publication to the Netherlands with no production delays arising from postal delivery times.

Similar pioneering efforts have seen the foundation of 'telecottages' in many rural areas of the United Kingdom. A 'telecottage' is a generic term for a rural information technology centre, which provides easy access to IT, usually in a public building and on an informal basis. The telecottage can provide formal and informal training, and can act as a catalyst for small enterprises by providing cost-effective access to equipment, as well as supporting the work of community groups.

Apart from public funding, this concept has found sponsorship in the United Kingdom from BT in the form of four Teleservice Centres, established as well-equipped telematic service centres; the first of these to begin activity was in the Shetland Islands in 1991. The willingness of a major telecommunications corporation to become so involved in stimulating the development of a networking infrastructure for information enterprises testifies to the potential possibilities for the future.

In Europe, the concept of teleworking was developed first in Scandinavia, spreading quickly to the United Kingdom, and is now strongly favoured by government and EC initiatives in France, Spain and Portugal. The Telecottage Association, formed to support the growth in teleworking through personal networks of groups and individuals by means of seminars and newsletters, estimates that there are about 590,000 self-employed teleworkers in the United Kingdom. Many of these people are professional workers to whom the production, use and exchange of information is vital to their work.

The recent acceptance of distance working indicates a trend towards more skilled information workers, and the replacement of traditional office work by advisory, and consultancy-based work which does not require full-time attendance at a particular geographical location to be carried out. This is demonstrated by the Telemedicine project in northern Norway, for example, which provides specialist medical services from a central hospital in Tromsoe to isolated local hospitals and health centres through the telecommunications network. This links together services such as pathology, radiology, and cardiology with access to medical databases and patient information systems for remote diagnosis, without requiring the patient to make a difficult journey to the central hospital facilities.

Generally, teleworking can take a number of different organisational forms:

— home-working, in which the workers are based at their own home, making few visits to an employer premises;
— telecentres, which offer new information technology facilities for workers from various different organisations;

— satellite work centres, which are owned by a large company but are geographically dispersed;
— flexible working, in which the work is carried out partly at the organisational premises and partly at home.

These new organisational forms imply changes in the overall structures for, organisational communications, and an increased emphasis on the development of networks which are capable of stretching beyond the physical confines of organisational premises alone.

Private network

The backbone of the private network is often provided by leased lines rented on the basis of sole use from the local telecommunications authority. The costs and conditions which are imposed on the lease differ quite widely between countries. Where lines are cheaper, as in the United Kingdom for example, a large corporation may now be able to justify a leased line on the basis of voice transmission only, using one Megastream line to replace several analogue phone lines, and be able to transmit data 'for free' on top of this usage since a fixed annual rent is paid. High bandwidth circuits such as these supply point to point connections, and are appropriate between sites which have a high data traffic flow. Dial-up lines may be used where small amounts of data are sent at infrequent intervals, possibly using parts of a public packet switched network.

Since 1989 organisations operating private networks are allowed to resell spare capacity on their bandwidth, so that linking in with an existing private network already in use elsewhere may be one option; for example, banks may make network capacity available to some of their corporate customers. While terrestrial lines are normally controlled by a telecommunications authority, since the liberalization of services nonterrestrial transmission offers a wider range of choices. Microwave links can be installed in line of sight between tall buildings, and satellite services can be employed to carry audio, video, and data services within a wide geographical area.

In the United States an 'open skies' policy, under which any qualified organisation can apply for a licence to operate a domestic satellite service, has been in operation since 1972; in the United Kingdom, however, the granting of full licences has been more reticent. Satellite capacity is available from a number of specialist data communications companies, and in Europe through the Eutelsat consortium of PTT authorities.

The pricing for Eutelsat usage is differentiated by member country with wide discrepancies in national rates; recently, clients have been able to book capacity through any member offering the best service. The development of very small aperture satellite transmission (VSAT) has lowered the relative costs of this medium, since a receive-only dish uses the same technology as satellite television, and can be installed with the same case without the need for formal planning permission. This can provide a low cost 'point-to-multi-point' data broadcasting, for fast updating of many sites simultaneously; and is also used as a stop-gap measure for establishing a network link quickly, or to link sites which are separated by difficult geographic terrain.

Cellular network radiophones can also be used for non-terrestrial data links, but are not yet ideal for this purpose. This method appears attractive for linking a portable personal computer fitted with integral modem into a corporate network from uncertain locations; however, the cellular channel is noisy, and the transition between cells introduces delays in which contact may easily be lost, preventing truly mobile data communications. Although the transmission of packet data over the VHF radio waveband is feasible, its widespread use has not yet developed in the United Kingdom; licences have only been granted to radio data companies for quite limited and specialized markets. The wide area networking elements also take on an international dimension if the organisation needs to link into sites in other countries.

Larger organisations have diverse information needs, and sometimes specialist but vital performance requirements, demanding the development of a networking strategy which is flexible and controllable. For information networking to support corporate communications, the organisation has three main choices.

1. To build a private network, using network elements from different sources.
2. To send data over one or other of the public data networks.
3. To hand over all network management aspects to a third party specializing in this field.

These choices have varying significance for different sizes and types of organisation operating in different fields; these disparate demands will lead to differing perceptions of the technology which is at the leading edge for a particular situation.

Smaller organisations, or those in which the information and technological infrastructure is less developed, may be well satisfied with options which are already considered obsolete by those in which infor-mation has a high strategic or mission importance. The use of public telecommunications in one organisation may have as far-reaching effects within that context, as are sought by another which is planning frame relay and broadband networking as replacements for X.25 and ISDN.

Some significant advantages of the use of public data services are given below:

1. The development of private networks demands the use of scarce personnel with technical expertise in networking skills, and a high capital investment; while using public networks leaves the organisation free to concentrate on its main activities without draining off resources.
2. Once a private network is developed it is hard to change, and expensive to upgrade with technological advances. Information activities may demand a high capacity at critical times, but may not justify this permanently (for example, with seasonal peaks in retail transactions); variable use of the public data network will smooth out peaks and troughs of this nature.
3. The broader scope of public services can develop targeted services for particular needs in a cost effective way, and save on the duplication of effort.
4. In a similar way, organisations can take advantage of the emergence of international standards through participation in a more general service, without the cost of individual development; for example, electronic data interchange standards for basic business documents.

The use of completely private networks, can have important attractions especially to a larger organisation which is able to amortise costs over a longer period.

1. The strategic importance of information to the organisation may demand control over the data at all stages, without fear of compromising security and confidentiality.
2. Control of the network enables technological decisions on speed and efficiency, the use of proprietary protocols, and flexible changes in response to need.

3. Control also extends to economic factors, where the unpredictable nature of changes in public services are avoided while spare capacity can be resold to other clients.

The third choice available to organisations is the use of third-party services to take over the management of all network facilities on its behalf. This removes the need for specialist expertise and keeps the technology up to date, while retaining some control and security, by making this the responsibility of an expert networking company. This is an attractive option to a medium sized organisation where communications is important for its business-but not of vital strategic importance-particularly if this involves the use of international connections and the consequent complexity of dealing with different national authorities. Network management companies may offer project management in the development of a network for a specific problem within a defined budget, or full *facilities management* of all networking arrangements.

Liberalization of telecommunications has encouraged the growth of management services from both private companies and the telecommunications carriers, while the increasing complexity of networking has made their services attractive to the client. The operators have often evolved from organisations which have established their own extensive private networks.

A major development in the short- to medium-term future will be a substantial growth in multimedia telecommunications in one form or another. In this way, multimedia information networks will correspond more closely to the experience of communication and information interchange in everyday life, with a flexible mix of sound, picture, and words. The exact nature of this experience, and its effect on information networking in general, remains to be determined.

A major preoccupation of national governments and regional associations is to build the infrastructure for these developments as quickly as possible (and preferably faster than their competitors). In the United States, for example, in an attempt to accelerate the extension of fibre optic cabling to the home and workplace on a massive scale, the Federal Communications Commission (FCC) decided in 1992 to allow the regional Bell holding companies to transmit video programmes over their telecommunications lines, in competition with the cable television companies. This attempt to create a communications infrastructure for the next decade is seen by many Americans as crucial to the continued economic dominance of the United States.

The FCC, for example, places much weight on multimedia devices such as high definition television (HDTV), a digital two-way interactive television set, as the vehicle for this information expansion, aiming at a 15-year deadline for complete HDTV conversion. The technological futurism is the subject of much political controversy and manoeuvring at the current time; it seems likely though, that the new presidential administration will lead out more liberalization to support competition-led innovation and technological advances in communications media, and there is a clear emphasis on the use of technology for economic development in the shaping of public policy statements.

One more immediate result is likely to be the more rapid development of the National Research and Education Network, sponsored for many years by Vice-President Al Gore. The building of NREN services will bring into focus many of the issues on information access and price, and of the emerging adjustments in role of all those involved in the information cycle. In Europe, a similar urgency has fuelled a number of projects sponsored by the European Commission to work towards the creation of integrated broadband communications systems by the latter part of this decade.

The RACE programme, funding research into advanced communications technology and services, indicates by its name some of its underlying objectives, and the ESPRIT programme has initiated the IDOMENEUS project to co-ordinate and improve European efforts in the development of new information environments in the area of interacting open media.

Adopting lessons learned from the French experience in the establishment of the Minitel system, the EC has initiated a number of pilot projects in fields ranging from banking and finance, manufacturing, transport, distribution, and health care; other projects include distributed multimedia publishing, and a broadband network based library for the petroleum and chemical industries, with a 1995 target date for the introduction of commercial services.

The existence of a technology, however, does not always guarantee its success. It is worth remembering that the Picture Phone was launched by AT&T at the World Fair of 1964. This was a first example of the videophone; in 1992, almost 30 years later, British Telecom launched a low-cost consumer videophone, which can be connected directly to the normal telephone socket; this has yet to make any substantial impact in the market-place.

A development which is likely to be of more significance, though, is the planned availability of audio-visual workstations based on the standard PC. Such a device will make the full integration of data and voice networks within the workplace a reality, and will open up a wider market for multimedia information services. Many of these exist in prototype form within the existing infrastructure, Multimedia electronic mail, for example, is now possible even in a limited text-based medium such as the Internet.

The multimedia information mail extensions (MIME) to the standard Internet mail protocol permit the inclusion of still images, group III fax images, compressed full motion video, and multipart playback sequences of mixed information types. Desktop videoconferencing, the ability to conduct meetings with a geographically remote person each at their own desk, has been established as a feasible communications technology, although so far finding only a niche rather than global market. The experience of this videoconferencing raises some key issues since it is clear that, as with most other information technologies, the technical issues are much less important than the social and organisational ones. Technical advances which have made the idea more feasible include the emergence of high bandwidth ISDN networks, video compression techniques, accepted standards, and powerful graphics-based workstations.

The degree of success in implementing this technology is determined rather by the extent to which it supports the way people work. The involves an understanding of the communications patterns between individuals and groups, and of their information needs and the uses to which information is put; of the way in which contacts with individuals and formal information sources assists the innovative process, and an appreciation of the interdependent balance between formal and informal communication.

Technology has often been used to support formal communication patterns, rather than the informal, and sometimes is intended to replace rather than support either. Multimedia communications systems cannot replace face-to-face contact any more than the telephone (although a similar argument was made against the telephone at its introduction). Thoughtful design may, however, be used to appropriately support existing human communication patterns. The Cruiser video-conferencing system designed by Bellcore, for example, uses the metaphor of a 'virtual hallway'—floor plan representing the groups of participants—along which a user may navigate, 'cruise' and interact with others in the process. For multimedia multi-user systems such as this, the interface must include some form of social protocol which enables decisions about the nature and style of desired interaction to be taken.

Many issues which will effectively delineate the shape of multimedia networking in the future remain as yet poorly understood and little explored. In some areas, however, there is more immediacy on concerns which are being raised by the substantial growth in network traffic and users, and the potential changes which can be perceived in the near future.

The growing importance of digital information and its availability over networks which demand physical and technical access create barriers which are increasingly insurmountable for many groups of potential users. While there is no space here to discuss the social role of information systems, there are a few examples of attempts to bypass these barriers in recent developments. The Cleveland FreeNet experiment, for example, is an attempt to increase access to Internet information to a wider audience. The vast amounts of information, and the worldwide nature of the Internet, also bring to the fore issues of intellectual property and copyright surrounding electronic information. Much of the information held on this network is freely available, as long as it is used for non-commercial purposes.

The subsequent use of information taken from computer networks cannot be controlled, however, once it has been downloaded from the original source. It may appear in many diverse guises, be re-partitioned, amalgamated, and reused, taking on a life of its own. Print-based copyright legislation does not translate easily to the electronic environment. A feature of the legislation to found the advanced NREN network requires the provision of charging mechanisms to be put in place, suggesting a trend towards more control over use and users.

The characteristics which make electronic information difficult to define and 'freeze' at one point in time also raise questions on the nature of bibliographic control and mapping of information resources. Electronic documents and journals which can be updated immediately, replacing the original copy, are difficult to define as a bibliographic entity which has a declared and fixed content, which can be cited for later use. The identification of various versions of a logical item becomes a complex (or perhaps impossible) task, as does preservation and archiving as a permanent record of publication. These problems also redound upon ethical issues involving the quality and accuracy of the document content. Electronic documents may easily be changed, or 'falsified' with changing intellectual fashions in a way that print fixed at one point in time cannot.

The unstructured and fluid process which allows a network user to make information available without recourse to formal publisher or refereeing process has great advantages in stimulating an innovative and creative dialectic, but at the cost of a large proportion of false, misleading, or incorrect information which must also be sorted through and rejected. Whilst the research community, in which much of this type of activity takes place at present, has evolved a fairly sophisticated code of practical ethics for network co-operation and exchange, it is doubtful that this will survive a broadening of access and the introduction of commercial interests.

The increasing ubiquity of the networking environment is raising questions about the relative responsibilities of those involved in the information transfer process. Traditionally, this process could be described in terms of five distinct roles: the information provider, who provides the original source material; the information host, who makes it available and accessible, 'publishing' in a print or electronic sense; the carrier or distributor, providing a channel for the information; the intermediary, traditional role for the information service professional; and the information user, the final consumer. This model has long ago begun to break down when applied to the networking environment.

The information provider is often the same as the information host; the common carrier, the telecommunications authority, provides information services in its own right; and the information user more often wishes to find and retrieve the information directly. Many people have begun to question the role of the publisher in the electronic environment: since the author can mount a document in its electronic form on a local computer (quite probably the format it was originally composed in) and the network facilities act as a distribution mechanism, it becomes harder to gauge the function of a traditional publisher. Although this is clearly not appropriate for many types of publishing, in some areas it is possible to see advantages.

For instance, the traditional venue for reporting research has been as a journal article in some summarized form; network publishing would allow a reader to optionally download original datasets and intermediate analysis, as well as authorial commentary, directly and without a time delay. The development of network publishing is likely to involve identifiable changing characteristics compared to the traditional activities:

— a growth in simulcast publishing, with one source file producing a variety of complementary versions in different formats;

— multimedia electronic publishing, integrating database, text, image, sound, and video;

— the use of information tools to skim, navigate, browse, and utilize these new media products;

— selective and customized publishing targeted at particular groups;

— a linking with the concept of a 'virtual library', where access and materials are not constrained by physical barriers.

The information user and the information provider potentially have a much more direct and interactive relationship, possibly to the extent that the information exchange cannot be completely separated from the communication process itself. This raises a question mark against the received role of the intermediary, as a filter between originator, distributor, and recipient.

As the growth in electronic information begins to demand a new philosophy of the nature and function of information so also the activities of the information professional must, in this setting at least, change and adapt.

No longer able to adopt a custodial role in managing and organizing the materials and artefacts of information, the librarian or information scientist must adopt a facilitating strategy, aimed at creating the conditions for a user to negotiate the information sphere successfully.

The librarian no longer 'owns' the information since it is not contained within any physical institution; and it cannot therefore be 'managed' in the same physical sense. The information user, however, must still negotiate an information space, now across a digital network as much as before within the confines of a library, in order to achieve a successful resolution to the information transfer process.

Bibliography

Baily, Charles W., Jr. "Network-Based Electronic Serials". *Information Technology and Libraries* 11 (March 1992).

Bates, M., System meets user: problems in matching subject search terms, *Information processing and management*, 13, 1977.

Bates, Marica J. 1979, Idea tactics. *Journal of American Society for Information Science* 30 (September).

Bates, Marica J. 1979b, Information search tactics. *Journal of the American Society for Information Science* 30 (July).

Belkin, N. J., T. Seeger and G. Wersing 1983, Distributed expert problem treatment as model for information system analysis and design. *Journal of Information Science.*

Borgman, Christine L. 1989, All users of information retrieval systems are not created equal. An exploration into individual difference, *Information Processing and Management.*

Buxton. A. B., and A. J. Meadows. 1977, The variation in the information content of titles of research paper with time and discipline. *Journal of Documentation* 33 (March).

Carrow, Deborah, and Joan Nugent. 1977, Comparison of free-text and index search abilities in an operating information system. In Information management in the 1980s: *Proceedings of the American Society for Information Science, 40th annual meeting, Sept, 26-Oct. 1. 1977.* White Plains, NY: Knowledge Indstry Publications.

Chuadamani, K.S., and R. Shalini. "Journal Acquisition-Cost Effectiveness Models." *Information Processing and Management.*

Derr, L. 1983, A conceptual analysis of information need. *Information Processing and Management.*

Dervin, B. and Nilan, M., 'Information needs and uses', American review of information science and technology, 21, 1986.

Doszkscs, Tamas E. 1983. CITE/NLM: Natural language searching in an online catalog. *Information Technology and Libraries.*

For a review of this post-Boolen IR research *see*: Bookstein, Abraham, 'Probability fuzzy-set applications to information retrieval', Annual review of information science and technology (ARIST), 20, 1985 and 'The potential of improvements in commercial document retrieval systems', *Information processing and management*, special issue, 24, 1988.

Foskett, A.C. 1982. The subject approach to information, 4th ed. London: Bingley.

Furnas, G. W., *et al.* 1984, Statistical sematics: Analysis of the potential performance of keyword information systems. In Human factors in computer systems, edited by John C. Thomas and Michael L. Schneider. Norwood, NJ: Ablex.

Heine, Michael H. 1980, The question as the fundamental variable in information science. In *Theory and application of information research: Proceedings of the second Internal research Forum on Information Science, Copenhagen, 1977*, edited by Ole Harbo and Leif Kajberg, London: Manshell.

Hildreth, C.R., 'To Boolean', Information technology and libraries, 2, 1983.

Ingwersen, P. 1984, Psychological aspects of Information retrieval. *Social Information Studies* 4 (April/July).

Kemp, D. Alasdair. 1976, The nature of knowledge: *An introduction for librarians.* London: Bingley.

Lancaster, F. W., Information retrieval systems: characteristics, testing, and evaluation, New York, John Wiley & Sons, 1968, 181-2l; *see* also: Oddy R. N., 'Information retrieval through man-machine dialogue', *The journal documentation*, 33 (1), 1977.

Line. Maurice B. 1974, Draft definitions: Information and Library needs, wants, demands and uses. Aslib Proceedings 26 (February).

Lockett, Mary W. "The Bradford Distribution: A Review of the Literature 1934-1987". *Library and Information Science Research* 11 (January-March 1989).

Mick, Colin K. 1980, Towards usable user studies. *Journal of American Society for Information Science* 31 (September).

Monsell, Stephen. 1981, Representations, processes, memory mechanisms: The basic components of cognition. *Journal of the American Society for Information Science* 32 (September).

Pratt, 19881, The information of the image. Noorwood, NJ: Ablex.

Salton, Gerard, "The use of extended Boolen logic in information retrieval", Proceedings of the Annual Meeting of the ACM SIGMOD, Boston, MA, 18-21 June 1984, SIGMOD record, 14(2), 1984.

Schabas, Ann H.1982, Post coordinate retrieval. *Journal of the American Society for the Information Science* 33 (January).

Smith, Linda. 1976, Artificial intelligence in information retrieval systems. *Information Processing and Management.*

Smith, Linda. 1980, Artificial intelligence applications in information systems. *Annual Review of Information Science and Technology.*

Svenonius, Elaine. 1986, Unanswered questions in the design of controlled vocabularies. *Journal of the American Society for Information Science.*

Taylor, R. S., 'Question negotiation and information seeking in libraries', *Collage and research libraries*, 29, 1968.

Titus, Elizabeth McKenney, Wallace C. Grant, and Lorrance J. Haticome. "Barcoding As a Tool for Collection Use Analysis: A Pilot Project." *Information Technology and Libraries* 13 (December 1994).

Index